THE **NEW**
MARK TWAIN
HANDBOOK

GARLAND REFERENCE LIBRARY
OF THE HUMANITIES
(VOL. 615)

THE **NEW** MARK TWAIN HANDBOOK

E. Hudson Long
J. R. LeMaster

GARLAND PUBLISHING INC. • NEW YORK & LONDON
1985

Library of Congress Cataloging-in-Publication Data

Long, E. Hudson (Eugene Hudson), 1908–
The new Mark Twain handbook.

(Garland reference library of the humanities ;
v. 615)
Enl. ed. of: Mark Twain handbook. 1957.
Bibliography: p.
Includes index.
1. Twain, Mark, 1835–1910.   2. Twain, Mark, 1835–
1910—Bibliography.   3. Authors, American—19th
century—Bibliography.   I. LeMaster, J. R., 1934–
II. Long, E. Hudson (Eugene Hudson), 1908–   Mark
Twain handbook.   III. Title.   IV. Series.
PS1331.L6   1985   818'.409   85-45124
ISBN 0-8240-8667-8 (alk. paper)

Cover design by Alison Lew

Printed on acid-free, 250-year-life paper
Manufactured in the United States of America

In memory of
Dixon Wecter

CONTENTS

PREFACE

The *Mark Twain Handbook* was published by Hendricks House in 1957 as a volume in the Handbooks of American Literature series under the general editorship of Gay Wilson Allen. In the twenty-eight years since the appearance of the *Mark Twain Handbook*, a great deal of scholarship has accumulated. More than a hundred books have been published along with hundreds of critical articles. A review of all that has been published, however, is beyond the scope of this study. Rather, we have tried to account for the most significant work that has been done. In the case of critical articles, we have used those published before 1957 liberally. But of the many published since 1957, few contribute new ideas to Twain scholarship or add information to what is already known. For that reason, as well as reasons having to do with the length of our study, we have used few critical articles published after 1957.

Our aim has been to produce a useful handbook. As was done in the *Mark Twain Handbook*, we have not only summarized Mark Twain scholarship but have also evaluated the various contributions. We have supplied notes at the end of each chapter, and the annotated bibliography at the end of each chapter consists of all works cited by page number as well as works discussed but not cited. Relying on the second edition of the *MLA Handbook* for matters of style, we have placed citations in the text, thereby eliminating the need for footnotes or endnotes.

Where possible, we have used the authorized edition in citing works by Twain. Except for the prefaces, pagination in the authorized edition appears to correspond to that of the uniform trade edition, the limp leather edition, and the Mississippi edition. As for further bibliography, we recommend Merle Johnson's *A Bibliography of the Works of Mark Twain* (1935). Reprinted in 1972, Johnson's book is still valuable to both the scholar and the student. For works about Twain we recommend Thomas A. Tenney's *Mark Twain: A*

Reference Guide (1977). Since 1977 Tenney has supplied annual supplements to his bibliography in *American Literary Realism 1870–1910*. *Mark Twain: A Reference Guide* is both exhaustive and valuable.

For the last twenty years the most important contributions to Twain scholarship have been published by the University of California Press. First, the press produced a uniform edition of Mark Twain's works, and then, through collaboration with the Center for Textual Studies at the University of Iowa, commenced publication of a projected series of twenty-five volumes known as the Iowa–California Edition—a major attempt to restore Twain's texts to conform to the author's original intentions. As represented by the supplements, by the explanatory notes, and by the textual notes of each volume of the series produced thus far, the quality of scholarship is impressive. Efforts in the Iowa–California Edition to purify Twain's texts are long overdue; they will contribute significantly to scholarship in the future.

Finally, we wish to express our appreciation to the staff of Moody Memorial Library at Baylor University for assistance in locating materials necessary to this study. We are grateful to Valerie Fraser, Jane Healey, Harriet Fadal, and Debbie Rhoads for assistance in preparing our manuscript for publication. And to the administration at Baylor University we are grateful for released time and a grant, without either of which this project would not have been possible.

EHL
JRL
June 27, 1985
Waco, Texas

ACKNOWLEDGMENTS

We wish to express our appreciation to Harper & Row for permission to quote from the following:

Mark Twain's Autobiography, Harper & Brothers, 1924.
Mark Twain's Letters, Harper & Brothers, 1917.
Mark Twain's Notebook, Harper & Brothers, 1935.
Albert Bigelow Paine, *Mark Twain: A Biography*, Harper & Brothers, 1912.

Chronological Table
Significant Events in Mark Twain's
Life, and Publication Dates

1835   Born at Florida, Missouri, November 30.

1839   The Clemens family moved to Hannibal, Missouri.

1847   Father, John Marshall Clemens, died in March.

1847   Worked as a printer on either the Hannibal *Journal*
          or *Gazette*, following his father's death.

1848-50   Probably worked for Joseph P. Ament as a printer on
          the Hannibal *Courier*. Worked perhaps until 1851.

1850-52   Orion Clemens started the *Western Union* in September,
          1850. In the spring of 1851 he combined it with the
          Hannibal *Weekly Dollar Journal* under the name Hannibal
          Journal and Western Union, which became the *Journal*
          in February, 1852. Sam helped his brother.

1852   "The Dandy Frightening the Squatter" appeared in the
          Carpet-Bag for May.

1853   Left Hannibal in June to go to St. Louis.

1853   August, in New York. Visited Philadelphia during the
          winter and corresponded for the Muscatine (Iowa)
          Journal.

1854   February, visited Washington, D.C.

1854   Summer, in Muscatine, Iowa, with his mother and Orion.
          Probably worked on Muscatine *Journal*.

1855   Winter and spring, in St. Louis. Joined Orion in
          Keokuk during the summer.

1856   Worked for his brother in Keokuk until fall. Left
          again for St. Louis.

1856   October 18, began the Thomas Jefferson Snodgrass
          letters for Keokuk (Iowa) *Daily Post*. Moved from
          St. Louis to Cincinnati.

1857   Lived in Cincinnati during the winter and met the
        Scotchman named Macfarlane.

1857   April, boarded the *Paul Jones* for New Orleans, intend-
        ing to go to South America, but met Horace Bixby, who
        agreed to teach him the river.

1858   Learned the river as a "cub" and piloted freighters.

1858   June, brother Henry killed in a steamboat explosion.
        Sam reproached himself because of a quarrel with the
        pilot which had caused him to be left behind instead
        of Henry.

1859   April 9, Samuel Clemens' pilot license granted.

1859   Wrote "Sergeant Fathom" burlesque of Isaiah Sellers,
        New Orleans (daily) *Crescent*, May 17.

1861   Outbreak of the Civil War put an end to piloting.
        January 21, first "Quintus Curtius Snodgrass" letter
        in New Orleans (daily) *Crescent*, the last appearing
        on March 30.

1861   June, "Campaign That Failed" service in Missouri.

1861   Twenty-one day journey by stagecoach to Carson City,
        Nevada, during late July and early August.

1862   The "Josh" letters for the *Virginia City Territorial
        Enterprise*, written between mid-February and the
        last of July.

1862   August, joined the staff of the *Enterprise*, to remain
        there until May, 1864.

1862   "The Petrified Man" hoax published in *Territorial
        Enterprise*, probably October 5; reprinted by *San
        Francisco Daily Evening Bulletin*, October 15.

1862   During November and December, reported the Second
        Territorial Legislature of Nevada from Carson City
        for the *Enterprise*.

1863   February 2, in a dispatch to the *Enterprise* from
        Carson City, first signed himself "Mark Twain."

1863   Early summer, first visit to San Francisco, in
        company with newspaperman Clement T. Rice (The Un-
        reliable).

1863   "The Empire City Massacre" hoax printed in *Territorial
        Enterprise*, October 28.

1863   December, met Artemus Ward, at Virginia City.

1864   January, elected "Governor" of the Third House by
        fellow newspapermen at Carson City.

1864   February 21, New York *Sunday Mercury* published
        "Those Blasted Children," Twain's first known
        Eastern publication. Reprinted by the San Fran-
        cisco *Golden Era*, March 27.

1864   May, became involved in a controversy with a rival
        editor, leading to a proposed duel, in violation of
        Nevada law, which caused Twain's exit to San Francisco.

1864   Summer and fall, worked for the San Francisco *Morning
        Call*, the *Golden Era*, and the *Californian*.

1864   Exposure of municipal corruption led to departure
        from San Francisco to the Tuolumne Hills in the
        Mother Lode Country in December.

1865   January, pocket mining at Angel's Camp. February,
        returned to San Francisco; wrote "Jim Smiley and His
        Jumping Frog."

1865   November 18, the "Jumping Frog" story printed in the
        New York *Saturday Press*. Supported himself in San
        Francisco by writing potboilers for the press.

1866   March 7, sailed for the Sandwich Islands to write a
        series of travel letters for the Sacramento *Union*;
        in Hawaii four months and a day.

1866   June 25, special dispatch on the burning of the
        clipper ship *Hornet* at sea.

1866   October 2, embarked on the lecture platform, talking
        on the Sandwich Islands at the San Francisco Academy
        of Music.

1866   December, sailed for New York, crossed the isthmus.

1867   January, arrived in New York.

1867   March and April, visited St. Louis, Hannibal, and
        Keokuk.

1867   May, *The Celebrated Jumping Frog of Calaveras County,
        and Other Sketches* published by C.H. Webb in New
        York.

1867   May 6, lectured successfully at Cooper Union in New
        York.

1867   June 8, sailed on the *Quaker City* for the Holy Land
        excursion as correspondent for the San Francisco
        Alta California.

1867   November 19, returned to New York.

1867   November, served briefly as private secretary to
            Senator William M. Stewart of Nevada.

1867   December 27, first meeting with Olivia Langdon.

1868   January 2 or 3, first date with Olivia, to hear
            Charles Dickens read.

1868   March, journeyed to California to secure publishing
            rights to his *Alta* correspondence. Lectured there
            during the spring and summer. July 6, sailed for
            New York.

1868   August, first visit with the Langdon family in
            Elmira.

1868   November and December, conducted strenuous lecture
            tour.

1869   February 4, became engaged to marry Olivia.

1869   July, *The Innocents Abroad* published.

1869   August, purchased a partnership in the Buffalo *Ex-
            press* through loan of $25,000 from Jervis Langdon.

1869   November and December, lectured under James Redpath's
            management.

1870   January, continued lecture tour.

1870   February 2, married Olivia Langdon.

1870   March, wrote for the New York *Galaxy*, until April,
            1871.

1870   July 5, hasty trip to Washington, photographed by
            Matthew Brady, and met General Grant.

1870   August 6, Jervis Langdon died.

1870   November 7, Langdon Clemens prematurely born in
            Buffalo.

1871   February, *Mark Twain's (Burlesque) Autobiography and
            First Romance* published in New York.

1871   Spring and summer, the Clemens family vacationed at
            Quarry Farm, Elmira, New York, henceforth to be
            their favorite summer retreat.

1871   October, moved to Hartford, Connecticut, and rented
            a house at Nook Farm.

1871   Fall lecture tour to finish paying debts caused by
            sacrifice of Buffalo interests.

1872   Lecture tour continued through early February.

1872   February, *Roughing It* published by the American
          Publishing Company.

1872   March 19, Olivia Susan (Susy) Clemens born.

1872   June 2, Langdon Clemens died (Twain's only son).

1872   August, sailed for England.

1872   November 9, honored at Lord Mayor's dinner in London.

1873   Summer spent in Britain and Europe with family.

1873   November-December, lectured in England.

1873   December, *The Gilded Age*, in collaboration with
          Charles Dudley Warner, published by the American
          Publishing Company.

1874   January, sailed home from England.

1874   June, Clara Clemens born.

1874   September, dramatized version of *The Gilded Age*
          opened in New York.

1875   *Old Times on the Mississippi* appeared in the *Atlantic
          Monthly*, January-June and August.

1875   July 21, *Sketches New and Old* published by the
          American Publishing Company.

1876   December, *The Adventures of Tom Sawyer* published
          by the American Publishing Company.

1877   April, production of a play *Ah Sin* in collaboration
          with Bret Harte, which opened in Washington, May 7.

1877   May 16, visited Bermuda with Rev. Joseph Twichell.

1877   September, *A True Story and the Recent Carnival of
          Crime* published by James R. Osgood.

1877   December 17, made Whittier birthday speech in Boston.

1878   March, *Punch, Brothers, Punch! and Other Sketches*
          published by Slote, Woodman and Company.

1878   August, walking tour with Twichell through the Black
          Forest.

1878-79   Lived abroad in Germany and Italy.

1880   March, *A Tramp Abroad* published by the American
          Publishing Company.

1880   June, the so-called "Cleveland Edition" of *1601*, or
          Conversation as It Was by the Social Fireside in the

	Time of the Tudors. The "West Point" edition seems to have been 1882.
1880	July 26, Jean Clemens born.
1881	November, visited Canada for a fortnight.
1882	January, *The Prince and the Pauper* published by James R. Osgood.
1882	April–May, trip down the Mississippi to New Orleans, and a return journey with Horace Bixby.
1882	June, *The Stolen White Elephant* published by James R. Osgood.
1883	May, *Life on the Mississippi* published by James R. Osgood.
1883	May, again visited Canada briefly.
1884	Summer, campaigned for Grover Cleveland.
1884	November–December, lecture tours with Cable.
1885	January, *Adventures of Huckleberry Finn* published by Charles L. Webster and Company.
1885	January–February, continued lecture tour with Cable.
1885	Fall, published General Grant's *Memoirs*.
1888	Master of Arts degree from Yale.
1889	December, *A Connecticut Yankee in King Arthur's Court* published by Charles L. Webster and Company.
1890	Summer, engrossed in the Paige typesetting machine.
1890	Autumn, Susy entered Bryn Mawr.
1891	June, family closed Hartford home and went to Europe.
1891–92	Winter in Berlin.
1892	March, *Merry Tales* published by Charles L. Webster and Company.
1892	May, *The American Claimant* published by Charles L. Webster and Company.
1893	February 25, the £*1,000,000 Bank-Note* published by Charles L. Webster and Company.
1893	Spring, family in Italy; Twain made trips to America to stave off failure of the Paige machine.
1894	Spring, *Tom Sawyer Abroad* published by Charles L. Webster and Company.

1894   April 18, Charles L. Webster and Company executed assignment papers, carrying Samuel Clemens into bankruptcy with it.

1894   Summer, Clemens' family remained in France; Twain visited the United States in July and August.

1894   November, *The Tragedy of Pudd'nhead Wilson and the Comedy Those Extraordinary Twins* published by the American Publishing Company.

1894   Winter in Paris.

1895   May, returned home, spent early summer at Quarry Farm.

1895   Mid-July, commenced the lecture trip which produced *Following the Equator.*

1896   May, *Personal Recollections of Joan of Arc* published by Harper.

1896   August 18, Susy, favorite child, died.

1896   November 17, *Tom Sawyer Abroad, Tom Sawyer, Detective, and Other Stories* published by Harper.

1896   Winter in London.

1897   March, *How to Tell a Story and Other Essays* published by Harper.

1897   November, *Following the Equator* published by the American Publishing Company.

1898   Last debts paid during the winter.

1900   May, *How to Tell a Story and Other Essays,* with new material added, published by the American Publishing Company.

1900   June, *The Man That Corrupted Hadleyburg and Other Stories and Essays* published by Harper.

1900   October, *English as She Is Taught* published by the Mutual Book Company of Boston.

1900   Autumn, returned to America, where he received a national welcome; took house at 14 West Tenth Street, New York.

1901   February, *To the Person Sitting in Darkness* published by the Anti-Imperialist League of New York.

1901   Summer on Saranac Lake; fall cruise to Nova Scotia on Henry Rogers' yacht.

1901   October 20, Yale conferred the Litt.D. degree on
          Clemens.

1902   April, *A Double Barrelled Detective Story* published
          by Harper.

1902   June, University of Missouri conferred LL.D. degree
          on Clemens.

1903   April, *My Debut as a Literary Person with Other
          Essays and Stories* published by the American Pub-
          lishing Company.

1903   October, Clemens family settled in Italy for Livy's
          health.

1904   April, *Extracts from Adam's Diary* published by Harper.

1904   June 5, Olivia Langdon Clemens died.

1904   September, *A Dog's Tale* published by Harper.

1905   September, *King Leopold's Soliloquy* published by the
          R.P. Warren Company of Boston.

1906   *Eve's Diary* and *The $30,000 Bequest and Other Stories*
          both published by Harper.

1907   February, *Christian Science* published by Harper.

1907   Oxford honored Clemens with the Litt.D. degree.

1907   October, *A Horse's Tale* published by Harper.

1909   April, *Is Shakespeare Dead?* published by Harper.

1909   *Extract from Captain Stormfield's Visit to Heaven*
          published by Harper.

1909   December 23, death of Jean.

1910   Mark Twain died April 21; buried at Elmira, New York.

1910   July, *Mark Twain's Speeches* published by Harper; a
          second edition issued in 1923.

1916   *The Mysterious Stranger* published by Harper.

1917   *What Is Man? and Other Essays* published by Harper.
          First published anonymously, August 20, 1906, at the
          De Vinne Press.

1917   *Mark Twain's Letters* published by Harper.

1919   *The Curious Republic of Gondour and Other Whimsical
          Sketches* published by Boni and Liveright.

1923   *Europe and Elsewhere* published by Harper.

the Later Years, and *Mark Twain's Letters to His Publishers, 1867-1894,* published by the University of California Press.

1969   *Clemens of the Call: Mark Twain in San Francisco, Mark Twain's Mysterious Stranger Manuscripts, Mark Twain's Correspondence with Henry Huttleston Rogers, 1893-1909,* and *Mark Twain's Hannibal, Huck and Tom* published by the University of California Press.

1972   *Mark Twain's Fables of Man* published by the University of California Press.

1973   *The Works of Mark Twain: What Is Man? and Other Philosophical Writings* published by the University of California Press.

1975-79 *Mark Twain's Notebooks and Journals,* volumes one through three, published by the University of California Press.

1979-81 *The Works of Mark Twain: Early Tales & Sketches,* volumes one and two, published by the University of California Press.

Chapter 1

THE GROWTH OF MARK TWAIN
BIOGRAPHY

Introduction

More than any other classic American writer, Mark Twain
assumes the proportions of a folk myth. He appeals to his
readers not only as an author but also as a personality, for
Samuel Clemens the man is often present in his books. Aside
from his fame as a novelist, Twain's position in letters rests
also upon works which are perhaps best described as fictionalized
biography. To his contemporaries, he was a personage—at his
death, known and honored throughout the world; yet with the
exception of a few discerning critics, Twain's age regarded him
primarily as a humorist and a striking personality. The affection given Mark Twain was even more to the man, popular and
beloved, than to a literary artist. Indeed, his writings
were so much a part of his life that it becomes difficult to
separate the two. So completely has Clemens been identified
with his work that it remains the fashion—as with Poe—to read
reflections of biography into his books. No other American
author seems to have left so complete (if perplexing) an account
of his own life, and some investigators have so often searched
for subtle or devious meanings where probably none exist that
the biography has sometimes suffered distortion.

At the same time that Samuel Clemens made the personality
of Mark Twain interesting to the world, he also represented
something distinctly American, for Twain was of the continental
United States, a product of the same region which produced
Abraham Lincoln. The first major writer to emerge west of the
Mississippi, he captured the American past, the idyll of the
small town before the machine age, and the enduring romance
of the great river. Besides, he was a born storyteller and a
successful entertainer, and with these qualities he endeared
himself to a vast, uncritical audience. As Clemens' position
in our literature continues to rise, it becomes increasingly
clear that Mark Twain possessed a profound knowledge of human

beings in many and varied phases of life. Samuel Clemens the
artist transmuted this into literature, and with an increasing
appreciation of his literary creations there has come an equal
interest in the mind of the man. Certain aspects of his life
present a "problem" to psychoanalytical biographers; and
critics, both friendly and unfriendly, have searched for the
secrets of his innermost thoughts. Thus arises the question:
was Mark Twain, in his own mind, afraid and a failure, or was
he courageous and secure, as adult as Melville or Hawthorne in
his realization of evil?

Samuel Clemens enjoyed the role assigned him by his own
generation; because he liked acting a part, he dramatized his
own life history by mingling actuality with fiction. Not the
way it was, but as it should have been, was generally the way
he told it; for Mark Twain, the creative artist, never let mere
fact interfere with the narrative. Consequently biographers,
although possessing a vast bulk of autobiographical material,
have faced the difficult task of disentangling fact from fancy.
Furthermore, with the paradox of Mark Twain the exuberant fun
maker, on one hand, in contrast to the utterer of bitter pessimism on the other, the critics have explored the details of
his intimate life for an explanation. In brief, Twain presents
the fascination of questions to be answered; and as a result,
criticism of his work has been invariably bound with a search
into biographical fact.

Mark Twain biography has grown, then, with our interest in
his work; and as his literary standing has risen, we have sought
explanations through a greater knowledge of his life. By a
process of simple accumulation of newly discovered facts, accurate knowledge of his backgrounds, and clearer insight into his
motives, the story unfolds more reliably. Mark Twain the legend,
the national figure, the great personality remains, but Mark
Twain the man as he was and the author of international scope
comes into focus. Whether Mark Twain stands at the apex of the
first cycle of our American literature, taking his place with
Whitman, Melville, and Hawthorne, or whether he marks the beginning of a new age in fiction, he remains a pivotal figure.
The change in attitude from that which dismissed Twain as a
"phunny phellow" to Dixon Wecter's solemn declaration that
Huckleberry Finn is "probably the greatest novel written in
this hemisphere" (*Mark Twain* 6) tells much of the growth of
modern literature and thought. What critics and biographers
have thought of Mark Twain, how their theories evolved, and
what they have concluded become interesting in evaluating the
actual facts of his life. Yet to sift the chaff of legend from
the grains of truth, we must first know why the different interpretations have arisen. Since each generation must solve
its specific problems, the writings of Samuel Langhorne Clemens

take on a new significance for the future, as they have increased our knowledge in the past. Whatever the trend in
scholarship, however, whether Mark Twain's value should appear
greatest as realist, satirist, or humanitarian, it was as a
humorist that he looked upon this life.

Beginnings of Biography

John Camden Hotten's account of Twain's life appeared in
1873. Prefixed to the *Choice Humorous Works of Mark Twain*, it
was republished in subsequent editions in London and helped to
introduce the American humorist to the British public. Hotten
quoted liberally from Twain's own account of his activities,
especially from *Roughing It*, to outline the career of a popular
humorist and successful entertainer. This bare sketch, padded
with anecdotes and with appreciations of Twain's humor taken
from current journals, is the first glimpse that the reading
public received of a life then seeming to hold no complexities.

The first separate biography of Samuel Clemens was *Mark
Twain: The Story of His Life and Work* (1892) by Will M. Clemens.
Despite three brief notes from Twain printed in the preface, he
neither liked the book nor approved of its author, especially
since many people mistook the man for a relative. For the
facts of Twain biography this story holds little value, but as
a source of materials that became part of the legend it is interesting. The American success story of the wild, reckless
boy who starts as a poor printer and becomes "a man of family
and a millionaire" unfolds (10).[1] Anecdotes are related, some
obviously fictitious, a few genuine. The figure created is
that of an entertainer who is also a serious thinker, and above
all practical in money matters. "He is a literary Midas" (194).
With a ready wit he extricates himself from embarrassing situations, entertains people for hours with his conversation, and
always enjoys a prank. Here are the legends and typical anecdotes such as have obscured Twain biography and made the facts
difficult to ascertain.

In 1898 Robert Barr contributed a brief, unimportant
character sketch to *McClure's Magazine* ("Character Sketch" 246-
51). The following year, however, *McClure's* published an excellent short biographical appraisal by Twain's nephew, Samuel E.
Moffett ("Biographical Sketch" 523-29).[2] Though written by a
relative, it is objective and not a family memoir. Twain himself liked this account of his life, which he considered accurate
and appropriate.

Testimony of Friends and Relatives

In September, 1910, William Dean Howells paid personal
tribute to his friend. Although not a complete biography, *My
Mark Twain* (1910) is an interesting record of intimate friendship between two leading literary figures. For its account
of Samuel Clemens during the final years, *My Mark Twain* remains an important book, the best of the writings produced by
his friends and associates. Howells does not minimize Twain's
eccentricities, but he is far more concerned with the fundamental values of the man. What some might term vanity, Howells
concedes to be love of the dramatic, a feeling for costume,
and a keen sense of pleasure in harmlessly shocking others.
"He had," says Howells, "the Southwestern, the Lincolnian,
the Elizabethan breadth of parlance, which I suppose one ought
not to call coarse without calling one's self prudish" (4).
There are intimate recollections; once Twain, wearing "white
cowskin slippers, with the hair out," did an imitation of a
"crippled colored uncle to the joy of all beholders." To
Howells it seemed that Twain possessed "the heart of a boy
with the head of a sage" (5).
    Often during walks, he and Mark Twain admired nature, talked
about books, and discussed their beliefs. Twain thought there
must be a conscious source of things, but "... he never went
back to anything like faith in the Christian theology, or the
notion of life after death, or in a conscious divinity" (32).
Howells records Mark Twain's views on racial equality, his
sympathy for the black race, and his desire to ameliorate
their condition; but Howells' statement that Mark had a black
butler "because he could not bear to order a white man about"
implies a distinct awareness of racial differences (34). The
same abhorrence that caused him to detest slavery made him
praise labor unions as the workingman's only hope of "standing
up like a man against money and the power of it" (43). From
these conversations, recalled by Howells, we gain a firsthand
knowledge of many private attitudes and deep convictions.
Memories of social visits reveal the lighter, though no less
intimate, nature of Clemens. In the parlor, at the dinner
table, or in the billiard room, many amusing or enlightening
incidents occurred, which Howells charmingly preserved.
    Not only is *My Mark Twain* a primary source book for the
later stages of Twain's life, but it is of interest as the
opinion of a contemporary who valued his work and presented a
critical appraisal that remains fresh. Here may be found the
answers to many of the so-called "problems" magnified by subsequent critics of Clemens' life and work.

As I Remember Them (1913), based on the days when Joe
Goodman, R.M. Daggett, Dan DeQuille, and Mark Twain were col-
leagues, preserves the personal recollections of a Virginia
City journalist, C.C. Goodwin. A frontier newspaper man who
became a judge, Goodwin vigorously recalled the fellowship and
excitement enjoyed by Twain on the Comstock when Western journalism first schooled him for a career. Interesting in its
portraits of Twain's associates--men from whom he learned
much--the book provides a vivid narrative of hearty times.
Not a biography of Clemens in any sense, *As I Remember Them*
preserves the associations and friendships contributing to
the development of Mark Twain--all told by one who knew them.

While vacationing in Bermuda, Elizabeth Wallace, a school-
teacher, met Mark Twain during his final years; she later
visited at Stormfield and corresponded with him. Her recollections in *Mark Twain and the Happy Island* (1913), reveal chiefly
the tender, considerate side of his nature. Wallace remembered
his attachment to children, particularly little girls, and his
entertaining conversations, occasionally enlivened by tirades
against the "general asininity of us all" (15). She recalled,
also, that Clemens nourished a "particularly tender spot in his
heart for all things English" (58). To her he was "the King,"
courteous, considerate, generous, and lovable, which the letters
included in this idyllic presentation seem to confirm.

Of Mark Twain's readers, none was more enthusiastic than
Brander Matthews, Columbia University English professor, literary historian, and critic. From the *Jumping Frog* in its original
edition, Matthews followed each succeeding volume, his conviction growing that Twain was a native humorist worthy to stand
beside the great figures of literature. This ardent interest,
stimulated by a personal meeting in 1883, matured into friendship. Matthews knew Twain's faults, and he has told them in
"Memories of Mark Twain" in *The Tocsin of Revolt* (1922). As a
member of the American Copyright League, Matthews found that
even a great humorist can sometimes take himself too seriously.
Other times he observed Mark's hair-trigger temper, which could
smolder steadily into hatred. But their friendship, despite a
few upsets, continued through years of banqueting, speeches,
and vacations filled with games--happy times when the author
acted like a boy.

These memories are interesting also because Twain confided
to Matthews how his books wrote themselves, stopping when the
tank of inspiration ran dry, and refusing to commence until it
filled again. Of equal interest is the account of Twain's
speeches, a few of which astonishingly failed because of an
unfortunate choice of subject. To Matthews, it seemed that
Samuel L. Clemens the man and Mark Twain the writer ever remained separate personalities, one the embodiment of ethical
integrity, the other the droll humorist.

A Lifetime with Mark Twain (1925) is the story of Katy
Leary, faithful and devoted servant for more than thirty
years in the Clemens household. Katy recalled the family before the fireplace after dinner, with Twain reading aloud from
Browning or Dickens; then about nine o'clock when the children
had gone to bed, the butler brought in "a pitcher of hot water
and a bottle of the best Scotch whiskey" for Twain, while Mrs.
Clemens took tea. "After they'd had the tea and the toddy,
they would set [sic] and talk and laugh--happy and contented;
and then they'd go to bed about ten o'clock, and that would
finish the day" (Lawton 9).

Through these intimate recollections we see the family
entertaining with dinner parties, play productions for the
children, or Mark Twain spinning stories. Henry Irving once
told Katy that Twain had "the makings of a very great actor in
him" (Lawton 36). Mrs. Clemens was beloved by her servant; if
Twain was ever "henpecked" by Livy, it escaped the eyes of Katy
Leary. Katy knew the Clemens family intimately through their
economic depression and their journeys abroad.

Unfortunately better known than Goodwin's book, *Gold Rush
Days with Mark Twain* (1930) is less reliable. And although at
publication the reviewers generally accepted it at face value,
the book actually is neither biography nor criticism. Originally published in pamphlet form as *Memories of Mark Twain and
Steve Gillis*, it is full of contradictions and inaccuracies,
for "Bill" Gillis as an old man remembered not only much that
never happened, but incorrectly nearly everything that did.[3]
It has no biographical value, and its only interest for the
reader of Mark Twain is that "Bill" Gillis was among those who
once had seen him.

Clara Clemens' *My Father, Mark Twain* (1931) is informal
biography, making no pretense at being a full-length study,
but it presents her father as his family knew him. It is an
important supplement to our biographical material, fresh, revealing, a picture of private life that could come from no
other source. Through the eyes of his daughter we see a more
intimate side of Twain's personality than was revealed by
Howells. Here is the private life of a father with his children, told by a daughter, who was often a close comrade. The
book, well illustrated from family photographs, makes available, also, a number of hitherto unpublished letters. Twain
appears first as the father of three little girls, whom he
always had time to entertain, and for whom he always showed
love and consideration. Like Howells, Clara Clemens remembers
his solicitation for anyone in distress. In fact, the general
picture of the home, while more intimate, is essentially the same
as that given by Howells. And the love story of Sam and Livy remains as Howells described it, and as Twain himself declared
it, from the time before his wedding when he wrote, "... I am

so happy I hardly know what to do with myself--and I bless you, and give honest gratitude to God that it is so" (13), until in remorse he referred to her as "she that was the life of my life" (253).

My Father, Mark Twain gives an account of Clemens' financial failure and his efforts to pay his debts that parallels the ones by Howells and Albert Bigelow Paine. The relationship of the author with his family, remembered by Clara Clemens, shows Twain delighting in his home and enjoying his friends. He exhibits a sensitive nature, upset by annoyances, frequently giving way to temper--essentially the same type of character that appeared to William Dean Howells.

The chief value of Clara Clemens' book is its picture of Mark Twain with his family, and the letters that are included intimately reveal Twain's devotion to Olivia. Though nothing more than a story of the Clemens home as it centered around Twain, this book is necessary to anyone seeking to deal with the problems created by Brooks and his followers.

Mark Twain, Business Man (1946) was written by Samuel Charles Webster as a vindication of his father Charles L. Webster, to whom Clemens seemed at times impossible in business dealings. More interesting to the student of Twain, however, is the information contributed about the Clemens family at the beginning of the Civil War. Webster gives the most complete portrait that we have of Mark Twain's mother, remembered at first hand by members of the family. Here, too, are letters more intimate than any published since Clara Clemens' book. Not only Jane Clemens, but Annie Moffett Webster, Pamela, Orion, and his wife, Mollie Stotts Clemens, receive their fullest treatment to that date. Webster traces the ancestry and background of Mark Twain's immediate family from its origins on both sides in Virginia through the migrations which ended in Hannibal.

Mark Twain, Business Man contains newly published letters from Twain in Nevada, some in a more gloomy mood than is generally associated with him at that period, because as Webster explains, the optimistic letters had already been published. Olivia Langdon later appears as her in-laws saw her. The Langdon family, so Mark's relatives recall, were not "conventional wealthy Victorians," but socially progressive with liberal ideas about relief for the indigent and racial problems (113). If there was anything about Olivia Langdon that the Clemens family disapproved of, there is no record of it here. Generous and broad-minded, she appears the wife Mark Twain thought her to be.

Though Webster's chief interest was the affairs of the publishing house, of which he has given us our fullest account, his main contributions concern family life; and his book corrects some of the previous statements made on that subject. He

reveals Twain's impulsive and difficult nature, recording how
Charles L. Webster even had to run personal errands for Twain
and his family. Webster corrects some statements by Paine and
the conclusions drawn from them by later writers.

Mark Twain, Business Man is a source book for the student
of Twain biography; there is material from memoirs and personal
letters of the Clemens family not available elsewhere. It is
by far the fullest picture of Twain's relatives, especially
Jane Clemens. The problems of the Civil War episode are made
clearer and the relationship between Twain and his business
associates, though generally unfavorable to Twain, is informative.

Mark Twain and I (1940) by Opie Read is a series of anecdotes of old-fashioned joke-book variety. Since Read knew
Clemens, some of the stories may be authentic, but one suspects
the touch of the storyteller in them all, and the book has no
biographical value.

Dorothy Quick's *Enchantment: A Little Girl's Friendship
with Mark Twain* (1961) is a story of Twain's special relationship to one of his Angel Fish who as a grown woman "tried to
write this book through the little girl's eyes" (219). The relationship began when Dorothy Quick, age eleven, met Mark
Twain, age seventy-two, aboard the S.S. *Minnetonka* in 1907.
It ended when Twain died in 1910, but Twain's influence did
not end. He encouraged Dorothy to become a writer, and she
did. A frequent guest at Twain's house, she brought youth and
a lively imagination to the relationship. Twain read to her,
told her stories, introduced her to famous people, and spent
as much time with her as he could. When he was on trips, they
corresponded. Dorothy writes, "It was fun going places with
Mark Twain and being made much of" (77). Affection between the
two was strong, and in her adult years Dorothy remembered Mark
Twain as a happy man. *Enchantment* is valuable because it is a
human interest story, a love story, and it pretends to be no
more than that.

Nearly everybody who knew Mark Twain has set down something
about him. Charles Warren Stoddard, one-time secretary, relates
his experiences on a lecture tour abroad with Mark in *Exits and
Entrances* (1903). Henry Watterson, good Kentuckian, recalls
pleasant times enlivened by bourbon in *"Marse Henry": An Autobiography* (1919). From the Western years, we have accounts by
friends like Dan DeQuille in "Reporting with Mark Twain"
(1893), and comments of Bret Harte. Hostile in tone were the
statements of Senator William M. Stewart, who in *Reminiscences
of Senator William M. Stewart of Nevada* (1908) related a number
of unpleasant incidents, objected strongly to his own characterization in *Roughing It*, and made accusations against Mark
which at this distance scarcely seem to hold water. In another

vein, S.J. Woolf described the celebrity who sat for his portrait in "Painting the Portrait of Mark Twain" (1910). And
the indefatigable seeker after reminiscences will find no lack
of contributors, but a wealth of material, most of it useful,
as for instance, the account by Professor William Lyon Phelps
in *Autobiography with Letters* (1939).

Authorized Biography

Albert Bigelow Paine's *Mark Twain: A Biography* (1912) contains too much information--whatever its faults--ever to be
entirely neglected. As secretary and companion during the
final years, authorized biographer, and Clemens' literary executor, Paine had the advantage of intimate association and first
access to extensive materials. Undertaking to tell everything,
he narrated the only full-length life yet written. No student
can afford to dispense with Paine, but one should have at hand
supplements and corrections from more scholarly--if at times
less entertaining--sources. Our chief quarrel with Paine
arises not alone from his Victorian manner of altering for propriety, but more for his acceptance of unreliable sources and
his failure at times to investigate primary materials. Yet he
erected a monumental biography to the man he honestly admired,
who always remained for him--as for other intimates--"the King."
In the preface to the twelfth edition of his book, in
1935, Paine defended himself against attack, chiefly from Bernard DeVoto. To the charge of inventing either incident or
dialogue, Paine replied that an abundance of both made such
methods unnecessary. Admitting the need for certain revisions
in his original edition, Paine explained the corrections, based
upon the investigations of the Rev. C.J. Armstrong of Hannibal.[4]
But these were his only emendations. How young Sam stood by
his father's coffin and made the promise so perturbing to the
imagination of Van Wyck Brooks, Paine defended, saying he took
the story from a record by Orion, who was present (1: xviii).[5]
And from inconclusive evidence a plea is even made for the
coonskin story and the "pocket mining incident." Paine, it
appears, never realized that he had ever failed in accuracy or
insight. For the writing of a life such favorable conditions
have rarely existed, and the book does entertain, since Paine
constructed a straightforward account, wherever possible per-
mitting Twain to speak for himself. Thus Twain, like David
Crockett before him, told stories that never happened. Tall
tales, of course, divert the general reader, but scholars have
inherited the problem of sifting the fictional passages from

the real biography. As more corrections are made, *Mark Twain:
A Biography* naturally diminishes as a source book.

Paine's desire to tell everything caused him to subordinate
Twain's literary career to the narrative of other activities.
The biographer, in brief, neither critic nor literary historian,
was unable to relate Twain's books to the tradition of native
American humor. He accepted anecdotes too readily, especially
for the California and Nevada periods, for which he principally
relied on the *Autobiography*. Finally, there is the Victorian
"window-dressing," the bowdlerization that put propriety above
virility. But despite the errors in Paine's book, most of it
is true to the character and personality of Mark Twain.

Autobiography, Notebooks, Letters, and Speeches

The *Autobiography* (1924) was dictated at intervals over a
period of years; Twain, who intended it should not be published
for a century, tried to be utterly frank and unconventional.[6]
The latter quality, however, appears chiefly in the unorthodox
manner of composition. As Twain dictated he chose whatever
subject happened momentarily to strike his fancy, regardless
of chronology or unity. Such method allows a wide variety of
subjects and furnishes entertaining table talk, anecdotes, and
reminiscences, but it does not produce a life story, artistically constructed. When Twain talks about his uncle's farm,
his boyhood, and his early surroundings, he forms graphic
descriptions, heightened by sense perceptions as fine as Spen-
ser's. These vivid memories of past experiences give the *Autobiography* its touches of poetic quality, but as a tour de force
it is unsustained. With the stipulation to hold publication
until long after his death, Twain declared that he was writing
from the grave (1: xv-xvi).[7] The two volumes selected for publication in 1925 by Albert Bigelow Paine reveal the rambling
method of composition, but show, too, the vitality of a mind
occupied with a variety of interests.

Though Twain fully intended to write the true story of
his inner life, actually it was not his nature to do so; for
the actor in him crowded the diarist from the stage. In the
passages about Livy and Susy, he came closest to self-revela-
tion. But Twain's version of the publication of General Grant's
memoirs, the fiasco of the typesetting machine, and his travels
on the lecture platform are not unadorned narrative; Twain remembered he was entertaining an audience. What actually gives
the book its place among important autobiographies is the
charm and insight with which Twain recounts the story of young

Sam Clemens: first the little boy, then the youth, and finally
the young man from Hannibal emerging as the literary artist.
In these passages, the *Autobiography* has poetic perception,
humor, and vivid descriptions, such rare stuff as Twain's best
fiction is made of.

Bernard DeVoto edited *Mark Twain in Eruption* (1940) to
rectify the omissions of Albert Bigelow Paine. From the unpublished papers of the Clemens literary estate, to which he
had succeeded Paine as executor, DeVoto selected anecdotes,
opinions, and reminiscences, most of them too personal for
previous publication, some too virulent. Like the *Autobiography*, this sequel is a rambling discourse upon people Twain
knew, events which caught his interest, and occasionally himself. For the sake of unity, DeVoto selected what he considered
relevant as well as what he considered interesting. Only slight
changes in grammar and punctuation were necessary, and here and
there the breaking up of an interminable sentence.

The attack upon Theodore Roosevelt, begun in the *Autobiography*, continues here more strongly, showing greater apprehen-
sion for the future of the nation. To Twain, there was little
good in the popular Teddy, whose elevation to the presidency
foreboded the end of the Republic and the inevitability of
"monarchy"--the only autocratic or dictatorial form of government Twain knew, hence his stock term for all absolute rule.
One section concerns Andrew Carnegie, whose conceit Twain
heartily disliked; and Carnegie's fellow plutocrats with their
hired politicians frequently receive the cutting lash of Twain's
wrathful tongue (105-06).

In a nostalgic mood, "Hannibal Days" recalls similar *Autobiography* passages as Twain depicts his school days, the old-
time minstrel show, and tells of an amusing experience with a
mesmerist that is worthy of Tom Sawyer. The antics of Jim
Wolfe, once plagued with cats, are here continued in two anecdotes of that extremely bashful boy, this time afflicted with
wasps (136-42). Twain's comments on the writing of his own
books and his experiences with publishers, some of whom he
thought dishonest, add little to the record. But in telling
of his own unfortunate business failures, Twain unburdens himself.

Mark Twain in Eruption contains scathing comments on his
contemporaries, wisely withheld by Paine, but printable today.
Of Bret Harte, Twain said, "He hadn't a sincere fiber in him.
I think he was incapable of emotion, for I think he had nothing
to feel with" (265). Mrs. Thomas Bailey Aldrich is dismissed
with: "I do not believe I could ever learn to like her except
on a raft at sea with no other provisions in sight" (293). Her
husband fared better, though Twain disliked his vanity, as he
did that of Edmund Clarence Stedman, who "... believed that the

sun merely rose to admire his poetry ..." (294). Others,
especially Bayard Taylor and Rudyard Kipling, Twain liked.

Various facets of Twain's thinking appear: he praises Grover
Cleveland, denounces Anglo-Saxon imperialism, recalls the admirable, narrative art of Jim Gillis in Jackass Gulch, and delights over his pastor's predicament with a profane hostler.
Finally, Twain returns to his customary indictment of the
human race in general, and restates his philosophy of inevitable
events, linked to a primal cause.

Charles Neider has edited an abbreviated *Autobiography of
Mark Twain* (1959), arranged in chronological order, which may
please the general reader; however, the serious student will
still be forced to consult the earlier autobiographical publications by Paine and DeVoto.

When A.B. Paine edited *Mark Twain's Notebook* (1935), he
left the impression that it was intimate autobiography with
nothing modified, nothing changed. "The entries," announced
Paine, "whatever their interest, or lack of it--are as he left
them, and they bring us about as near as we shall ever get to
this remarkable man, easily the most remarkable of his time"
(xi). Paine is probably right in saying that Twain was never
deliberately salacious or indecent, only occasionally frank
and rough. The excerpts Paine published are random jottings
about whatever Mark found momentarily of interest. Twain talked
to himself--freeing his mind by "blowing off steam" in his note-
book--and many subjects are denounced more strongly in private
than in print. Yet Paine has kept the safety valve in place;
and although here and there some steam escapes, the full blast
remains to be published.[8] Twain never did keep a consistent or
orderly diary, for he claimed that he was discouraged by a
youthful attempt which ended daily: "Got up, washed, went to
bed" (1). His journal is neither formal nor regular, because
Twain was always jotting down sudden thoughts and occasional
feelings. Beginning with some very brief notes on the Mississippi River, written when Clemens was learning piloting, Paine
next prints a few entries made by Twain in the West.

During his trip to the Sandwich Islands Twain began making
humorous maxims: "Never refuse to do a kindness unless the act
would work great injury to yourself, and never refuse to take
a drink--under any circumstances" (12). Once in Honolulu,
Twain is delighted with the islands, but notes: "More missionaries and more row made about saving these 60000 [*sic*] people
than would take to convert hell itself" (21). On his way back to
San Francisco and during the subsequent voyage to New York,
Captain Ned Wakeman began taking shape in his mind as literary
material. And comments appear characteristic of the later
Twain.

During his travels Twain pauses with notebook to free his mind. Creative ideas appear sporadically. Notes made in 1883 suggest possible plots: "Write the Second Advent, with full details--lots of Irish disciples--Paddy Ryan for Judas and other disciples. Star in the East. People want to know how wise men could see it move while sober. John interviewed" (167). While writing the *Connecticut Yankee*, Twain filled his diary with invectives against monarchy and established church, equaled only by his privately expressed contempt for Paige of the typesetting machine. Then across the continent, through Europe, and over India, the journal moves toward the final years.

Mark Twain: Life As I Find It (1961), edited by Charles Neider, is a collection of tales, essays, and sketches not easily available, and although interesting the material is not of real import. However, *Mark Twain's Notebooks and Journals*, published thus far in three volumes, is an effort to present the entries in Twain's notebooks and journals in the order in which they were written. Volume one, published in 1975 and edited by Frederick Anderson, Michael B. Frank, and Kenneth M. Sanderson, covers the years 1855-1873. Also published in 1975, volume two, covering the years 1877-1883, was edited by Frederick Anderson, Lin Salamo, and Bernard L. Stein. Published in 1973 and covering the years 1883-1891, volume three was edited by Robert Pack Browning, Michael B. Frank, and Lin Salamo.

In *Mark Twain's Notebook* (1935), marking the centenary of Twain's birth, Albert Bigelow Paine published less than a fourth of Mark's journal entries; and in his prefatory remarks in volume one of *Mark Twain's Notebooks and Journals* (1975) Frederick Anderson writes, "Now, on the occasion of the full publication of the complex documents from which Paine drew his earlier version, it seems appropriate to evaluate Paine's editorial labors against current standards of textual scholarship" (vii). The evaluation shows, among other things, that Paine misrepresented the scope of his collection. Forty-five of the forty-nine notebooks known to exist are in the Mark Twain Papers, and as for the value of *Mark Twain's Notebooks and Journals*, the introduction to the first volume probably states it best: "The erratic nature of the notebooks, with their diverse and often almost compulsive record of minute matters, allows us access far closer than more formal documents to the movements of a man's mind at a distant time" (1: 10).

Mark Twain was a good talker. Sought as an after-dinner speaker, welcomed around the world as a lecturer, he made all kinds of addresses on innumerable occasions. In 1910 Mark Twain's selected speeches were published with an introduction by William Dean Howells; later Albert Bigelow Paine added to

and rearranged them. This second collection, *Mark Twain's
Speeches* (1923), is separated into three periods, the first
beginning with San Francisco covers his early career; the second
the middle years; and the final period presents the national
figure, sought for advice and applauded for his humor. Mark
Twain's speechmaking career remains to be told, but investigators are steadily adding speeches to those already collected.
Once, at least, in the Whittier birthday dinner speech, an
interesting fiasco occurred. Yet even then, Howells, who was
present, later wrote: "I never heard Clemens speak when I
thought he had quite failed" (ix). Those fortunate enough actually to hear Mark Twain declare that his printed speeches
can never produce the same effect. A great actor, Twain held
his audience through dramatic art and personal magnetism.
Something of that colorful personality shows in the speeches;
otherwise they add little to biographical interpretation.

Of more recent vintage, and consisting partially of speeches,
Mark Twain Speaks for Himself (1978), edited by Paul Fatout,
ranges from 1862 to 1909. In these newspaper accounts, letters, speeches, and interviews Clemens expresses himself on a
variety of subjects. Here we follow Twain from California to
his success in the East. While the topics are generally those
of the moment, Twain's reactions are interesting.

Albert Bigelow Paine's edition of *Mark Twain's Letters*
(1917), like all his work on Twain, is carefully selected and
bowdlerized. But it is a necessary addition, being--as Paine
regarded it--a supplement to the personal side of Mark Twain.
Unaware of other writing existing from Clemens' youth, Paine
began his collection with the fragment of a letter, from when
Sam was seventeen (1: 21-22). The letters continued in chronological order until a few days before Twain's death. Whenever
it seemed necessary, Paine added a word of explanation. The
early letters show the Pepysian art that enabled Mark to pre-
serve such bits of social history as the customs on the Philadelphia "bus" (1: 28). His concern over the well-being of his
relatives appears early, too, and we find him taking his mother
on a visit to New Orleans.

Paine omits the Civil War period to take Sam directly out
West from the Mississippi River. Desire for sudden wealth
made young Clemens first a miner; then as frontier journalist,
he describes his associates, literary and otherwise (1: 94-96).[9]
These letters further reveal Clemens' ability to portray people
and depict places; as biography they document his whereabouts,
activities, and friends.

As Twain progressed in the literary world, the letters tell
of his friendship for Howells, whom he selected as mentor.
Correspondence with Howells, Twichell, and Aldrich increased,
while he wrote to other authors on both sides of the Atlantic.

To Andrew Lang, Twain confided that he had never sought to
"help cultivate the cultivated classes," but had always
written for the "masses," not to instruct but always to entertain them (2: 527). The letters literally circle the earth,
for the Clemens family was on the move as Twain's fortunes
varied, with a return to the lecture platform the only ready
solution. Happiness and success, sorrow and disaster, follow
each other, but they are not here so intimately revealed as in
later sources. Paine intended *Mark Twain's Letters* as a supplement to his biography, and so they remain.

A letter from Clemens to Mary Hallock Foote in 1887 was
published in facsimile by Benjamin DeCasseres as *When Huck
Finn Went Highbrow* (1934). For forty-two weeks Twain read the
poetry of Robert Browning to a Browning class composed of
women, and in addition to revealing Twain's enthusiasm for
Browning, DeCasseres records a pleasant memory of seeing Clemens
in 1908 leading a group of delighted youngsters into a children's matinee at the Empire Theatre to see Maude Adams in
Peter Pan.

Mark Twain's Letter to Will Bowen (1938), written from
Buffalo, February 6, 1870, addresses his old friend from Hannibal in a nostalgic mood. Twain remembered schoolday incidents,
some about people and places later utilized in *Tom Sawyer*.
Like a happy boy, Clemens confided his good fortune in his
new home and recent bride, saying, "She is the very most perfect gem of womankind that ever I saw in my life--& I will
stand by that remark till I die" (10). This letter was reprinted in *Mark Twain's Letters to Will Bowen* (1941), a collection of sixteen letters to "My First, & Oldest & Dearest
Friend," written intermittently from 1866 to 1900.[10] A member
of Tom Sawyer's gang, Will Bowen was one of three boys whose
combined characteristics furnished Twain the material for Tom
himself (3).[11] The origin of *The Adventures of Tom Sawyer*
appears first in these letters (16-21).[12] They reveal, also,
the friendship of Sam Clemens for a boyhood chum, from whom he
was not separated, despite distance, time, or circumstance.
Twain fondly reminisced over school days, boyhood pranks, and
old places, yet in a subsequent letter bluntly stated his
aversion for maudlin sentiment over the past, disparaging the
sentimental as unworthy of a man.

An interesting volume of Clemens' correspondence, *Mark
Twain to Mrs. Fairbanks* (1949), edited by Dixon Wecter, shows
young Sam Clemens seeking advice from Mary Mason Fairbanks,
discussing his literary ambitions, and confiding details of
his none-too-easy courtship of Livy. These letters tell much
of Samuel Clemens' change from the wild humorist, out of the
West, into the author, settled with his family in Hartford in
1871. Since Mrs. Fairbanks, who served as mentor during the

Quaker City excursion, remained a valued friend until the end,
they are an important biographical link. Dixon Wecter identi-
fies a number of the "Innocents," who are named for us (xiii-
xiv, xvii-xviii, 84). Biographical errors, also, are correc-
ted; for instance in the chronology of Clemens' courtship of
Livy (36). Wecter also cites Twain's awareness of social
abuses, as in Mark's "Open Letter to Commodore Vanderbilt,"
where that old millionaire is advised to "go and surprise the
whole country by doing something right" (81). There is more
about the financial aid and sound business guidance given
Clemens by Jervis Langdon, and it was he (so we learn) who
suggested Buffalo rather than Cleveland as the place to start
in journalism, while he concretely backed Twain with $25,000,
half of it advanced in cash (102). There is also more Twain
humor, of course: when the coachman, Patrick McAleer, came
dressed in a more expensive coat than his own, Twain wrote,
"It did not seem to me that a man's coachman ought to wear a
finer coat than himself, & so, under way, I swapped coats with
Patrick and--" (124).

Twain's pessimism, early in evidence, is expressed on the
death of a Mr. Benedict, revealing that the death of his own
little son, five years before, was still a source of grief.
Finally there is the unfortunate story of Mark's complete
separation from his old friend, Dan Slote, with whom he fell
out over a business deal (247).

The Love Letters of Mark Twain (1949), also edited by
Dixon Wecter, is one of the most revealing biographical items
to appear since the Paine biography. Here is the intimate
record of a noble love story, a perfect marriage equaled only
by the life of Robert and Elizabeth Browning. *The Love Letters
of Mark Twain* proves useful, too, in setting the biographical
facts straight. Mark's first "date" with Livy is here verified
as January 2 or 3, 1868 (6). The character of the Langdon
household--actually somewhere between the "stagnant fresh-water
aristocracy" of Van Wyck Brooks and the "progressive, even
iconoclastic" society of Max Eastman--seems distinctly liberal
in some of its social sympathies, yet at the same time "pious-
provincial" in certain standards of daily life (8).

This book permits a more penetrating insight into Mark
Twain's personal sorrows than was previously available. Susy's
illness and Jean's epilepsy were of course known, but never so
clearly; *The Love Letters of Mark Twain* is important for emphasis as well as for new materials. Above all, these letters
present the love story of Samuel Clemens and Olivia Langdon,
ideally based upon mutual devotion and enduring in complete
physical and spiritual compatibility. Furthermore, these
letters should help to destroy the myth of the feminine tyrant
invented by Van Wyck Brooks--if anything is left of that

mythical creation, following the refutations of DeVoto, Wagenknecht, and Ferguson.

The last letter in the two volumes of the *Mark Twain-
Howells Letters* (1960), edited by Henry Nash Smith and William
M. Gibson, is numbered 672, but almost half the letters were
previously published in *Life in Letters of William Dean
Howells* (1: xix). The letters in the present collection are
remarkable in a number of respects, not the least of which is
that they record forty years of friendship between two great
American writers. The letters are replete with expressions
of mutual sympathy, empathy, admiration, and love. The two
writers did not always agree, as evidenced by their differences
over the Cleveland-Blaine campaign for the presidency, but the
letters would have it that they were always friends. Clemens
was essential to Howells, coaching him in the art of platform
reading, and Howells was essential to Clemens as editor and
advisor, curbing the excesses of a funny man often given to
invective and slapstick.

The Howells and Clemens families constitute a major theme
throughout the letters. One cannot help but be impressed by
the frequent expressions of love and concern for spouses and
children, and particularly in those instances motivated by
family illness and death. The reader is also impressed by
Clemens' obsession with gadgetry and his dream of acquiring
immense wealth. Besides writing, publishing, and copyrighting,
other interests shared by the two writers were humor, drama,
travel, lecturing, religion, and international affairs. More
than anything else the two volumes of *Mark Twain-Howells Letters* constitute a record of how Twain and Howells complemented
each other.

When Lewis Leary edited and documented *Mark Twain's Letters to Mary* (1961), he filled in the background with newspaper
accounts. The volume contains letters from Twain to Mary
Rogers, daughter-in-law of the Standard Oil executive Henry
Rogers, Clemens' friend and benefactor. The material is interesting because it is so arranged as to form a narrative of
the last ten years of Twain's life. Of even more interest,
however, is the material in *Susy and Mark Twain: Family Dialogues* (1965), edited by Edith Salsbury from letters, manuscripts, and journals, because it gives the reader an intimate
story of the Clemens family. Through dialogues twenty-five
happy years appear, ending with the devastating impact of
Susy's tragic death, which deepened Twain's pessimism.

Mark Twain's Letters to His Publishers, 1867-1894 (1967),
contains texts of 290 letters, of which the texts of twenty-
three are reprinted from *Mark Twain, Business Man*, and five
from *Mark Twain's Letters*. The quarter of a century covered
by the letters, 1867-1894, was the most productive time in

Mark Twain's career, and the letters are generously supplemented by editor Hamlin Hill with information taken from notebooks and documents of various kinds. Between 1867 and 1894 Twain had five major publishers, and they all came into his disfavor at one time or another. One learns much from these letters about Twain's commitment to the American Publishing Company, subscription publishing, and what Hill calls "the world of high if slightly soiled finance" (69). One learns much about Twain's "thirst for investment, business, wild gambles and wilder schemes" (70). Perhaps of most importance, however, is that in these letters one sees Mark Twain revealing a part of his life "that was essential both to his view of himself and to any reader's comprehension of his complex personality" (8).

As part of an effort by the University of California Press to publish a uniform edition of the Mark Twain Papers, *Mark Twain's Correspondence with Henry Huttleston Rogers, 1893-1909* (1969), edited and with an introduction by Lewis Leary, is valuable in documenting significant events in Twain's personal and business life. Consisting of 464 annotated letters, the volume, contends Leary, should be viewed as "a continuation of *Mark Twain's Letters to His Publishers, 1867-1894*, edited by Hamlin Hill" (v). It continues the story of Twain's business transactions from the time he met Rogers in the autumn of 1893 until the death of Rogers in May of 1909. It also contains the story of a friendship of equal duration. The Standard Oil executive and the writer complemented each other, and the present volume contains a record of their symbiotic relationship.

Formal Biography

Although Archibald Henderson knew Mark Twain, his contribution to biographical material is not a personal memoir or reminiscence, but more an attempt to summarize the man and his work. *Mark Twain* (1911), by Archibald Henderson, begins the formal biography of Clemens. Henderson attempted a biographical appraisal and critical interpretation, which it has been the fashion to dismiss as curiously devoted to the thesis that Mark Twain was a Southern gentleman. Obviously, Henderson does emphasize the Southern influence, but it is also true that many students of Twain have forgotten that he came from Kentucky and Virginia ancestry.

Henderson's critical appraisals are, nevertheless, sometimes penetrating. Convinced that "Mark Twain was a great

American who comprehensively incorporated and realized his
own country and his own age as no American has so completely
done before him," Henderson called him, "a philosopher and
sociologist who intuitively understood the secret springs of
human motive and impulse ..." (xi). It is to Mark Twain the
world author--not the native American humorist--that this
professor paid his respects. In separate chapters, Henderson
treated the man, the humorist, the world-famed genius, and
the philosopher-moralist-sociologist. Although not a full-
length biography, or a complete critical analysis, this book
does point in the direction taken by such later scholars as
Ferguson and Wagenknecht.

   Mark Twain, Son of Missouri (1934) by Minnie M. Brashear
is an important work on Mark Twain's boyhood and the influences that went into his development until he became a pilot.
A specialized study, it added factual information about
Clemens' youth and his earliest writings. The description
of Hannibal, its citizens and environment, is the fullest
prior to Dixon Wecter's *Sam Clemens of Hannibal*. Brashear
emphasizes, too, the influence exerted on little Sam by Uncle
John Quarles and his farm. Pointing out that Clemens grew up
in a democratic western atmosphere, which prevented his being
entirely a Southerner, she states, nevertheless, that the
Southern tradition, which was present, affected his temperament and personality.

   The epic quality which appears in Twain's writings Brashear
believes to derive in part from his early environment when the
frontier was pushing onward to California. Clemens drew sources
from original elements because "He knew both what was good and
what was bad in a western town of heroic aspiration ..." (75),
for which he became the spokesman.

   Brashear has added new facts to our knowledge of Twain's
early writing. She discloses that the editorial controversy
involving young Sam was not caused by poking fun at a rival
editor for being jilted in love (as generally supposed) but
resulted instead from an editorial about mad dogs. Brashear
utilizes Hannibal papers, published from 1839 to 1853, to
divide the Hannibal *Journal* writings which can be assigned
with certainty to Twain into four groups.

   Brashear studied the formative elements in Sam Clemens'
early life, especially the first twenty-five years, and
through a careful and complete investigation into the Hannibal
of that day gave us a new interpretation of its general culture. Especially valuable is the chapter "The Shadow of
Europe"; equally important is "Sam Clemens' Reading," which es-
tablishes that he had access to Shakespeare, Milton, Cervantes,
Goldsmith, and the Bible. By destroying unreliable concepts
of Twain's early environment Brashear directed attention to a

neglected aspect of Twain scholarship, one later to be treated
even more fully by Dixon Wecter.

The best general, comprehensive evaluation of Mark Twain
appearing up to the centenary of his birth is Edward Wagenknecht's *Mark Twain: The Man and His Work* (1935); this volume
sums up succinctly all that was then known. Wagenknecht did
not attempt to write a detailed biography, his purpose being
an appraisal through careful examination of all the evidence.
The book appeared too early in 1935 to make use of the *Notebook* edited by Paine or the revised edition of Merle Johnson's
Bibliography, but these would not have altered any conclusions.
To Wagenknecht, "Mark Twain was an actor who appeared beneath
the proscenium arch of the heavens in many different roles"
(3). Appearing as Tom Sawyer, he preserved through memory the
idyll of his youth, as Colonel Sellers he experienced many
dreams and hopes, as the Connecticut Yankee he spoke his Americanism with humor and with satire, and as Joan of Arc he cham-
pioned chivalry and idealism. Wagenknecht clearly shows that
while Mark Twain was a realist on the one hand, he was, also,
equally the idealist on the other.

Wagenknecht sketches the outlines of Mark Twain's youth
and early manhood; when the facts are inadequate or missing,
he makes no pretense, but admits it. He emphasizes the importance of the wide variety of experiences in Twain's life, and
explains that Twain was unusually close to his materials, so
much so that his life and his work may be one (5). From boyhood came the descriptions later found in the poetic passages
of his works, of which Wagenknecht says, "Not even 'The Eve
of St. Agnes' is richer in sense-impressions than those descriptions" (7). From the findings of Brashear and the Reverend
C.J. Armstrong, Wagenknecht gives a brief but accurate description of Hannibal and the Clemens family. He rejects the theory
that Clemens was happiest as a pilot, pointing out that he did
not return to the river when he had the opportunity, and he
quotes from Twain himself to bolster his position (11).

Twain's development as a man of letters is traced from the
newspaper offices of the West to the "world of eastern respect-
ability." We see the home, built in Hartford in 1874, where
he lived with his family for "seventeen happy years," and
Quarry Farm near Elmira, where during the summer "much of Mark
Twain's best writing was done" (14).

Wagenknecht, however, agrees with Brooks that Mark Twain
sought to attract attention as a character, rather than as an
artist--that "... he did not take himself very seriously as a
man of letters" (17). But his interpretations differ from
those of Brooks, though he does agree that Clemens, reacting
as he did to the world, lived inwardly rather than outwardly.
In spite of Clemens' reading, Wagenknecht claims that "Mark

Twain pays comparatively little attention to the recognized
classics, to the giants of letters" (34). It is from the
literature of the frontier that he developed, for the "frontier
itself existed as literature," and Twain appears here as the
inheritor and the fulfillment of this tradition, not as the
creator of something new. Indeed, the frontier is credited
with setting Mark apart from other literary men of his day,
such as Howells and James. His imagination was stimulated
by the forest and the river; through the black slaves he felt
the imagination of a primitive race, absorbing a distinct
folklore element into his nature. "Yet he never copies blind-
ly," says Wagenknecht; "... whatever he used was transformed,
recharactered, transmuted into art" (53).

Wagenknecht attributes the pessimism of Twain's last years
to his tenderness, his idealism, his hopes and dreams for the
human race, which led him to expect mankind to be less cruel,
mean, and degraded than it actually was. During his boyhood
in Hannibal, Sam Clemens encountered horrible incidents, he
saw all shades of life on the river boats, he observed the
human animal in the mining camps; and what he knew of the
more civilized aspects of life did not alter his convictions
that while there are noble human individuals the race as a
whole is despicable. Wagenknecht states it:

> The griefs and sorrows of Mark Twain's personal life
> pass over then, as by a natural transition, into his
> sympathy for humanity, impelling him powerfully in the
> direction of pessimism as he contemplates the wrongs
> that humanity has to bear. (229).

Mark Twain emerges from this volume a generous, kind man,
intelligent but undisciplined. An artist with poetic qualities,
Twain appears something of a seer, skeptical of the future from
his observation of the present and his study of the past,
finally more sad than hopeful. Revised and updated in 1961
and again in 1967, this sound evaluation of both the man and
his work has not been entirely superseded by any subsequent
volume.

Mark Twain's Western Years (1938) by Ivan Benson is the
standard work on that period of Clemens' biography. Benson
has examined material previously unavailable, including a
number of writings not reprinted, and his study shows the important influence of Samuel Clemens' life in Nevada and California upon his literary career. On the *Enterprise* Clemens
first took up writing as a sole means of support; it was then
that he adopted his later-famed pseudonym; and there, too,
he first began to address more than just a local audience.
From Nevada Sam Clemens, writing as Mark Twain, developed into
a personality, and through the medium of the newspapers gave

vent to his natural inclinations to amuse, shock, and satirize.
Clemens had written humorous sketches like the Snodgrass correspondence, and travel letters for the Muscatine *Journal*, and
he had engaged in editorial controversy and personal satire--
all before leaving for Nevada. But in the West he abandoned
entirely the misspellings and conventionalities of his earlier
pieces.

Benson traces Mark's career as a silver miner, motivated
by the same desire to strike it rich that actuated the others.
Pseudoscientific conjectures and interpretations receive no sympathy in this book, which presents Sam Clemens as a normal
young man, enjoying the freedom of the West, and the excitement of possible wealth. The duality of roughness and tenderness, noted by other Twain biographers, appears. As a reporter
on the *Territorial Enterprise* of Virginia City, Twain was influenced by his associates: Joe Goodman, editor of the paper,
"whose kindly guidance, skillful tutorship, and understanding
friendship followed Mark Twain beyond the Comstock into later
years" (68); William Wright (Dan DeQuille), Sam's boon companion, who then showed greater promise than Clemens; Rollin M.
Daggett, a courageous man, never hesitating to express honest
convictions in print; Steve Gillis, "king jokester of a tribe
of Comstock joking giants," who was a printer on the paper;
and Denis McCarthy, part owner of the *Enterprise*, later to be
Mark Twain's business manager on the 1866 lecture tour.

After successively trying his hand as printer, pilot, and
miner, explains Benson, Sam Clemens finally in the West settled upon writing as a career. The West, alone, allowed him
the free expression to develop the personality since associated
with his pen name throughout the world. Benson has carefully
examined the facts of Samuel Clemens' adoption of "Mark Twain"
as a pseudonym with the conclusion that the story remembered
by Mark actually never happened (81). *Mark Twain's Western
Years* shows how Clemens' associates in Virginia City aided
him to become a journalist; there, too, Artemus Ward advised
him to get his writings printed in the East if possible.

Showing Twain's development into a professional writer,
Benson invalidates several stories printed by Paine, such as
the Comstock duel (112), for example. This volume includes a
valuable bibliography of Mark Twain's writings in the newspapers
and magazines of Nevada and California, from 1861 through 1866,
and a number of early items are reprinted in the appendix.

Although Franklin Walker's *San Francisco's Literary Frontier* (1939) is a history of the literature produced in San
Francisco and its vicinity from the Gold Rush of 1849 to the
opening of the railroad in 1869, the pattern of the book is
biographical. Walker traces Twain's career as a pilot, the
military experience, which resulted in his coming West, Twain's

journalistic career in Washoe, his mining experience, and finally the story of his San Francisco days. Not only do Artemus Ward, Bret Harte, and Twain's newspaper cronies appear, but also Adah Menken in *Mazeppa*, the literary Bohemians, and much that went with them. Walker, moreover, reveals the taste of Twain's audience through a discussion of the San Francisco publications. A significant "moralistic strain" now emerged in Twain's features written for the *Territorial Enterprise* and sent as daily letters from San Francisco (196). Mark Twain became a satirist and a reformer.

Though succumbing to a fad for spiritualism, Twain managed to escape a literary rage, designated by Walker as "A Rash of Poetry." Twain was genuinely popular; he was one of the boys. When he finally left California for his Old World excursion, it was as the "Wild Humorist of the Pacific Slope," who reported on Europe for the readers of the *Alta California*, affirming their convictions and sharing their irreverence. As an exposition of Twain's literary progress, *San Francisco's Literary Frontier* is a valuable chapter in the story of Mark Twain's Western years.

In no sense a scholarly contribution, Cyril Clemens' anecdotal narrative, *Young Sam Clemens* (1942), is an unpretentious study of the years until 1866. Because the author visited places where Twain once lived and where people who knew young Sam Clemens were happy to remember him, the story is fresh and often amusing. But instead of biography, the book perpetuates legend.

DeLancey Ferguson's *Mark Twain: Man and Legend* (1943) is a sane and scholarly treatment of all that was then known or conjectured about Mark Twain as a man and writer; it is the best book in its field. In the eight years following the publication of Wagenknecht's book much was added to the Twain canon, which Ferguson has evaluated and augmented through his own research. The only fault of this volume for the student is that it omits footnotes. Though designed for the general reader, Ferguson's work is so sound in a scholarly sense and his conclusions so sane that we must regret the loss of adequate annotation. The chief original contribution is a description of the manuscript of *Huckleberry Finn*, which the author has examined carefully (217-30). But the book's greatest value is that DeLancey Ferguson has carefully read Mark Twain's writings and all the research produced upon them; he has minutely studied the problems of Twain biography to make a judicious presentation. Passing lightly over Mark's nonliterary activities, Ferguson treats him principally as a man of letters, telling how Twain wrote his books and why he wrote them as he did. Ferguson prefers to deal with facts instead of theories; thus the problems of influences on Sam Clemens from his boyhood,

the effect of the West on his literary style, whether or not
Livy and Howells exerted a good influence on his art, the final
pessimism--all are carefully considered. For the first time
since 1935 Twain is again in the hands of a critic competent
to evaluate his writings against the background of English and
American literature to which they belong.

Although *The Big Bonanza* was first issued in the fall of
1876, its reappearance with an informative introduction by
Oscar Lewis (1947) makes available a storehouse of information
on the country that turned Sam Clemens into Mark Twain. Mark's
associate on the Virginia City *Territorial Enterprise*, his
roommate and intimate friend, Dan DeQuille (whose true name
was William Wright), knew Nevada. In *The Big Bonanza*, written
years later with Twain's encouragement, Dan retold the anecdotes and reminiscences of the discovery and history of the
Comstock Lode. Here are the delightful stories of "Old Virginia," "Pancake" Comstock, and his wife who wouldn't stay
bought, the polite Frenchman who escaped roasting, and a host
of other characters and their escapades. Unlike the writing
which he and Twain did in their youth, *The Big Bonanza* distinguishes between imagination and fact. With all of the
humor and burlesque, there is the actual history of the Lode
and how it was worked. Although the book sold well only in
the West, its worth has long since been recognized by historians for its fresh and vivid atmosphere of the fabulous
mines. Published for the first time in the introduction are
several letters by Mark Twain, chiefly of interest in showing
his loyalty to old pals from Washoe. Though not Twain biography
this is a book rich in background materials of Twain's life in
Nevada.

A very specialized study of the same period, Effie Mona
Mack's *Mark Twain in Nevada* (1947) is a full account of Mark's
three years there, which emphasizes the conclusions already
formed by Ivan Benson. Mack adds the social background to
Roughing It in minute details. Her study shows that *Roughing
It* faithfully presents in fact and spirit the character and
customs of the early days of Nevada. While there is nothing
new, for instance, in telling how Joseph Thompson Goodman was
the discoverer of Mark Twain, and how Dan DeQuille served as
mentor, Mack's purpose is to show that Sam Clemens owed more
to Virginia City than to San Francisco. More completely than
anyone else, she has gone through the available records and
newspapers, and she traces in detail these formative years.
But there is more of Nevada than of Mark Twain, and excellent
as the book remains as a guide and supplement to *Roughing It*,
its primary value is social history. Mack unfortunately relied too much on Paine's "official life" and on Clemens' own
mingling of fancy and reality, but she has given proper em-

phasis to the Comstock Lode and Washoe in the making of the essential Twain.

Even more specialized is *Mark Twain and Hawaii* (1947) by Walter Francis Frear, whose long residence in the islands fitted him admirably for this exhaustive study of Mark Twain's four months and a day there. Frear demonstrates that the importance of the visit was out of all proportion to its length, for it was the interstice between Clemens' years of preparation and the following years of success. Always an oasis or happy memory to Twain, the islands exerted an influence greater than mere pleasant retrospective value, for his writings there show a style in transition from the crude, briefer compositions of frontier journalism to the more formal manner of the future. And Hawaii brought Twain to a new profession, later to prove financial salvation--lecturing. Frear has not merely treated the visit to Hawaii, the journey and return, but in a lengthy volume explores all its influences, together with Twain's continuing references throughout a lifetime.

Though not a biography *The Literary Apprenticeship of Mark Twain* (1950) by Edgar M. Branch presents a chronological interpretation of Samuel Clemens' development as a writer. The early Hannibal sketches, while possessing no true literary value, are important nevertheless for their "comic disposition," which Branch credits with placing "Sam Clemens squarely in the stream of American realism" (21). The colloquial nature of these apprentice pieces naturally required character portrayal through ordinary, everyday language, as well as the presentation of native subjects. And in fact the "speech rhythms of the vernacular" continued through the travel letters written by the printer and pilot, despite the intrusion of occasional bits of "elegance" (26). With the Thomas Jefferson Snodgrass letters, both crude and imitative, we find young Sam "more consciously in the tradition of American humor," merging numerous features of Sut Lovingood, Simon Suggs, and Jack Downing; interesting indeed is the continuity pointed out by Branch between the "unlettered, first person speech" of Snodgrass in 1856 and the "masterful language" of Huck Finn in 1884 (43). The earlier Snodgrass' successor, Quintus Curtius, who discarded the misspellings and bad grammar of his predecessor, reveals (if nothing more) sound comments on "the militaristic reversal of human values" (55).

It is as reporter in Washoe that Branch finds Twain "highly personal, exaggerated, and comic," working to cause guffaws, perpetrating hoaxes, indulging in burlesque, and ridiculing with satire. Moreover, it was in 1865 that a sense of his past began to appear in Clemens' writings; then, too, Washoe comedy was utilized, not alone for laughter, but in the in-

terest of truth, for if Twain the Nevadian had produced laughter, the Californian became, also, the "Moralist of the Main."
Observing that the Sandwich Island letters had value as pre-
liminary training for *The Innocents*, Branch (unlike Frear)
does not regard them as anything more. But with the sailing
of the *Quaker City* Twain's apprenticeship was over: "He was
launched on a long voyage and a long career" (194).[13]

   Mark Twain as a Literary Artist (1950) by Gladys Carmen
Bellamy demonstrates that Twain was much more the conscious
craftsman than is generally believed. While admitting that
Clemens was never a "self-conscious" artist in the sense that
Henry James was, Miss Bellamy follows Walter Blair and Lionel
Trilling in claiming that he was more "conscious" in his literary activity than frequently admitted. The book employs something of the Van Wyck Brooks thesis that Twain failed to
achieve complete artistic success, but the reason advanced
is that he failed to secure "a comprehensive grasp of writing
discipline"; indeed, the "importance of form in writing" and
"concern with technique" were fully realized by Clemens, who
unfortunately nearly always failed to reach them (34).

   Bellamy categorizes Clemens' fundamental ideas into four
"primary bases" of thought: "moralism, determinism, pessimism,
and patheticism" (64), which she then discusses. "The burlesque satire of the early Mark Twain touched not only the
fashions, the manners, and the ideals of the Western Gilded
Age, but its ethics as well" (85), Bellamy tells us, for she
does not follow Brooks in believing that Clemens surrendered
his integrity to the frontier. Yet she finds the moralist at
cross purposes with the determinist, and frequently with the
artist, for she states, "In other words, life cannot be prized
unless its content is valuable. And here the moralist in
Mark Twain suffers a defeat; he tries to save mankind to a
life which he often paints as despicable and futile" (118).
It is in burlesque that Bellamy finds Twain an artist, for
she disagrees with Brooks that the artist was undone by the
humorist. Instead, she reaches the conclusion that "most of
his early writings are not true humor but satire," and she
declares, "It was unfortunate for Mark Twain as an artist that
his attention was centered on the limitations of mankind rather
than on the possibilities" (154).

   Kenneth R. Andrews' *Nook Farm: Mark Twain's Hartford
Circle* (1950) considers the social and intellectual milieu of
the two happiest decades of Samuel Clemens' married life.
Andrews has made the most complete study thus far of the
friends and neighbors comprising a close-knit group in Hartford's choice residential district. Here at Nook Farm Clemens
lived lavishly, enjoyed the devotion of his family, the respect
of his friends, and the admiration of his widely increasing

reading public. Surrounded by a cultural environment he
definitely aspired to, Samuel Clemens soon became one of its
leaders. Even religion proved no deterrence, for the genial
congregationalism of Horace Bushnell, which had replaced dour
Calvinism, permeated the community. The religion of love
preached by Beecher was soon followed by the message of ethics
and wide humanity voiced by his successors. "Through the
years, then," says Andrews, "Burton, Parker, and Twichell
presided more and more over a 'religious' activity turned
secular as memory of the old theology grew dim" (50). Joseph
Twichell, Charles Dudley Warner, and their neighbors are considered in relation to each other and for the influence they
exerted on Twain's thought. It was a pleasant life, as retold
by Andrews' detailed study.

Henry Seidel Canby's *Turn West, Turn East* (1951) presents
Mark Twain and Henry James in terms of the two great, opposing
forces in American culture--the ties binding us to Europe and
the contrasting pull of frontier expansion. Yet in many ways
Canby shows Twain and James to be opposite sides of the same
coin, possessing the same basic values in their concern for
the integrity of the individual confronted with a moral problem, whether it be a Huck Finn or an Isabel Archer. Fundamentally Twain and James dealt with the existence of good and
evil, and each in his own way was a humorist. Dissimilar as
their methods seem, Canby says, "Yet Mark, like Henry, might
have got his formula from the great Russian Turgenev, who was
contemporary with both. All three selected the situations
most likely to express the central figure of a story--which is
more valuable in the kind of stories all three wrote than plot"
(159). While adding no new material, this sensible study reveals the similar qualities, so often typically American, which
the two authors contributed to world literature through their
respective art.

Dixon Wecter's *Sam Clemens of Hannibal* (1952) was begun as
part of what surely would have been the definitive biography
of Mark Twain, a project cut short by Wecter's sudden death
while serving as literary executor of the Clemens estate.
Based on a full examination of Twain's unpublished manuscripts,
plus a careful investigation of family papers, court records,
census reports, and newspapers, Wecter's fragmentary study
gives more information about Samuel Clemens to the age of
eighteen than any other source; for he has recreated Hannibal
street by street and house by house. Here is the most complete
account of Clemens' ancestry, the fullest narrative of his
father and mother, and the most detailed description of their
daily home life and community activities. And certain matters
are illuminated. The autopsy performed on his father, which
the boy witnessed through a keyhole, left Sam Clemens with one

of the shocking memories of his life, too carefully guarded
ever to be mentioned, except to Orion. Even in his notebook,
years later, Twain veiled the facts by saying it was his
uncle's postmortem (116). This shock, no doubt, contributed
to Sam's sleepwalking on the night of his father's funeral.

Sam Clemens of Hannibal, also, adds richly to our knowledge of young Sam's schooling, religious training, and the
folkways which guided his later conduct, as well as revealing
more of the autobiographical element in Twain's fiction. Interesting, too, is the use Wecter makes of the uncompleted forms
of *The Mysterious Stranger* and tales of Tom and Huck to show
that as the dream of boyhood faded the disillusioned Mark
Twain was unable to finish them. Though there are few revisions in this story of Twain's youth, there are numerous
important matters of emphasis given.

In *Twins of Genius* (1953) Guy A. Cardwell has written a
complete account of Mark Twain's association with George W.
Cable, especially during the winter of 1884-85, when they
toured the country, giving readings from their books. Cardwell has collected the press notices, and he includes all the
available letters, exchanged by Twain and Cable from July
1881 through October 1906, except those already printed. It
seems that each influenced the other, though perhaps Twain at
the time derived more from the tour through their discussions
of social justice and problems of human relationships then
existing in the South.

The Adventures of Mark Twain (1954) by Jerry Allen is
partly narrative and partly Twain's own autobiography and fiction. Allen has brought a great deal together from many
scattered sources to make one of the most readable books about
Twain, but like him she has embroidered biographical facts
with his fiction. The whitewashing of the fence in *Tom Sawyer*
appears as part of the biography, and certain facts now dis-
credited by scholarship, such as the story of Isaiah Sellers
and Clemens' pen name, are retained. But the book, especially
the last half, is rich in background material, and Allen de-
votes considerable space to Twain's social criticisms of these
later years. Her studies of the sociological import of
Huckleberry Finn and *A Connecticut Yankee* are a useful contribution. The student, however, will regret the lack of any
documentation.

The Art, Humor, and Humanity of Mark Twain (1959), edited
by Minnie M. Brashear and Robert M. Rodney, presents autobiographical insights into Clemens' life which the editors
use as a means of reflecting upon his career and thinking.
The major emphasis is upon Mark Twain's essential humanity.
On the other hand, Arlin Turner's *Mark Twain and George Washington Cable* (1960) is based upon letters, many hitherto un-

printed, written during the Twain-Cable lecture tour.   The
two authors expressed themselves frankly about each other,
providing interesting biographical material.

One of the more fascinating accounts of Mark Twain and his
family is Caroline Thomas Harnsberger's *Mark Twain, Family
Man* (1960).   For her work, she has drawn heavily on Paine's
biography (1912), Clara Clemens' *My Father, Mark Twain* (1931),
and Dixon Wecter's edition of *The Love Letters of Mark Twain*
(1947).   She depicts Twain as a loving husband and a doting
father, one whose marriage was close to perfect and one whose
children were both praised and reprimanded according to the
acceptability of their behavior.   Although Harnsberger's book
at times seems to be more about Clara Clemens, whom she knew,
than it is about Mark Twain, it is well illustrated with family
photographs and brings together information important to Twain
biography.

Given the popularity of pictorial biographies, it is not
surprising that two excellent pictorial biographies of Samuel
Clemens exist.   *Mark Twain Himself* (1960), produced by Milton
Meltzer, and *Mark Twain and His World* (1974), by Justin Kaplan, are attractively illustrated and contain reliable texts.

Paul Fatout's *Mark Twain on the Lecture Circuit* (1960)
is biographical in the sense that Fatout concerns himself with
chronicling Mark Twain's career as a speaker, beginning with
his debut as a public speaker in Hannibal and ending with his
last public appearance, which took place when Twain delivered
the commencement address at St. Timothy's School in Catons-
ville, Maryland, on June 10, 1909.   Fatout discusses such influences on Twain's becoming a public speaker as Artemus Ward and
Bret Harte.   He also examines a number of speaking engagements
in their entirety, that is, beginning with advanced publicity
and ending with responses as recorded in newspapers and other
sources.   The major service Fatout performs for the reader,
however, is more biographical than analytical.

Frank Baldanza's *Mark Twain* (1961) purports to be an introduction to and interpretation of the life and works of Mark
Twain: "The aim has been to provide a succinct and thorough
survey of his life that takes into account all the biographical
research that has been done since A.B. Paine's monumental
authorized biography" (v).   Intended for the nonspecialist,
Mark Twain contains a wealth of information, but the distinc-
tiveness of the book lies in its unique organization.   Samuel
Clemens the man and Mark Twain the writer are discussed in
the first two chapters with the remainder of the book devoted
to discussion of the works, but not in the usual chronological
order.   Baldanza treats the autobiographical, the travel, the
historical, the juvenile, the American, and the polemical
writings as units in themselves.   Furthermore, he discusses

one book at a time, chapter by chapter, and such a painstaking
method is bound to prove beneficial to the general reader.
Mark Twain is a welcome addition to general studies; Baldanza's
critical comments afford the kind of assistance the general
reader needs.

Hamlin Hill's *Mark Twain and Elisha Bliss* (1964) examines
Twain's relationship to Elisha Bliss and the American Publishing Company. The view put forth is that Twain's decision to
become a literary author, as opposed to remaining a journalist,
and his performance as an author were largely determined by
his association with Elisha Bliss and the American Publishing
Company. When Twain expanded the *Alta California* letters into
Innocents Abroad, Bliss examined the results and made suggestions. When Twain produced *Roughing It*, using largely the same
method, for the first time he was creating a long narrative.
Writes Hill, "*Roughing It* was a success, then, and the writing
and publishing of it and *Innocents* were instrumental in the
humorist's shift from journalism to literature" (67). The implication is that without Bliss and the American Publishing
Company Mark Twain would likely never have become a man of
literature. By contrast, Bret Harte's influence on Samuel
Clemens, as depicted in Margaret Duckett's *Mark Twain and
Bret Harte* (1964), seems not to have ended so well. A friendship which began in San Francisco ended bitterly at Hartford;
and while Harte enjoyed success in Boston circles, Clemens was
regarded as a literary comedian. Tracing the careers of both
writers, Duckett throws considerable light upon the relationship of the two men. What actually caused Clemens' hatred of
Harte, however, is not known, and readers can still make their
own judgments.

Somewhat Freudian in approach, Justin Kaplan's *Mr. Clemens
and Mark Twain* (1966) begins when Mark is already thirty-one
and a journalist in San Francisco. As for the early years,
Kaplan contends that Mark is his own best biographer. Positing
Twain's discovery of the usable past as the central drama of
his literary life, Kaplan sees him transforming the past into
literature but always in response to a period of forty years or
so following the Civil War. Kaplan cites Paine's biography as
indispensable; he also cites the Twain-Howells correspondence
published in two volumes in 1960 as having already done much
of the work for anyone who would write a biography of Twain.
Kaplan sees his role as biographer as primarily one of syn-
thesis, and in that role he has done a credible job. The biography of Mark Twain is obviously too large to be written in
424 pages, but Kaplan piles detail on detail giving his reader
a fast-paced narrative of the writer's life.

In *The Trouble Begins at Eight* (1968), Fred Lorch considers
the role of the speaker's platform in the transformation of

Twain's estimate of himself from a regional journalist-lecturer to a distinguished American both at home and abroad. Examining the tours and the tour lectures, Lorch focuses upon Twain's rise to fame, upon the various elements which contributed to Twain's success, and upon Twain's attitudes toward himself as humorist and lecturer. Of great interest to the reader is Lorch's analysis of Twain's platform manners and techniques in Chapter Fifteen as well as audience response to those manners and techniques in Chapter Sixteen. However, the chief value of Lorch's book remains biographical rather than analytical. In a related book, *Mark Twain at Large* (1969), Arthur L. Scott attempts to ascertain "Mark Twain's travels and his opinions concerning the entire foreign scene" (vii). Beginning with Twain's pleasure cruise around the Mediterranean in 1867, and ending with his final trip to Europe in 1903, Scott follows Mark Twain the traveler recording Twain's likes and dislikes about foreign cultures during the thirty years between the first and last trips. At the outset the dominant image is that of the American West facing the Old World, but the final image is that of an American ambassador-at-large interpreting American culture to the world.

In *Mark Twain: God's Fool* (1973), Hamlin Hill deals with the final decades of Clemens' life. It is a sad story of an old man in failing health and at odds with his daughters. Eventually Clemens was caught in a battle between his daughters and his secretary and her husband, during which it was discovered that the two trusted employees had gained legal control of Clemens' estate. The control was quickly rescinded. Against this unknown background many notable visitors came to Stormfield to pay their respects to Mark Twain. Hill has worked with a great deal of new material, unknown to earlier biographers. In his literary biography of Clemens, *The Authentic Mark Twain* (1984), Everett Emerson also treats the last years. Emerson examines the entire literary career, beginning with the early letters. He pays particular attention to Twain's working the *Alta* letters into *The Innocents Abroad*, the composition of which Twain viewed, according to Emerson, as the culmination in his struggle to become a "member of the literary profession" (42). As for the last years, Emerson contends that Twain's identity problem intensified. Tending toward manic-depressive behavior, Twain's greatest problem as a writer was coping with himself, contends Emerson. In spite of his problems, or perhaps because of them, Mark Twain remains one of America's great writers, and the reason may lie in the fact that in almost everything he wrote "something attractive is to be found" (277).

Van Wyck Brooks and the
Psychological Approach

When Van Wyck Brooks wrote *The Ordeal of Mark Twain*
(1920) he raised questions, some still unanswered, and started
a dispute, which soon became bitter. Indeed, much since
written about Twain has been mainly an attack upon Brooks'
theories, or even upon Brooks himself for having advanced
them. *The Ordeal of Mark Twain* divided Twain biographers into
rival camps, yet it is really not a biography in the strict
sense of being a "life"; actually it is a psychological study.
Other authors were being examined in the same manner, for it
was then the fashion. Brooks starts out with a set of theories,
and as usual with theorists, he uses what will fill his needs
and ignores what does not. Despite this, he has reached certain conclusions that still appear valid. In addition, he
shows at times a penetrating insight into Twain's character.
The book is by no means as valueless as some critics would have
us believe. DeVoto and Benson have both attacked Brooks with
so much vigor that the attack becomes almost personal, while
Ferguson, appealing to common sense, simply rejects the theories.
Whether or not one agrees with Brooks, one cannot accept
Paine's advice to DeVoto to ignore him; for he has raised too
many issues about Mark Twain and the America that produced
him, despite the obvious limitations of his approach, to be
ignored.
     Much of the book is pseudoscience, an attempt to substi-
tute psychological theorizing for common sense, and a tendency
to make something mysterious out of the obvious. The purpose
is to explain the bitter pessimism that developed in Twain's
mind, the despair which made him regard man as the meanest of
animals and life as a tragic mistake. How could one who had
achieved such popularity and success, the affection of his
countrymen, and the acclaim of the world, have felt as Mark
Twain did about life? Not content with an objective explanation, Brooks insists upon "some far more personal root ...
some far more intimate chagrin" (20). Searching for a "deep
malady of the soul" Brooks even convinces himself that Twain's
delight in billiards, which led him to beg for one more game
at four o'clock in the morning, is really not enthusiastic
playing, but actually a fear of being alone. Mark could not
face himself; "... he had transgressed some inalienable life
demand," becoming a frustrated personality, a victim of arrested
development, of which he was not entirely conscious, but which
crushed the spirit of the artist in him. Declaring that Twain
lives today in only two or three books, Brooks further asserts
that his appeal is largely to rudimentary minds. It is not so

much the accomplishment that interests Brooks as the conjecture of what might have been. Brooks accurately points out
many of Twain's traits, but misunderstands the reason for their
being. Twain had a nature alike barbaric and sweet; he had a
passion for the limelight; he possessed an inner humility;
there was a great deal of comic impudence in him; he lacked
an inner control over his own boundless energy in creative
efforts; during his final years he developed a mechanistic
philosophy. From this, Brooks condemns Twain as a "frustrated
spirit, a victim of arrested development," saying, "... the
poet, the artist in him, consequently had withered into the
cynic and the whole man had become a spiritual valetudinarian"
(40-41).

The theory then elaborated is that the only period of life
in which Sam Clemens was really happy was during his four
years as pilot on the Mississippi. We are told, "... the earlier pages of *Life on the Mississippi*, in which he pictures
it, are the most poetic, the most perfectly fused and expressive
that he ever wrote" (43). Having found himself in a pilot's
career, Clemens is supposed to have lost himself when he left
it. Brooks calls the world into which the author was born
"drab and tragic." The entire social setting of life in Hannibal is made to appear close to the backwoods underprivileged
found in Erskine Caldwell. Without giving proof enough to
satisfy most Twain investigators, Brooks declares that little
Sam was born a predestined artist. First, his environment
is declared to be ugly and soul-destroying; next, his mother
is charged with warping him beyond hope. Because Sam Clemens,
standing beside his father's coffin, promised his mother that
if she would not send him back to school, he would be a better
boy, Brooks believes he thereby forsook the artist inherent
within. From then on he must follow the mirage of wealth.
Only as a pilot could Sam reconcile his opposing wishes: to
be an artist and to win his mother's approval, an approbation
which was the same as that of the pioneer society to which she
belonged. In condemning Jane Clemens' influence upon her son,
The Ordeal of Mark Twain denounces pioneer society in general.
As a pilot Sam was successful financially, winning the praise
of his family and neighbors, while at the same time he was an
individual. "It is an outburst of pure aesthetic feeling,
produced by a supreme exercise of personal craftsmanship" (68),
says Brooks. Moreover, here is a fertile field for observation and schooling. "He will not always be a pilot; he is an
artist born; some day he is going to be a writer" (73). But
this is all shattered by the Civil War, when Sam Clemens, after
four years as a pilot devoted to the ideal of craftsmanship,
is suddenly thrown into a world obsessed with exploitation.
There was one standard for success: the accumulation of wealth.

The West fares no better in this narrative than the Midwest. There Mark encountered the "promoter's instinct,"
which Brooks illustrates with the story of Jim Gillis, who
refused to admit that California plums were too acid to eat.
Unable to stand apart from his Washoe associates, Clemens
capitulated to his environment. Since it was impossible for
him to secure wealth and prestige, while remaining at the
same time an artist with creative instinct, he abandoned his
own aspirations, descending to the level of his associates.

But not until he fought an inner battle, according to
Brooks, who reads chagrin into Twain's manner of entering the
Enterprise office to join the staff. For in becoming a humorist, Twain felt that he was "compromising rather than ful-
filling his own soul" (111). From then on Mark thought of his
writing as only a product, another way to earn money; it was
never an artistic creation. Taking no pride in his work,
Mark could never be happy as he had been while a pilot. That
his creative instinct was still in rebellion, Brooks deduces
from his deprecatory remarks about the "Jumping Frog," yet
Mark capitulated nevertheless to the "gregarious, acquisitive
instinct of the success-loving pioneer" (117).

With Clemens' marriage to Olivia Langdon, the wife supersedes the mother for Brooks as the blight upon his art, and
Elmira is pictured as a place without moral freedom or intellectual culture: "A provincial fresh-water aristocracy, resting on a basis of angular sectarianism, imposed its own type
upon all the rest of society, forcing all to submit to it or
to imitate it" (139). Just as he had surrendered in Hannibal
and in the West, Twain submitted here, producing not the
literature he wished to write, but only the kind of books accepted by his wife and Elmira. This then, was the ordeal, an
artist who wished to create beauty through the truthful expression of his individuality, selling his birthright to earn
wealth and popularity.

The defects inherent in such a study readily become apparent; Brooks has attempted to psychoanalyze a dead man,
which at best can produce only conjectural results. It is
not surprising, then, that Brooks' method is often inadequate.
There are other defects in this study as well: there is no
basic knowledge of either the Mississippi Valley or the Far
West; there is a general disparagement of all humor, and
finally there are a good many conclusions based on evidence
spun from imagination.

Although he does not continue Brooks' attack on Twain,
Stephen Leacock was influenced by it. His *Mark Twain* (1933),
in partial acceptance, deplores the influence first of the
mother, then later the wife. While stating that the East
exerted a bad influence on Twain, he ignores Brooks to commend

the environment of Hannibal and the West.   Indeed for Leacock, "The West made Mark Twain" (21).   With a gusto that
could not be dampened, Twain continued to write *for* the East,
but not *of* it.   Leacock admits that Mark was held to those
bounds considered respectable by Livy, Joe Twichell, and
Howells, that after all it was the Victorian age, but finally
concludes, "They did their loving best to ruin his work--and
failed; that's all" (64).   As a humorist, Twain became a
national figure and a legend; to Leacock, a successful humorist himself, Twain's desire to be taken as a serious writer
is simply a natural trait of human nature.   In the stories of
Tom and Huck Leacock feels Mark was at his best; after pointing out the faults in both works, he says of the latter:

> But the bulk of the book is marvellous.   The vision of
> American institutions--above all, of slavery--as seen
> through the unsullied mind of little Huck; the pathos
> and charm of the Negro race shining through the soul of
> Nigger Jim--the western scene, the frontier people--it
> is the epic of a vanished America. (86)

In short, Leacock agrees with Brooks that Mark Twain was
hindered, but unlike Brooks, he believes that Twain rose above
these obstacles.   There is an appreciation of the best of
Twain's work, especially his humor, although Leacock fails as
critic when he turns to the writings of the later years and
to the historical narratives.   As biography this book is not
important; as a comment by a fellow humorist it is interesting.

Edgar Lee Masters, under the influence of the Brooks thesis, continued the negative approach in *Mark Twain: A Portrait*
(1938).   The man emerging from Masters' study is not admirable.
Although he took his biographical material from Paine, adding
nothing of his own, and ignoring subsequent contributions,
Masters nevertheless presents a radically different figure.
To the Paine material he added Brooks' frustration theory,
but this time with a Midwestern accent.   Agreeing that Twain
was thwarted, Masters seeks the explanation in cultural up-
rooting.   The implication is that Twain should have stayed in
Missouri.   But chiefly he finds fault with his subject for
not having entered into the class struggle.   Perhaps Masters
himself had come under the influence of the dialectical
materialists, so popular in the thirties, and he infers that
Mark's career was blighted because political and economic
ideas were relegated to the background in his fiction.   If
Mark Twain had always written with a social, political, or
economic purpose, then Masters would have felt that he was
living up to his full stature as an artist.   While agreeing
with Brooks that Twain failed as a satirist, he blames the
failure on Mark's having neither the mind nor the character

for the task. The Brooks postulate of a loveless household,
and the baleful influence of Jane Clemens and Calvinism,
causes Masters to accept the episode of contracting measles
as a turning point in life, an attempt "to be done with the
suspense and the terror" (18).

   In *The Times of Melville and Whitman* (1947) Brooks continued his assertion that the "frontier was generally stagnant
in its formal culture" (78). His treatment of the far West,
however, shows a modified attitude; no longer is it a place
of artistic frustration, for Brooks must now admit, "Mark Twain
was the seriocomic Homer of this old primitive Western World,
its first pathfinder in letters, its historian and poet" (300).
Yet Brooks persists in saying that Clemens had little pride in
literature, preferring piloting (453), that he was primarily
interested in making money (459), and that he suppressed
honest opinion to secure public approbation (462). Notwithstanding, *The Times of Melville and Whitman* evidences an appreciation of Twain's folk art and Brooks no longer condemns
humor. To understand the changed attitudes, one needs to know
the attack waged on Brooks' theories by Bernard DeVoto.

                    DeVoto and the Rebuttal

   Before the controversy developed which was to turn Mark
Twain biographers into divergent factions, John Macy--who
later would reaffirm his views--wrote a sensible essay in
The Spirit of American Literature (1913). Anticipating, as it
were, the pseudoscientific insistence upon Twain's limitations
through environmental influence, Macy affirmed that he was a
humorist, naturally and by preference, a writer who must be
approached as such (250). Twain, neither a victim of censorship, nor a sufferer from frustration, meditated like Swift
on human folly, seeing life with breadth and penetration.
Then seriously intent upon truth, he humorously approached
mankind, generally tolerant, sometimes affectionate, but with
true chivalry scorning the false, mean, and cruel. Macy in-
terprets the final pessimism as ethical and materialistic
determinism, in a word explaining it: "Character is fate" (275).

   Mark Twain had universal proportions and an interest in
most of the vital problems of humanity, says Macy, who admitting
the unimportance of his philosophy as such reaffirms his wide
range, depth of insight, and his knowledge of good and evil.
For Twain's work, taken in total, constitutes of mankind the
"greatest canvas that any American has painted" (275). Later
in *The Story of the World's Literature* (1925) Macy, with the

theories of Van Wyck Brooks before him, denies them, stating
that Mark's wings were never clipped, either by personal
associates, or anything inherent in American life. Indeed
Macy declares, "He said all he had to say, he knew how to say
it, and circumstances fostered his genius" (532).

In a succinct account of Mark Twain, C. Hartley Grattan
also took issue with the pseudoscientific appraisals. He admitted that the humorist had a volatile temperament and possessed a wide range of feeling; Mark was "an idealist of a
most uncompromising sort," who was swept to the heights by
the noble and sublime, but plunged into despair by the horrors
mankind committed ("Mark Twain" 276). Though primarily a
critical essay, this piece is one of the most valid summations
of Mark Twain's characteristics. Twain, an improviser in both
life and literature, lacked the discipline which made Henry
James a great structurist, but he had, on the other hand, an
accumulation of deep and varied experiences. "So volatile a
temperament and so comprehensive an experience have rarely
been housed in one man" (275), concludes Grattan, who finds
this the logical explanation for the unevenness of Twain's
work. Of Brooks' theory Grattan observes, "No civilization
can be so arranged that it will detect and coddle genius from
the cradle to the grave" (277). He admits that Mark often
gave himself up to the moneymaking of the Gilded Age, but
nevertheless contends that "... he was strong enough to reject
it insofar as it violated his ideals of decency and honor"
(277).[14]

Bernard DeVoto wrote *Mark Twain's America* (1935) to refute
the charges of Van Wyck Brooks against Clemens and his environment. It is not a biography, but as the author intended, a
preface to Twain's writings. For the student, it is the most
important book since Paine's official life. DeVoto examines
historically the country into which young Sam Clemens was born
and the influences which went into his development. Himself a
product of the West, a student of the frontier and its literature, DeVoto presents Clemens as the natural heir of frontier
culture: the folk stories of the pioneer, black lore, together
with the formative influence of the native humorists. DeVoto
demonstrates the presence of beauty in frontier life and shows
the poetic quality imparted to Mark Twain's prose by the
forest and the prairie. There is the epic sweep, the length
and breadth of the great river, which also afforded opportunity
to watch an entire civilization passing in review. Twain's
debt to the earlier humorists of the old Southwest is discussed
and for the first time brought clearly into focus.

But DeVoto's account of the frontier is not all poetry;
there is violence with the horrors of gang warfare, the "But-
cherknife boys," the Murrells, who murdered, plundered, and

terrorized. Vice in all forms flourished in the river towns
and on the steamboats; prostitution ranged from the parlor
houses to the "cribs"--everything from plumes and silk to rags
and filth. There was gambling, accompanied by all degrees of
card sharks and confidence men. These phases of life were a
part of Mark Twain's America, part of the influences that made
Mark Twain. As a corrective to Brooks, DeVoto wastes no time
on what Mark Twain might have said: "I have no interest beyond
his books. My effort has been to perceive where and how they
issue from American life" (xi). The purpose is to bring discussion back to what Mark Twain actually wrote, away from sup-
positions and theories. As the book is not a complete biography, its chief concern is the Midwestern and Far Western
phases, by which time DeVoto believes Mark Twain was fully
developed; thus there is brief treatment of the final years.
To DeVoto, Samuel Clemens was a normal boy, who grew up naturally with no desire to be anything other than he was. A flaw in
the permanent value of the book is that so much space is consumed in refutation of the psychoanalytic theories about Twain,
arguments which needed demolishing, but now no longer seem
worthy of the importance given them.

Fred Lewis Pattee, even as John Macy, seemed to anticipate
something of the approaching Brooks-DeVoto controversy in his
A History of American Literature Since 1870 (1915). He valued
highly the Hannibal background, and states, "His books nowhere
rise into the pure serene of literature unless touched at some
point by this magic stream that flowed so marvelously through
his boyhood. The two discoverers of the Mississippi were
De Soto and Mark Twain" (48). After his education on the river,
Twain then entered upon what Pattee--rejecting any thought of
corrupting influence--regarded as the graduate course of the
Western years. For him there are three Mark Twains: "the droll
comedian ... indignant protester ... romancer"--and it is the
third, who caught the "sunset glow" of a vanished phase of
America, the age of Mississippi steamboats and Western gold
rush days, who lives as a great artist (58).

In a later study for the American Writers Series, *Mark
Twain: Representative Selections* (1935), Pattee did not reverse
his opinions, but gave them fuller expression. Aware of the
vogue enjoyed by Brooks, he rejected all the theories expounded
as Twain's ordeal; Pattee dismissed the charges against Jane
Clemens and Olivia by terming their exponents "theory-riding
Freudists." He repudiates, too, the deprecation of Hannibal
and Washoe, for Pattee insisted that here Twain found inspiration for his finest work. That the East prevented his complete
realization of that early inspiration Pattee dismissed as "Nonsense! Twaddle!" (Introduction xxvii). The proper approach to
Mark Twain's work is through his humor, says Pattee; Clemens'

sensitive conscience and complex emotional attitude do not
necessarily make a frustrated Shelley. Of Twain's position
in literature Pattee is not so enthusiastic, but regardless of
critical estimate, he insists upon Mark Twain as the product
of an environment fortunate for his talents, and his greatest
talent was the gift of making people laugh.

A sound, informative volume, *Mark Twain at Work* (1942), is
a limited but important study of Twain's methods of writing.
Bernard DeVoto has explained something of Twain's habits of
composition and solutions of difficulties. Clemens' episodic
methods are apparent in his attempts to use the materials of
Tom Sawyer, the first of these being the "Boy's Manuscript"
in which Tom's adventures are performed by Billy Rogers (5).[15]
Indeed the seed from which the central action of *Tom Sawyer*
developed--"random and clumsy scenes"--began first as burlesque,
and with little attention to "minutiae." It was not until
Twain turned to memories of youth, picturing the idyll of boyhood, preserving the nostalgic dream, that he hit upon the key
to greatness. Yet *Tom Sawyer* developed only after several false
starts, and after some of the same materials--the description
of the society amid which Sam Clemens matured--had been utilized
in *The Gilded Age*. DeVoto's discussion of *Huckleberry Finn*
shows how Twain undervalued the effort, even pigeonholed it,
as the momentum of initial enthusiasm slowed to a halt. Elsewhere Clemens explained a similar break in writing *Tom Sawyer*:
"... my tank had run dry; it was empty; the stock of materials
in it was exhausted; the story could not go on without materials;
it could not be wrought out of nothing" (*Eruption* 197). Thus
the author worked, declaring that whenever he struck a snag,
he had merely to wait, even if for two or three years, until
the tank of inspiration again filled.

DeVoto believes that Twain laid *Huckleberry Finn* aside
during the summer of 1876, because in his original idea to
continue *Tom Sawyer* there was no "dynamic purpose." Though
achieving some great passages, Clemens lost interest, letting
Huck fall by the wayside while he regaled Joe Twichell with
1601 and collaborated with Bret Harte on *Ah Sin*. For six years
Huck remained on the shelf; meanwhile Clemens busied himself
with *A Tramp Abroad* and *The Prince and the Pauper*. Not until
Twain revisited the river to collect materials for *Life on the
Mississippi* did he again turn to *Huck*; in fact the river book
was partly a rehearsal of materials. DeVoto says, "His trip
down the river had refilled the tank; he was ready to work again"
(*Mark Twain at Work* 63). Twain's unpublished notebooks reveal
how he selected certain subjects, discarded some, altered
others, or used them intact--all resulting in a masterpiece.

The final essay entitled "The Symbols of Despair" DeVoto
calls "a chapter, hitherto unwritten, in the biography of Mark

Twain," one "agonizing as personal history" (*Mark Twain at Work* 105). DeVoto believes Twain was so deeply hurt by his personal disasters that the wound affected the artist as much as the man. Hence came the urge to write, not only to alleviate his grief but also "to vindicate himself as a writer, to restore the image [of himself] that had been impaired" (*Mark Twain at Work* 110).

Of course, the legacy known as the Brooks-DeVoto controversy became a popular subject among Twain scholars. Once more debated than it is now, the controversy, nevertheless, has remained with us. For evidence of the extent to which it has remained with us, one need only examine such books as *A Casebook on Mark Twain's Wound* (1962), edited by Lewis Leary. *A Casebook on Mark Twain's Wound* is a study of the Brooks-DeVoto controversy containing essays on both sides. Whether one reads Justin Kaplan's *Mr. Clemens and Mark Twain* (1966) or Everett Emerson's *The Authentic Mark Twain* (1984), he is ever aware of the Brooks-DeVoto controversy lurking in the background.

NOTES

1. This narration of Mark Twain's life by Will Clemens is antedated only by the brief account from Hotten in his pirated *Choice Humorous Works* (London, 1873, revised 1888) and by a sixteen-page pamphlet, circa 1886, by an unknown author, and distributed free to purchasers of Duke's Mixture Smoking Tobacco. Twain arranged with Chatto and Windus, the publisher of *Choice Humorous Works*, for a near-duplicate book of Hotten's edition of 1873, having the same title.

2. This later appeared as "Mark Twain: A Biographical Sketch" in *The $30,000 Bequest and Other Stories*, and in recent editions of Twain is available in *In Defense of Harriet Shelley*. The author, a favorite nephew of Twain's, was the subject of the essay "Samuel Erasmus Moffett" in *Europe and Elsewhere*.

3. The original pamphlet was published by *The Banner*, Sonora, California, in 1924.

4. Briefly these were as follows: Mark Twain's father was not elected clerk of the Surrogate Court, but died before the election; Sam was not apprenticed to Ament right after his father's death, the apprenticeship starting a year or so later; the title of "To Mary in H--l" is amended to "To Miss Katie of H--l."

5. Paine's *Mark Twain: A Biography* was originally published in three volumes in 1912 by Harper & Brothers, then issued in four volumes. The Centenary Edition (Harper, 1935) contains four volumes in two. Page numbers are the same in all editions.

6. Twain himself passed portions of the *Autobiography* for appearance during his life; see "Chapters from My Autobiography," *North American Review* September, 1906 and December, 1907. Paine left about one-fifth of this material uncollected, and he frequently revised that which he arranged for publication. See DeLancey Ferguson, "The Uncollected Portions of Mark Twain's Autobiography," *American Literature* 8 (1936): 37–46.

7. The *Autobiography* as edited by Paine was carefully selected to prevent anything shocking or too frank from appearing. More of the material has been released in recent years.

8. The manuscripts in the papers of the Mark Twain Estate show that what Paine selected for publication is an indication of what Twain confided to his journal, but not the culmination.

9. Paine prints Artemus Ward's letters of advice to Clemens, but unfortunately he does not have Sam's replies.

10. The final letter is addressed to Mrs. Bowen after Will's death.

11. Paine thought the other two were John Briggs and Sam Clemens (*Biography* I: 54).

12. Particularly the letters of January 25, 1868, and February 6, 1870, which contain some material later used in the "Boy's Manuscript" of 1870 or 1871.

13. *The Literary Apprenticeship of Mark Twain* concludes with a chapter on the fulfillment of the artist in *Huckleberry Finn*.

14. DeVoto called Grattan's essay on Mark Twain "the finest treatment of him in print" (*Mark Twain's America*, 218).

15. DeVoto dates "Boy's Manuscript" about 1870 and prints it in *Mark Twain at Work* (25–44).

WORKS CITED

Allen, Jerry. *The Adventures of Mark Twain*. Boston: Little,
    Brown, 1954. Based partly on Twain's fiction.

Andrews, Kenneth R. *Nook Farm: Mark Twain's Hartford Circle*.
    Cambridge: Harvard U. Press, 1950. A full treatment of
    Clemens' friends and associates during the Hartford years.

Baldanza, Frank. *Mark Twain*. New York: Barnes and Noble,
    1961. Effective critical analysis.

Barr, Robert. "Samuel L. Clemens, 'Mark Twain': A Character
    Sketch." *McClure's Magazine* 10 (1898): 246-51.

Bellamy, Gladys Carmen. *Mark Twain as a Literary Artist*.
    Norman: U. of Oklahoma Press, 1950. Useful and provoca-
    tive. Mainly critical rather than biographical.

Benson, Ivan. *Mark Twain's Western Years*. Stanford: Stanford
    U. Press, 1938. The standard work on Twain's life and
    writings in the West. Contains material not printed be-
    fore.

Branch, Edgar Marquess. *The Literary Apprenticeship of Mark
    Twain*. Urbana: U. of Illinois Press, 1950. More critical
    than biographical. A highly useful addition to Twain
    scholarship.

Brashear, Minnie M. *Mark Twain, Son of Missouri*. Chapel Hill:
    U. of North Carolina Press, 1934. Invaluable for the
    period covered. Takes Clemens up to his departure for
    the river. Prints new material.

Brashear, Minnie M. and Robert M. Rodney, eds. *The Art, Humor,
    and Humanity of Mark Twain*. Norman: U. of Oklahoma Press,
    1959. Emphasizes Twain's essential humanity.

Brooks, Van Wyck. *The Ordeal of Mark Twain*. Rev. ed. New
    York: Dutton, 1933. The revised edition varies slightly
    from the 1920 edition. A book often penetrating in re-
    vealing Twain's sensitivity and artistic nature, but lack-
    ing in understanding of frontier environment. Of no value
    as conclusion, but helpful as suggestion.

————. *The Times of Melville and Whitman*. New York: Dutton,
    1947. Contains much about Twain. Interesting mostly for
    Brooks' enlightened revisions of his former attitude toward
    the frontier.

Canby, Henry Seidel. *Turn West, Turn East: Mark Twain and
    Henry James*. Boston: Houghton Mifflin, 1951. Contrasts
    Twain and James to show the basic Americanism of both.

Cardwell, Guy A. *Twins of Genius*. East Lansing: Michigan
State College Press, 1953. A detailed study of the relationship between Twain and George W. Cable, containing
a number of unpublished letters.

Clemens, Clara. *My Father, Mark Twain*. New York: Harper &
Brothers, 1931. A valuable intimate picture by Clemens'
daughter.

Clemens, Cyril. *Young Sam Clemens*. Portland: Tebbetts,
1942. Adds nothing to our knowledge of Clemens.

Clemens, Will M. *Mark Twain: The Story of His Life and Work*.
San Francisco: Clemens, 1892. Of no value, but of interest
as the first book of Twain biography.

DeCasseres, Benjamin. *When Huck Finn Went Highbrow*. New
York: Madigan, 1934. Tells of Twain's admiration for
Browning's poetry.

DeQuille, Dan [William Wright]. *The Big Bonanza*. New York:
Knopf, 1947. An important book on Virginia City and the
Comstock Lode, written by Twain's oldest friend on the
Territorial Enterprise. Splendid for the Western back-
ground.

―――. "Reporting with Mark Twain." *California Illustrated*
(1893): 170-78.

DeVoto, Bernard. *Mark Twain's America*. Boston: Little,
Brown, 1935. Reprint of the 1932 edition. The best book
on the background that produced Clemens. Indispensable.

―――. *Mark Twain at Work*. Cambridge: Harvard U. Press,
1942. Not biography, but an important account of how
Clemens wrote, and a penetrating analysis of his pessimism.

Duckett, Margaret. *Mark Twain and Bret Harte*. Norman: U. of
Oklahoma Press, 1964. Treats the careers of both artists.

Emerson, Everett. *The Authentic Mark Twain*. Philadelphia:
U. of Pennsylvania Press, 1984. Literary biography.

Fatout, Paul. *Mark Twain on the Lecture Circuit*. 1960. Glouces-
ter: Smith, 1966. Chronicles Twain's career as a speaker.

Ferguson, DeLancey. *Mark Twain: Man and Legend*. Indianapolis:
Bobbs-Merrill, 1943. The best single volume on Twain at
the time.

―――. "The Uncollected Portions of Mark Twain's Autobiography." *American Literature* 8 (1936): 37-46.

Frear, Walter Francis. *Mark Twain and Hawaii*. Chicago: Lake-
side, 1947. A definitive treatment of Twain's visit to
the Sandwich Islands and its influences.

Gillis, William R. *Gold Rush Days with Mark Twain.* New York:
Boni, 1930. Inaccurate. Of no biographical value.

————. *Memories of Mark Twain and Steve Gillis: A Record of
Mining Experiences.* Sonora: *The Banner*, 1924.

Goodwin, C.C. *As I Remember Them.* Salt Lake City: Special
Committee of Salt Lake City Commercial Club, 1913.

Grattan, C. Hartley. "Mark Twain." *American Writers on American Literature, by Thirty-seven Contemporary Writers.* Ed.
John Macy. New York: Liveright, 1931. 274-84. The best
essay on Twain in print until superseded by Dixon Wecter's
The Literary History of the United States. Still of value.

Harnsberger, Caroline Thomas. *Mark Twain, Family Man.* New
York: Citadel, 1960. Well illustrated with family photographs.

Henderson, Archibald. *Mark Twain.* New York: Stokes, 1911.
Contains excellent bibliography covering 1869 to 1910.
Especially useful for foreign criticism.

Hill, Hamlin. *Mark Twain and Elisha Bliss.* Columbia: U. of
Missouri Press, 1964. Good discussion of Bliss-Twain relationship.

————. *Mark Twain: God's Fool.* New York: Harper & Row, 1973.
New biographical material.

Hotten, John Camden. Introduction. *Choice Humorous Works of
Mark Twain.* London: Chatto & Windus, 1873. Rev. 1888.
The first sketch of Twain's life. Anecdotal and full of
inaccuracies.

Howells, William Dean. *My Mark Twain.* New York: Harper &
Brothers, 1910. Clemens as seen by a friend and fellow
writer. An important contribution to Twain biography.

Kaplan, Justin. *Mark Twain and His World.* New York: Simon
and Schuster, 1974. Pictorial biography.

————. *Mr. Clemens and Mark Twain.* New York: Simon and
Schuster, 1966. Begins when Twain is thirty-one years
old.

Lawton, Mary. *A Lifetime with Mark Twain.* New York: Harcourt,
Brace, 1925. The memories of Katy Leary, a servant in the
Clemens household for thirty years. An interesting con-
tribution.

Leacock, Stephen. *Mark Twain.* New York: Appleton, 1933.
Not important, but interesting as an account of Twain
by another fine humorist.

Leary, Lewis, ed. *A Casebook on Mark Twain's Wound.* New York:
Crowell, 1962. Treats the Brooks-DeVoto controversy.

Long, E. Hudson. *Mark Twain Handbook*. New York: Hendricks
    House, 1957. Biography, criticism, bibliography to 1957.

Lorch, Fred. *The Trouble Begins at Eight*. Ames: Iowa State
    U. Press, 1968. Excellent treatment of Twain as a lecturer.

Mack, Effie Mona. *Mark Twain in Nevada*. New York: Scribner's,
    1947. A full account of Clemens during the days of the
    Comstock Lode, though containing more about Nevada than
    about Twain.

Macy, John. "Mark Twain." *The Spirit of American Literature*.
    Garden City: Doubleday, 1913. 248-77.

————. *The Story of the World's Literature*. New York: Live-
    right, 1925.

Masters, Edgar Lee. *Mark Twain: A Portrait*. New York: Scrib-
    ner's, 1938. Repeats all the fallacies of the Brooks
    theory. Of no value to the student of Twain.

Matthews, Brander. "Memories of Mark Twain." *The Tocsin of
    Revolt*. New York: Scribner's, 1922. 255-94.

Meltzer, Milton. *Mark Twain Himself*. New York: Crowell,
    1960. Pictorial biography.

Moffet, Samuel Erasmus. "Mark Twain: A Biographical Sketch."
    McClure's Magazine 13 (1899): 523-29. Reprinted in *The
    $30,000 Bequest and Other Stories*. By Mark Twain. New
    York: Harper & Brothers, 1906.

Paine, Albert Bigelow. *Mark Twain: A Biography*. Centenary
    Edition. 2 vols. New York: Harper & Brothers, 1935.
    The authorized life. Still an indispensable storehouse
    of information despite the need for corrections.

Pattee, Fred Lewis. *A History of American Literature Since
    1870*. New York: Century, 1915.

————, ed. Introduction. *Mark Twain: Representative Selec-
    tions*. By Mark Twain. New York: American, 1935. xi-lii.

Phelps, William Lyon. *Autobiography with Letters*. New York:
    Oxford U. Press, 1939.

Quick, Dorothy. *Enchantment: A Little Girl's Friendship with
    Mark Twain*. Norman: U. of Oklahoma Press, 1961. Human
    interest story.

Read, Opie. *Mark Twain and I*. Chicago: Reilly, 1940.

Scott, Arthur L. *Mark Twain at Large*. Chicago: Regency,
    1969. Twain on foreign cultures.

Stewart, William M. *Reminiscences of Senator William M. Stewart of Nevada.* Ed. George Rothwell Brown. New York: Neale, 1908.

Stoddard, Charles Warren. *Exits and Entrances.* Boston: Lothrop, 1903.

Turner, Arlin. *Mark Twain and George Washington Cable.* East Lansing: Michigan State U. Press, 1960. Adds information.

Twain, Mark [Samuel Langhorne Clemens]. *The Autobiography of Mark Twain, Including Chapters Now Published for the First Time.* Ed. Charles Neider. New York: Harper & Brothers, 1959. A shorter version of the original.

————. *The Love Letters of Mark Twain.* Ed. Dixon Wecter. New York: Harper & Brothers, 1949. A valuable addition to the facts of Twain biography as well as a depiction of an ideal love story.

————. *Mark Twain–Howells Letters: The Correspondence of Samuel L. Clemens and William D. Howells, 1872-1910.* Eds. Henry Nash Smith and William M. Gibson. 2 vols. Cambridge: Belknap Press of Harvard U. Press, 1960.

————. *Mark Twain in Eruption: Hitherto Unpublished Pages about Men and Events.* Ed. Bernard DeVoto. New York: Harper & Brothers, 1940. Autobiographical papers from the Clemens Literary Estate. A valuable contribution to our knowledge of Twain's mind and thought.

————. *Mark Twain: Life as I Find It.* Ed. Charles Neider. Garden City: Hanover, 1961.

————. *Mark Twain Speaks for Himself.* Ed. Paul Fatout. West Lafayette: Purdue U. Press, 1978.

————. *Mark Twain to Mrs. Fairbanks.* Ed. Dixon Wecter. San Marino: Huntington Library, 1949. Interesting, intimate correspondence.

————. *Mark Twain's Autobiography.* Ed. Albert Bigelow Paine. 2 vols. New York: Harper & Brothers, 1924. Selected from Twain's autobiographical papers.

————. *Mark Twain's Correspondence with Henry Huttleston Rogers, 1893-1909.* Ed. Lewis Leary. Berkeley: U. of California Press, 1969.

————. *Mark Twain's Letter to Will Bowen, Buffalo, February Sixth, 1870.* San Francisco: Book Club of California, 1938. Changed slightly when added to collection of Twain's letters to Bowen.

————. *Mark Twain's Letters.* Ed. Albert Bigelow Paine. 2 vols. New York: Harper & Brothers, 1917. A two-volume collection of letters, but by no means complete.

————. *Mark Twain's Letters to His Publishers, 1867–1894.* Ed. Hamlin Hill. Berkeley: U. of California Press, 1967.

————. *Mark Twain's Letters to Mary.* Ed. Lewis Leary. New York: Columbia U. Press, 1961. Additional biographical information.

————. *Mark Twain's Letters to Will Bowen, "My First, & Oldest & Dearest Friend."* Austin: U. of Texas Press, 1941. Sixteen letters from Twain to Bowen. Interesting for reminiscences about Hannibal.

————. *Mark Twain's Notebook.* Ed. Albert Bigelow Paine. New York: Harper & Brothers, 1935. Selections from Twain's journals. Brief and sketchy.

————. *Mark Twain's Notebooks and Journals.* 3 vols. Eds. vol. 1 (1855–73) Frederick Anderson, Michael B. Frank, and Kenneth Sanderson. Eds. vol. 2 (1877–83) Anderson, Lin Salamo, and Bernard L. Stein. Eds. vol. 3 (1883–91) Robert Pack Browning, Frank, and Salamo. Berkeley: U. of California Press, 1975–79.

————. *Mark Twain's Speeches.* Ed. Albert Bigelow Paine. New York: Harper & Brothers, 1923. A selection of Twain's speeches, but not complete.

————. "Samuel Erasmus Moffett." *Europe and Elsewhere.* By Twain. New York: Harper and Brothers, 1923. 351–54.

————. *Susy and Mark Twain: Family Dialogues.* Ed. Edith Colgate Salsbury. New York: Harper & Row, 1965.

Wagenknecht, Edward. *Mark Twain: The Man and His Work.* New Haven: Yale U. Press, 1935. Rev. 1961 and 1967. Best single book to 1935 on Twain's life and work.

Walker, Franklin. *San Francisco's Literary Frontier.* New York: Knopf, 1939. Sheds light on Twain's activities in California.

Wallace, Elizabeth. *Mark Twain and the Happy Island.* Chicago: McClurg, 1913. A charming picture of Clemens' visits to Bermuda.

Watterson, Henry. *"Marse Henry": An Autobiography.* New York: Doran, 1919.

Webster, Samuel Charles. *Mark Twain, Business Man.* Boston: Little, Brown, 1946. Adds biographical information about the early years of Twain, as well as the business transactions. An important contribution.

Wecter, Dixon. *Mark Twain*. San Marino: Huntington Library, 1947.

————. *Sam Clemens of Hannibal*. Boston: Houghton Mifflin, 1952. Definitive study of Clemens' youth. Invaluable for the influence of Hannibal on Twain's mature art.

Woolf, S.J. "Painting the Portrait of Mark Twain." *Colliers* 14 May 1910: 42-44.

Chapter 2

BACKGROUNDS

Hannibal

"My parents," wrote Mark Twain, "removed to Missouri in
the early 'thirties; I do not remember just when, for I was
not born then and cared nothing for such things" (*Autobiography* 1: 94). Located at the forks of Salt River (since become proverbial), Florida was a mere village in Monroe County,
scarcely two hundred miles away from Indian territory. Here
on November 30, 1835, the impartial bestower of genius, that
once touched a farmer's cot in Alloway, selected the small
home on one of Florida's two black muddy streets. Until the
age of four the boy, christened Samuel Langhorne Clemens,
lived amid the rude houses, mostly of logs, backed against
the cornfields with rail fences on either side. A log church,
puncheon-floored, beneath which hogs slept until disturbed
by the dogs, served on week days as a schoolhouse. The village boasted two stores, one owned by Sam's uncle, John A.
Quarles, where a man who made a purchase was entitled to draw
a drink of whisky from the barrel, or a boy was given half a
handful of sugar. Existence was primitive and purchases came
cheap. Business, however, was expected to expand with the
community, but unfortunately Florida refused to grow. Soon
the Clemens family moved again, pushed onward by financial
necessity and the hope of better conditions. They were not
movers by nature, but Hannibal offered promise of improved
fortunes for the family. Here John Marshall Clemens became a
leading citizen, serving on committees for municipal improvement, while he dreamed of riches to accrue someday from the
Tennessee land.

Hannibal, somnolent on the West bank of the Mississippi,
actually held no opportunities for wealth. Yet around it
rushed the tides of Western expansion as the continent opened
before the optimistic pioneers courageously pushing forward,
intent upon their fortunes. At its very door the great Mississippi presented a never-ending spectacle, continuously

varied. While viewing the drama, however, the little town
was not a participant; actually Hannibal was a marketplace
for nearby farmers. Thus Sam Clemens' youth began in idyllic,
antebellum days, amid a preindustrial society, for the in-
dustrial revolution and the sectional conflict leading to
civil war were yet to intrude upon Hannibal in the days of
Tom Sawyer.

By inheritence Sam Clemens was a Southerner. John Marshall
Clemens came from Virginia, bringing with him the ideals of
gentlefolk (Ferguson 15). Not wealthy himself, he belonged to
the class of small planter or professional man, in which tradition he fitted himself for the law. The Clemenses, though
not important in Virginia, were minor slaveholders, part of
John Clemens' inheritance being three slaves. Forced by his
father's death to assume male-headship of the family when only
seven years old, he became self-supporting. Circumstances
then took the family into Kentucky--the first move calculated
to relieve financial pressure. There young Clemens fell in
love with and married Jane Lampton, whose family, also from
Virginia, claimed kinship with the Earls of Durham. Upon
moving to Kentucky the Lamptons intermarried with the Montgomery and Casey families. Soon they were faced with fighting
Indians; Kentucky annals record how the sister of Twain's
great-grandmother narrowly escaped being captured by Indians
(Wecter 20-21).

From his father Sam Clemens inherited his intellect and
his integrity. Never a financial success, the elder Clemens
was instead a valued citizen of each community into which he
moved. Although visions of wealth never materialized, he continued the search, and he worked hard. By temperamental en-
dowment Sam possessed his father's desire for success, his
participation in civic affairs, a natural pessimistic strain,
joined by "free-thinking," and most fortunately of all, that
fine sense of justice, an abiding interest in right and wrong,
which placed all of Mark Twain's thought and action upon a
high plane of integrity and honor. The influence of John Marshall Clemens upon his son has only recently been fully appreciated, largely because Twain seldom spoke of him. When
he did refer to his father, the author called him "austere,"
and though incorporated in a jest, such a passage as "My father
and I were always on the most distant terms when I was a boy--
a sort of armed neutrality so to speak," seems to reveal the
true relationship ("A Memory" 12). The influence of Jane
Clemens, however, has been fully recognized, though at times
not wisely.

Van Wyck Brooks may be dismissed in the light of testimony
from more reliable witnesses. As Annie Webster put it, "I
can't imagine where they got the idea that Grandma was so pious

and strait-laced" (qtd. in Webster 226). Frustration theories
aside, Jane Clemens, Kentucky belle, loved to dance, dress
stylishly in bright colors, and she enjoyed a joke; to her we
may attribute Sam's similar traits. Of course, she attended
church and believed in God; and she tried to rear her son
religiously. Our most recent investigators dismiss the idea
of Jane Clemens as a pernicious influence. She was an attractive woman, energetic, fond of life, and at times eccentric--
nothing more. We may agree with the critics who derive Mark
Twain's humor from his mother, and we may add his love for
colorful clothes, but we should not forget to place full emphasis upon the qualities inherited from his father.[1]

The marriage of John Clemens and Jane Lampton was not
loveless, as sometimes misrepresented. Samuel C. Webster has
destroyed the basis for such charges by revealing Jane Clemens'
senility at the time she suggested it in old age, telling a
story her granddaughter suspected was appropriated from another
person's experience (224). The home life appears to have been
happy and normal. Unlike the families of Poe and Whitman there
is no indication of anything even bordering on the embarrassing.
The family, we must admit, was hard up; and it was because of
necessity that Orion at the age of fourteen became apprenticed
to a printer--a step down for the son of a lawyer (Ferguson
21-22). But aside from a natural desire to get on in the
world--shared by every healthy person not congenitally lazy--
the family seemed unscarred by its financial difficulties.
Orion, Pamela, Sam, and Henry were normal children, enjoying
a mutual affection, possessing the usual small jealousies,
but growing up sane, healthy, and with no more inhibitions
than those of any law-abiding citizen. Through his father
and mother Sam fortunately received the inheritance of their
English ancestry, transformed through pioneer environment--
Anglo-Saxon customs adapted to the Mississippi Valley, where
the violence of the frontier contrasted with the culture trans-
ported from Virginia.

Hannibal was a slaveholding community; more than half of
its citizens were Southerners. But actually slaves in Hannibal
were few, as there were no plantations on the delta scale,
only small farms on which the hands worked directly under
their owners. In the village itself the blacks were mostly
household servants, happily regarded as such, and consequently
treated better than the gangs of slaves impersonally supervised
by overseers. Yet blacks were not recognized as individuals;
they were property, regarded as Huck looked upon Jim, despite
his personal affection. For Huck's conscience, which plagued
him about his duty to Jim's owner, rather than to the slave and
his family, was actually the conscience of a region. Yet
Hannibal was not geographically of the Old South; it differed,
despite its customs and its stock (Branch 188-95).

Across the Alleghenies the stream of Southern culture from
the tidewater of the early republic adapted itself to the Mississippi Valley. Amid other soil and climate, confronted by
new conditions, it effected a changed way of life, retaining
parts of the old, but receiving a new identity. Physically
this society became essentially frontier, embracing equali-
tarianism and individualism, yet with social demarcations.

That slavery was an evil never dawned upon Hannibal consciousness. Young Sam regarded all the blacks as friends--
so did the rest of Tom Sawyer's band--and with slave boys of
his own age romped and played. "We were comrades," said
Twain, "and yet not comrades; color and condition interposed
a subtle line which both parties were conscious of and which
rendered complete fusion impossible" (*Autobiography* 1: 100).
Both slave and master regarded the relationship with equanimity.
Certain things were frowned upon: it was not often that black
families were separated, the practice being generally limited
to the settlement of estates. Cruelty to a slave, indeed,
brought such retributive unpopularity that it remained rare.
If little Sam ever saw a slave auction he never remembered it,
although, as he later admitted, it may have been because the
spectacle was not unusual. The sight of a chained slave, however, was another matter, for the sad faces of some once seen
lived too vividly in his memory to have arisen from a common
occurrence.

Although oriented toward the river, Hannibal retained a
lifeline to the East, for with slavery the settlers brought
also certain intellectual pursuits and something of cavalier
manners. There was a town library; four different bookstores
advertised in the newspapers. Books and magazines in fact
were plentiful, often of the best. Readers procured journals
published by Putnam, Harper, Godey, and Graham, while Shakespeare, Milton, and Shelley were for sale on the bookshelves,
along with volumes in French, Latin, and Greek. The Bible,
of course, was known to all, but the classics were read too,
and current literature, especially the typical humorous writings
of the region, was plentiful.

Then the surrounding woods with its wild flowers, animals,
and birds provided education of still another sort. There one
could hunt, fish, or just dream away the calm summer days, for
most days were calm, despite flares of violence, such as did
occur. The eternal cruelties and passions were present there
as elsewhere, breaking forth in perennial crimes; yet for the
most part existence was happy. During two or three months
each year Sam visited the farm of his uncle, John A. Quarles.
Situated four miles from Florida, the farm was worked by about
twenty blacks; one of them, old "Aunt" Hannah, the children
believed to be a thousand years old, while the slaves insisted

she had talked with Moses and credited her thin hair to fright at seeing Pharaoh drown.

There was an orchard, tobacco fields, and a limpid brook, deeply shaded among the trees for wading. Here, also, were swimming pools, more desirable because forbidden. And little Sam played to his heart's delight, climbing the hickory and walnut trees to gather nuts in season, swinging on strands of bark stripped from hickory saplings, or if strawberries were ripe picking them "in the crisp freshness of the early morning, while the dew beads still sparkled upon the grass and the woods were ringing with the first songs of the birds" (*Autobiography* 1: 106). All entered into his consciousness as the natural delight of the English countryside had impressed itself upon Wordsworth during rapturous boyhood. With night, entertainment shifted to the slave quarters, or the house servants gathered about the open fireplace to tell old tales of African fantasy. While a little boy quivered with mingled fright and delight, Uncle Ned spun a bloodcurdling tale to reach the climactic moment of the "Golden Arm."[2]

These old Southern customs of plantation and slave, it must be remembered, existed in a frontier environment. However peaceful Hannibal might be, situated as it was, there was no isolation from intruding violence and crime. Twain remembered the man Fairfax, magnanimously sparing a creature who had just tried to murder him with a pistol that misfired; the Corsican chasing his daughter with a flogging rope; poor old Smarr, shot down in the main street at midday and dying beneath the oppressive weight of a huge family Bible open on his breast; the slave killed by a lump of slag for a slight offense; the stabbing of the "young Californian emigrant" with a bowie knife; the helpless uncle whose nephews held him and repeatedly tried to kill him with a revolver which misfired; and the drunken ruffian shot down by a widow defending her home (*Autobiography* 1: 82, 118, 131-32). The sight of a pistol blazing or knife flashing, followed by the red blood gushing from a death wound, was actuality to Sam Clemens. But violence though prevalent was not prevailing, and as in the realism of Howells, happiness, not sorrow, was the general rule.

Mark Twain's papers, at the University of California, contain a lengthy list of Hannibal residents, notations about them, and comments on what became of them. If sentimentality must be ascribed to those people generally, they were also endowed with idealism, for Twain remembered their being more interested in deeds of honor than in making money. In the cynicism of old age he charged the new desire for wealth above honor to changes wrought by the 'forty-nine gold rush. Yet the Hannibal of earlier days as recorded in unpublished manuscripts contained its unpleasant side. Commenting on Zola's

La Terre Twain declared the vicious and abnormal minority in
any American village to be our American equivalent of its
naturalistic passages, for insanity, murder, rape, and
fanaticism were present in his own Hannibal. A manuscript
titled "Villagers of 1840-43" outlines several characters who
anticipate the villagers of Sherwood Anderson; one such, a
bridegroom, fails to appear for his wedding, and after pro-
longed search is discovered fully dressed like a bride, locked
dead in the family vault.[3] Thus Sam Clemens was aware of the
abnormal fringe of humanity, as were Sherwood Anderson, William
Faulkner, and Eugene O'Neill. But in the world of Mark Twain
as in that of Shakespeare and Chaucer the fringe never becomes
the whole cloth; minorities are seen perspectively, not magnified. These manuscripts, for our purpose, are important as
proof, nevertheless, that the abnormal was seen and recognized.

In brief, the boy Sam Clemens observed with alert eyes,
and from an orchestra seat, as it were, viewed the drama in
his town and on the Mississippi. Indigent raftsmen, fast
packets of commerce, luxurious side-wheelers, gay showboats
floated past in a fleeting world, romantic to the imagination,
yet real and endless. They brought glimpses of a cosmopolitan-
ism which though not of Hannibal was at least seen by the residents, and seeing was believing. The little town, meanwhile,
continued to be stirred by the Westward movement without being
swept into its rush. St. Louis was only eighty miles away,
and all within its orbit felt tremors from the expansion,
which brought the customs and manners of other places.
Whether from the river traffic or westbound emigrants, extremes
of wealth and poverty and diversity of race were evident. In
a way, then, Sam Clemens from early youth was a citizen of the
world, not just of Hannibal, and though remaining truly regional he was saved from ignorant provincialism. Viewing
society vertically through many strata, knowing whites, both
high and low, blacks, Indians, and half-breeds, the boy was
schooled during his most impressionable years through a broad
view of humanity, which helped to produce the world author.

Such education naturally continued through a lifetime as
Twain became a part of all he met, encountering probably a
greater diversity of experience than any other American author;
yet his formal schooling ended when he was about twelve--not
at all, it should be mentioned, to his regret. After John
Marshall Clemens' death the boy became an apprentice in a
printer's shop. Until the winter of 1850-51, when he went to
work for his brother Orion on the Hannibal *Journal*, first
called *Western Union* (Brashear 97)[4], Sam learned the newspaper
trade from Joseph P. Ament, owner of the *Missouri Courier*.
Under his brother's tutelage Sam rose to subeditor, but first
he served as printer, then learned how to write (Armstrong

485-501). The newspapers and periodical exchanges received
at the office were filled with humorous anecdotes, burlesque
characterizations, and hilarious satires--all brimming with
exaggerations and understatements. Such writing flourished
in American journalism for three decades before the Civil
War: tales of bear hunters, rivermen, country parsons, gamb-
lers, and trappers told with vigorous, sometimes clamorous,
fun. Still in his teens Sam became a part of this tradition,
in fact, even contributed to it. Franklin J. Meine says that
the young printer became "saturated with this frontier humor"
(*Tall Tales* xv). Actually Sam needed no books to acquaint
him with jokes and pranks, for he and his associates were constantly indulging in them. Frontier humor was a part of life;
the authors simply touched it up for literary consumption.
Of course, for the tall tales, the legendary exploits of a
mythical Mike Fink or a fictionalized version of Davy Crockett,
they drew the longbow as far as it would go. The bigger the
"whopper" the better. But most of the stories of Simon Suggs,
Sut Lovingood, and Major Jones have authenticity as social
history, and their narrative method furnished Sam Clemens his
model.

When Orion from financial necessity journeyed to Tennessee
in an effort to sell the Clemens' land there, Sam took charge
of the paper, thus starting his literary career. But Orion
returned unsuccessful, and the subeditor decided to look about
for pastures greener with currency. His writings in Hannibal,
though generally funny, are of interest only because Sam
Clemens wrote them; there is nothing to suggest the artist
of the future.

Mark Twain, when applying his theories to himself, liked
to trace developments from a sudden twist of events; one such
was the bleak, windy afternoon on the Hannibal streets when a
scattering wind swept into his hands the fragment from some
story of Joan of Arc. So stirred was the young printer's
imagination by this glimpse at history that from a broken bit
of dialogue he suddenly began to try his hand at sketching
characters and plots (Paine 1: 81-82). Among the exchanges
coming into Orion's office was the *Carpet-Bag*, published in
Boston by Benjamin P. Shillaber, creator of the Widow Partington, whose humorous comments reached an amused audience
throughout the nation. On May 1, 1852, the *Carpet-Bag* carried a slight, humorous sketch called "The Dandy Frightening
the Squatter," signed "S.L.C.," Sam's earliest known appearance
in print (if we except the squibs attributed to him in the
Hannibal papers) and therefore Mark Twain's first story (Meine
445).

The next year Sam left Hannibal, lured partly, no doubt,
by news of the Crystal Palace Fair in New York, which had

aroused Hannibal interest. If Sam had desired the river or
Western migration there was little to hinder him, but thinking
of himself as a newspaperman he turned his eyes toward the
Atlantic.

Wanderings

Although Sam Clemens soon found work in New York as a
printer and continued to report back home on his progress,
within less than two months he went to Philadelphia. October 26, 1853, found him writing to Orion in Hannibal, unaware
that his brother had moved to Iowa and bought an interest in
the Muscatine *Journal*. There the first forwarded letter was
published promptly as "Philadelphia Correspondence," to be
followed with others requested by Orion. Though these letters
gave Sam a chance to practice descriptive writing, they contain little humor, and read like travel reports. They are,
however, clear, straightforward, and free of verbosity.
February 18, 1854, Sam was in Washington, where he found expression for his humor in a few sly digs at Congress (*Muscatine Journal* 18-22). Then he decided to head homeward, joining
his mother and Orion in Muscatine during the late summer.
     Nobody knows how long he remained there before going to
St. Louis. We may assume that Sam worked for Orion on the
Journal, finding the earnings scarce and life rather dull by
contrast with the cities. Soon he was off again to St.
Louis, spending the winter and spring of 1855 there, before
returning home, this time to Keokuk, where Orion had moved
with his brother Henry.
     Now Sam seemed completely happy. With Orion married and
their mother located in St. Louis, he lived as he pleased in
his own quarters at Orion's job office. Popularity was instan-
taneous, and with congenial companions of his own age Sam
was content there about a year and a half. But there was too
much of John Marshall Clemens in his son to allow pleasure to
dominate his actions indefinitely. Working hard and receiving
little for it, Sam despite his irresponsible state of happiness
thought about advancement. Wanderlust seized him as he began
to imagine fortune awaiting him in South America.
     Then fate again entered the scene. A wind favorable to
Sam blew a piece of paper down Main Street; when he stooped
to pick it up, there was a fifty dollar bill. Whether he
waited four days for the owner to claim it or left that same
day we may never know, but with cash in hand he quickly made
plans (*Autobiography* 2: 288). Success with the Muscatine

Journal letters naturally suggested newspaper correspondence
as a means of securing money for his projected trip to Brazil,
and Sam arranged for a series of travel letters for which
George Rees, editor of the Keokuk *Post*, agreed to pay five
dollars each. The first letter was written from St. Louis,
October 18, 1856; then two more followed from Cincinnati
during the winter (Lorch, "Mark Twain in Iowa" 438).[5] Sam
adopted the customary pseudonym and illiterate spelling; as
Thomas Jefferson Snodgrass he recounted the misadventures of
a bumpkin who is ejected from a theater because he thinks the
play is real, makes a spectacle of himself on his first train
ride, and trying to do a young woman a favor is left holding
a basket containing a baby. When Sam upped his rates on the
editor, however, the arrangement was terminated, and Thomas
Jefferson Snodgrass' "Dierrea" was never added to the shelf
of world travel books.

But the winter in Cincinnati was to prove important for
notable association. Although his given name has escaped
Twain scholars, all attest the influence of a "Scotchman named
Macfarlane" (Paine 1: 112-15).[6] At the cheap boardinghouse
where Sam lodged, this humorless man, twice his age, exerted
an irresistible intellectual appeal. His trade Sam never
learned, but Macfarlane's hands were hardened by toil; his
mind, however, was a storehouse of knowledge gleaned from
serious reading in philosophy, history, and science. And Macfarlane, like O. Henry, knew the dictionary by heart; not once
was Sam able to discover a word unfamiliar to Macfarlane.
Prior to Darwin's publication of *The Origin of Species* this
independent thinker advanced a similar theory, except that he
went further: although life had developed on an ascending
scale from a primal seed to man, there the development had
stopped and retrogression set in. In lengthy discussions
lasting through the evening the Scotchman expounded his philosophy: man he contended had the only bad heart in the animal
kingdom; his alone contained malice, envy, and vice; man's
intellect was depraved; and consequently man was the moral
inferior of the animals. Readers of *What Is Man?* will recognize Macfarlane's lasting influence on the ultimate philosophy
evolved by Mark Twain.

For that influence alone the winter in Cincinnati remains
memorable, but there is aught else. With cessation of the
Snodgrass letters Sam temporarily abandoned literature to re-
vive his dream of cocoa hunter on the Amazon, a dream growing
brighter with the returning spring. April, 1857, found him
boarding the *Paul Jones*, bound for New Orleans, and then to
South America. But presence on the boat revived an older
boyhood dream, the ambition of every Hannibal youth to be a
pilot. The result was swift; Horace Bixby, one of the pilots,

knew the Bowen boys, Will, Sam, and Bart, all of whom had become pilots in realization of the dream Sam Clemens once
shared with them as pranking youngsters. By the time the
boat reached its destination Bixby had agreed to take Sam
Clemens on as a pilot, "learn" him the river, and on credit
at that (Paine 1: 117-20).

The Pilot

It was a deal, and Sam turned to his task innocent of the
multitude of minute details waiting to confound him. Along
with the river's changing shape, assuming shadows by starlight,
straightening its banks in pitch-dark, and fading away with
the gray mist, the pilot had to know the *real* shape so accurately that he could steer ahead, certain of his course regardless
of weather or time of day. No sooner did the cub master this
problem than he was staggered by the discovery that he must
remember shoal soundings and water marks, exactly as to spot
and trip.

No wonder Sam felt that piloting strained the memory as
nothing else on earth. But the reward was worth it; a pilot
earned from a hundred and fifty to two hundred and fifty
dollars per month, he was highly respected, and he ruled the
boat. As to what kind of pilot Sam became, conjecture has
been raised. Although he had only praise for his former pupil
when interviewed by Albert Bigelow Paine, Horace Bixby later
disparaged him: "He knew the Mississippi River like a book,
but he lacked confidence.... No sir, Sam Clemens knew the
river, but being a coward, he was a failure as a pilot" (qtd.
in Hutcherson 354).

The incident recounted in *Life on the Mississippi* of how
Bixby destroyed his cub's confidence, causing him to stop the
boat in a clear channel through fear of wrecking her, occurred while Sam was learning, but that seems to be how Bixby
remembered him. Sam's record, however, proclaims success
rather than failure; for he wrote from St. Louis in 1859,
when many young pilots were unemployed, that he was on the
City of Memphis, a large and difficult boat to handle. And
the Tom Sawyer in his nature delighted to allow a glimpse of
a hundred dollar bill in his wallet, while noting the chagrin
of those who had predicted his failure at the wheel (*Letters*
1: 43-44). Whatever pilots delighting in daredevil exploits
may have thought of his abilities, Sam continued in his profession, turning his wheel until traffic was ended by the war,
drawing good wages, and never having any serious mishaps.

Until his license was granted April 9, 1859, he must have continued as a cub, although it appears that he also piloted a freight boat without a license, such practice being lawful (Brownell, "License" 1-3). A picture of the *John J. Roe*, once piloted by Twain, shows it to have been a freighter. It was the passenger steamer, however, that appealed to Sam, who enjoyed the "glass temple" pilothouse with its "red and gold window-curtains," furniture with leather cushions, servants to supply "tarts and ices and coffee," and the glittering, gilded accommodations of the staterooms and saloon.

With his boyhood ambition realized, Sam now had plenty of money, and the family looked to him for aid and advice. But the river, a source of danger, even as it was a purveyor of wealth, held terrors as well as pomp and glory. Occasional steamboat explosions, horrible with scaldings, burned flesh, and mangled bodies, inflicted injury and death upon helpless passengers and crew. While still a cub, Sam Clemens himself came close to such catastrophe; an explosion on the steamer *Pennsylvania* killed his brother Henry. Because of a quarrel with a tyrannical pilot named Brown, Sam was put ashore from the *Pennsylvania* to follow on another boat. Henry, blown clear of the wreck by the explosion, although injured internally, bravely swam back to rescue others until his own lungs collapsed from the scalding steam. In his grief Sam reproached himself for the disaster, for he had previously urged his brother to help save the passengers in case of accident. It was he, not Henry, who had been put ashore to safety after the fight in the pilothouse, though both were involved. Finally in the hospital at Memphis he accidentally gave Henry an overdose of morphine. Sam blamed himself, but he also questioned the fates. Suppose he had not had the quarrel with its resulting events, or another pilot had been found to replace Brown, as the captain of the *Pennsylvania* had wished. The tragedy preyed on his mind, until unable to sleep at night, he confided to Orion his self-condemnations. For the first time he felt the mood of Melville, for chance and fate had brought tragedy to which he had unintentionally contributed. However youthful he may have been in temperament in later years, from the time of Henry's death, Clemens began to age in appearance. But he continued on the river, returning as steersman for kindly George Ealer, the idolator of Shakespeare. Securing his license, Sam finally became partner to his old mentor, Horace Bixby. On the *City of Memphis*, "the largest boat in the trade and the hardest to pilot," he must have performed satisfactorily, for we find him happy in his berth and hoping to save about a hundred dollars a month from his salary (*Letters* 1: 43).

Gradually Sam returned to his accustomed gaiety, "dissipating on a ten dollar dinner at a French *restaurant*--breathe it not unto Ma!" (*Letters* 1: 48). And on a trip which he gave his mother he outraged her Victorian sensibilities by hugging and kissing the girls and dancing the schottische (*Letters* 1: 46-47). Visiting in St. Louis, he teased his little niece until she complained to her parents that although everybody else understood about Moses and the bullrushes, she could never make Uncle Sam understand that Moses was not the keeper of the secondhand store on Market Street (Webster 39). And he enjoyed playing the piano.

As a pilot Sam Clemens tasted the sweets of success. It was his first triumph, financially and individually. Naturally while learning the river he had been forced by necessity to give up all thoughts of writing. Now that he had mastered his lessons and achieved boyhood's great ambition, Clemens found himself with leisure time. In 1859 the eternal humorist in Mark Twain found opportunity for expression. Captain Isaiah Sellers, a retired pilot with an inexhaustible memory, who contributed bits of river information to the New Orleans *Picayune*, wrote with an oracular assurance and egotistical manner, irritating to the younger pilots. Sam Clemens, annoyed by having present experiences continually depreciated by comparison with the past, even by one holding the longest service record on the river, seized a chance to retaliate. When Captain Sellers with an air of infallibility estimated the rise of a flood, basing his prediction on memory of experiences since 1815, Sam replied with a satire in the *Daily Crescent* (May 17, 1859).

Although Sam later thought that Sellers' articles were signed "Mark Twain" and that his own burlesque broke the old Captain's heart, there is no such evidence.[7] As Leisy suggests, the probable explanation is that the use of the name "Fathom" by Clemens caused him to confuse it in memory with the similar river term for the same sounding, "Mark Twain." Paine, who thought Sellers had used the name, believed Sam took it to make amends for a thoughtless injury (1: 150). But a careful investigation has destroyed this myth, and if there is any connection between Sellers and "Mark Twain" it is an indirect one confused in memory. As Sellers never used the name, Clemens could not have borrowed it from him. The old captain served a more immediate purpose, however, in bringing Sam Clemens momentarily again to newspaper writing.

But apparently he wrote nothing else, although the satire was generally appreciated by his cronies. Clemens' good salary enabled him to assist his relatives, and he continued to have fun, while improving himself with such cultural offerings as Church's painting "Heart of the Andes," which he took his sister Pamela to see in St. Louis (*Letters* 1: 46). Sam's letters

reveal that he had been reading Hood, Goldsmith, and Cervantes.
Although the country was on its tragic way to the War Between
the States, there is nothing in Clemens' letters or diary to
indicate it.

When the war started, Horace Bixby, who declared for the
Union, remembered that Sam had gone in the opposite direction.
Though little is known, it appears Sam accompanied another
pilot, named Montgomery, in supporting the Southern cause.
Dixon Wecter suggests that Clemens may have joined the Louisiana Guards in the winter of 1860-61. The conjecture arises
from the contents of a series of ten letters written for the
New Orleans *Daily Crescent* from January 21 through March 30
of 1861.[8] In the first letter, Sam, again using the name
"Snodgrass"--now changed from "Thomas Jefferson" to "Quintus
Curtius"--narrates in mock-heroic style the discomforts of a
bloodless expedition to capture Baton Rouge, in ignorance that
the Federal garrison had already capitulated. Throughout the
letters Sam satirized regimentation, parodied army discipline,
and burlesqued the awkward efforts of the recruits. The first
five letters are devoted entirely to humorous comments on getting
used to military life, but the sixth takes Snodgrass to see the
sights, recounting to his friend Brown a series of adventures
in restaurant and theater, similar to those of his predecessor,
Thomas Jefferson Snodgrass. The seventh letter, "Snodgrass
Dines with Old Abe," displays the derisive attitude of the
Confederates toward the Yankee President. The last three letters return to the difficulties of the civilian to adjust himself to his newly acquired military existence. If Sam Clemens
was not actually a member of this military aggregation, at
least he was familiar enough with its problems to write accurate
burlesque and satire. Yet his interest in the war appears
slight, for four days after Lincoln issued his call for troops
on April 15, 1861, Sam arrived in St. Louis from New Orleans,
where he left the volunteers he had so humorously depicted.
On the next day Orion received official notification of his
appointment as Territorial Secretary of Nevada. If there had
been conflicting opinions of loyalty among the pilots, even as
among most citizens of the border states, the same was true in
the Clemens family, for while Orion was an out-and-out abolitionist, his mother had a horror of "Black Republicans" (Webster 64).
Amid the excitement of impending hostility Sam found time, however, to embark upon Masonry, passing to a Fellowcraft degree
on the same day, June 12, 1861, that Governor Jackson called
the Missouri state militia into active service. At this time
Sam returned to Hannibal, formerly pro-Southern, but now con-
trolled by Union Home Guards. With several graduates of "Tom
Sawyer's band," among them Sam Bowen and Ed Stevens, he helped
to organize a Confederate battalion, a movement carried out

secretly to prevent arrest by the Federals (Paine 1: 164).
Already apprehensive lest he be forced into Union service and
made to pilot Federal steamboats at the point of a pistol,
Sam entered enthusiastically upon this new venture. There
was no formal enlistment, no oath of allegiance, and no discipline, the men electing their officers subject to dismissal.
As DeLancey Ferguson has indicated, Missouri was filled with
such groups, many disintegrating like this one, some even becoming outlaw gangs, such as Quantrill's, to rob and murder
(62). Mark Twain told his own story later in "The Private
History of a Campaign That Failed," adding his usual fictional
embroidery to the facts. Whether disillusioned by mud, briars,
and encounters with bulldogs, or weary from saddle boils and
sprained ankles, Sam Clemens was out of the army and back in
St. Louis taking a Master Mason's degree on July 10, 1861
(Lorch, "Campaign" 462). The charge has been leveled that
Clemens was a deserter from the colors, that he went West to
avoid the draft. But Professor Lorch seems to have stated the
problem sensibly and fairly:

> Orion had received what appeared to be, and was, a
> promising political appointment.... But while Orion had
> a good office he lacked the money to go to it, except
> such as he may have arranged to borrow. Sam still had
> money, saved from his earnings on the river. With the
> probable aid of his mother and sister, Orion urged Sam
> to go with him, partly for company, partly for financial
> aid, and partly to wean Sam from his Rebel sympathies.
> ("Campaign" 464)

When the Union forces occupied the surrounding countryside
after routing a Rebel army under General Sterling Price, many
hastily organized Confederates, such as the Home Guards, became
demoralized and filtered home, there being no power to hold
them. Sam Clemens' desire to retire from a group which was
never a part of the Confederate Army was not desertion. Neither
does it appear that he hoped to secure sudden wealth by joining
Orion, for employment and a chance to see the country were more
probably the magnets.

Agreeing to be the Secretary's secretary, Sam, without
assignment of duties or salary, paid both fares ($150 apiece),
and they were off in late July, 1861, on the twenty-day journey
immortalized in *Roughing It*. DeLancey Ferguson, however, believes that the secretaryship was a bit of Mark's customary
embroidery, that the real reasons for the trip were a desire
for adventure and Orion's determination to stop Sam's Confederate activities, something an ardent Unionist and abolitionist
could regard only with horror (65).

On July 18, the brothers traveled by steamboat from St.
Louis to St. Joseph, where cowhide boots and flannel shirts

replaced their former attire. Leaving by Overland stage,
July 26, they reached Carson City, Nevada, on August 14. So
completely had they affected the slouchy appearance of frontier
dress that the reception committee for the new Secretary was
dismayed. Brooks seized upon this change of costume to indicate loss of artistic integrity, but Ferguson seems closer to
Mark Twain when observing, "Tom Sawyer could always be counted
on to play a role to the limit" (66). Now Sam Clemens was in
the West, a frontier unique in time and place, where just
twelve years after the gold rush fortunes were still being
made, suddenly and when least expected.[9] Sam like everyone
else caught the fever, but like the majority he got nothing
but excitement. Though the theme of rich prospects runs through
all of Clemens' letters from Nevada--prospects which had captured Orion's imagination too--the later dedication of *Roughing
It* to Calvin H. Higbie "in memory of the curious time when we
two were millionaires for ten days" is nostalgic innacuracy.
The story told in *Roughing It* is, moreover, a composite account
put together for fiction.[10] But it was, no doubt, the disappointment suffered through the failure of the Monitor and
Wide West claims which extinguished Clemens' hopes of a fortune
from the mines. In partnership with Orion, Sam staked out a
claim at Esmeralda, going to work upon it, while Orion furnished
funds. By now, as his own resources were nearly exhausted,
he depended upon his brother until his prospecting and mining
efforts should pay off. Meanwhile, in his spare time Sam again
took up his pen, for a sore back and blistered hands were all
the mine yielded. On May 11, 1862, he mentions to Orion some
letters, written for the *Enterprise*--burlesque sketches, says
Paine, which were signed "Josh" (*Letters* 1: 81). Soon thereafter all hopes for wealth at Esmeralda dwindled into unpaid
debts. But the editor of the *Enterprise*, Joe Goodman--urged
by Barstow, a business manager with a weather eye for what
readers wanted--liked Sam's contributions enough to offer him
a job at twenty-five dollars a week. Though badly in need of
money, Clemens did not jump at the offer; instead he went away
for a week or so, leaving at midnight. Why or what for, nobody knows. Speculations run from Paine's statement that he
went into the wilderness for a communication with his soul to
DeLancey Ferguson's pragmatic guess that he may have heard of
a new bonanza and was investigating secretly to avoid a stam-
pede. Whatever the reason, he decided to give up mining, and
he had no desire for his old profession, for in a letter to
Pamela he declared, "I never expect to do any more piloting at
any price" (*Letters* 1: 85). Destiny was in the West, leading
him at last to the one occupation he should nevermore forsake.

Arriving one hot, dusty August afternoon, after a hundred-
and-thirty-mile walk to Virginia City, Sam entered the *Enterprise* office, where he dropped his pack, sank into a chair,

and absently declared: "My starboard leg seems to be unshipped.
I'd like about one hundred yards of line; I think I am falling
to pieces." Then he added: "I want to see Mr. Barstow, or
Mr. Goodman. My name is Clemens, and I've come to write for
the paper" (qtd. in Paine 1: 205). It was typical of his
humor: the irrelevant beginning, the pause for suspense, and
then the dramatic line.

Now Samuel Clemens, ex-printer, ex-pilot, ex-Confederate
irregular, ex-miner and prospector, was come into his own.
Shortly to emerge as "Mark Twain," he was never again to be
other than a professional man of letters, earning his liveli-
hood by his pen, from this climactic moment until the end of
his triumphant career.

Although the Comstock Lode derived its name from Henry
T.P. Comstock, the real discoverers were two miners, Peter
O'Riley and Patrick McLaughlin, who struck the ore at the top
of what became the famous Ophir Mine. Whether Comstock had
secured previous knowledge of the deposit or not has never
been settled--circumstances indicate that he did. At any
rate, O'Riley and McLaughlin unhappily found their strike to
be on land owned by Comstock, who promptly declared himself in
for a share. From then on, it was Comstock who was conspicu-
ously present around the Ophir, electing himself superintendent,
ostentatiously greeting all visitors, and doing so much talking
that people came to regard the lode as his, while the real
discoverers were quickly forgotten. Soon a village began to
form on the site of Comstock's land, first called Ophir, then
changing names several times, to be finally christened by
James Fennimore, better known as "Old Virginia," who enjoying
a customary spree, lurched to the ground with broken whisky
bottle and the cry, "I baptize this ground Virginia." The
name stuck, although it came to be called Virginia City (De-
Quille 32).

When Sam Clemens arrived, Virginia City was a rough, masculine community, loud and strong, fond of coarse humor and
straight whisky. Next to mining, in fact, its most lucrative
enterprise was saloon-keeping. Colorful, fascinating, boisterous, Virginia City had its sordid side also in the gambling
halls and numerous houses of prostitution, ranging from "ladies
of the evening" in abodes of tapestried walls down to the cheap-
est harlots in the cribs--practically the only women, by the
way, to be found in this masculine territory. True there was
a theater but its influence was more diverting than cultural,
for although it did offer Jenny Lind with her Swedish nightin-
gale songs and Artemus Ward with humorous lectures, the big
hit at Piper's Opera House was Adah Isaacs Menken in *Mazeppa*,
combining Byron, melodrama, and nudity to produce one of the
most effective presentations of sex appeal ever displayed on
the American stage.

On its better side Virginia City was lively, fresh,
healthy, and fearless, a place where rugged, vigorous men
lived according to a code, akin in its cardinal insistence
upon loyalty, honesty, and fairness to the chivalry of the
Old South, freshly acclimatized into Western setting and garb.
No college could have offered the curriculum of human nature
furnished by Sam's job with the *Enterprise*, for no faculty
could have educated him as did the men in that office. All
were exceptional, and what is more important in the career
of Sam Clemens, they helped him to develop those inherent
qualities, which through his associations on the newspaper
naturally grew into those of Mark Twain. From Joe Goodman,
his discoverer, Sam not only got his chance to live by his
pen, but he learned the force of informed, fearless writing.
Dan DeQuille, the best humorous writer on the coast, was his
constant companion, a model to follow, and a friendly guide.
It was in the manner of Dan that Twain began to achieve his
first success beyond the local boundary. Rollin M. Daggett,
founder of the *Golden Era*, later U.S. Minister to Hawaii, then
writing courageous satires for the *Enterprise*, taught Sam
something about fighting corruption. Little Steve Gillis,
one of the printers, weighing only ninety-five pounds, but
brave as a gamecock, who acted later as second in the Comstock
duel and accompanied him to San Francisco, was responsible
for the memorable visit to Jackass Hill. Denis McCarthy, part
owner of the paper, became Mark's business manager when the
lecture tour of 1866 was inaugurated (Benson 69-71).

The *Territorial Enterprise*, started by Joseph Goodman and
Denis McCarthy, had progressed in two years from shoestring
beginnings to its own building with the latest in presses and
compositors hired from San Francisco. William Wright (celebrated on the coast under the name of "Dan DeQuille"), chief reporter and feature writer, took Sam home with him, starting an
enduring friendship. If Goodman can be called the discoverer
of Mark Twain through his appreciation of the "Josh letters,"
to DeQuille goes the credit of breaking him in. In fact, it
was due to the need of a substitute for Dan, who was soon to
take a vacation, that Clemens was hired. Actually the new
writer had plenty of leeway, Goodman's policy being simply a
matter of getting facts and printing them in full--then letting the devil take the hindmost. Feuds thus arising were more
interesting than the news reports starting them. As DeLancey
Ferguson has emphasized, readers of the *Enterprise* were ac-
quainted with the news before the paper came from the press;
therefore aside from tips on business deals, what appealed most
was the lampoon or the hoax, or lacking that, then a good feud
in print (79-80).

Sam, the once "Dog-be-deviled Citizen" of Hannibal journalism, needed no instruction in starting a feud or creating a

lampoon. Now he was to learn the hoax, a favorite of Western humor, at which DeQuille was past master. But his first hoax about a "Petrified Man" appearing in the *Territorial Enterprise*, October 5, 1862, is indebted to "John Phoenix," the nom de plume of George Horatio Derby, who had died the previous year (Benson 175). Phoenix had written a hoax about finding living specimens of highly unusual animals in Washington territory. Although no evidence exists that it was anywhere taken seriously, the mere fact that the New York *Spirit of the Times* reprinted it without calling it humorous was seized upon in California to indicate a serious reception. From this incident the belief on the coast persisted that Western humorists could fool Eastern and European readers with outlandish tales presented as facts. There is no evidence that Clemens' "A Washoe Joke" about a petrified man was ever taken seriously anywhere, although Mark Twain ten years later improved the story and claimed it a successful hoax. But it was popular with Western readers, just as it is amusing today, and Twain probably recalled the legend about how John Phoenix "gulled" the East (Bellamy 29-43).

During the last two months of 1862 Clemens convinced Goodman that he possessed the ability to report on the Second Territorial Legislature of Nevada, which met at Carson City. As the *Enterprise* correspondent had just resigned to become legislative clerk, Goodman, despite Sam's ignorance of such matters, decided to give him a chance. The first letters sent back to the paper anonymously contained a number of blunders, arising from a lack of parliamentary knowledge, which Clement T. Rice, a skillful reporter for the rival Virginia City *Union*, quickly made the object of jest. Immediately Sam rejoined that Rice's articles might be parliamentarily correct, but in all other respects were a mass of misstatement, so far from the facts that he dubbed their author "The Unreliable" (Paine 1: 219-20). From then on, Sam never referred to Rice by any other term, a practice which delighted the newspaper fraternity of the coast, to whom Rice became "The Unreliable" for life. Sensing the value of journalistic warfare to keep them before the public, Rice and Clemens, although good friends socially, assumed the feud for their papers.

With his letters being copied up and down the coast, Sam began to wish for more than anonymity, realizing that if he wished to develop his stature as a personality his letters should be associated with a name. Goodman agreed, and on February 2, 1863, Samuel Clemens first signed the name of Mark Twain to one of his Carson City letters to the *Enterprise*.[11]

Upon arrival at Carson City, Sam had again "become the glass of fashion that he had been on the river" (Paine 1: 221).

He made his home with Orion, whose wife and little daughter
had arrived from the States, and who as acting governor of the
Territory was a person of importance. And Twain himself, now
popular in his profession, was never again to leave the limelight. While depending upon his pen, he continued to dabble
in mining stock, successfully augmenting his income. He could
renew the old habit of sending money home, several letters
revealing an enclosure of twenty dollars, for no matter how
much his enjoyment in Carson City or Virginia City, he did
not forget his Missouri relatives.

In May, 1863, Twain and the "Unreliable" Rice visited San
Francisco, where a hearty welcome from its citizens and many
visitors from Washoe began a round of high, wide, and handsome
entertainment. Twain was having the time of his life, and on
October 28, 1863, he wrote another hoax for the *Enterprise*,
traditionally known as "The Empire City Massacre" or "The
Dutch Nick Massacre." Like the story of the petrified man
thumbing his nose, the account of its general acceptance as
fact was later vivified and enlarged upon by Twain. But it
delighted Western readers, who reveled in the gory details
that blinded them to the hints that a hoax was being perpetrated. The story created a sensation having nothing to do
with Twain's real purpose of condemning the San Francisco
waterworks for "cooking" a dividend. When the truth was discovered, the papers which had printed it rebuked Twain to such
an extent that he was disturbed by the unexpected reaction,
for it appears that he had overstepped the line even for
Washoe (Lillard 198-203).

In December, 1863, Clemens met Artemus Ward, master platform performer, who exerted a double influence on his future
career: first, by demonstrating how a first-rate humorist successfully delivered a lecture, and secondly, by offering encouraging advice which Clemens had the good sense to follow.
For three weeks Artemus remained in Virginia City, enjoying
the companionship of Clemens and the others with whom he wined
and dined until the early mornings. It was an association of
mutual fellowship and esteem, and following Ward's departure
Clemens heeded his advice by preparing a bit of Comstock humor
for Eastern consumption.[12] Probably written in San Francisco
during the summer of 1863, "Those Blasted Children" was published in the New York *Sunday Mercury*, February 21, 1864, the
first product of Twain's pen to appear in an Eastern journal.
It was soon reprinted by the *Golden Era*--proof that Twain's
satire was funny on either coast.

When Joe Goodman, during a temporary absence, entrusted
Twain with editorship of the *Enterprise*, an unfortunate verbal
warfare ensued, reminiscent of the cub days on Orion's Hannibal
paper, but this time, unfortunately, not so easily settled.

As Twain narrates in *Roughing It*, a sack of flour was auctioned
to raise money for the Sanitary Fund, the Civil War equivalent
of the Red Cross, sponsored by the ladies of Carson City (2:
24-31). Still Southern enough to indulge in anti-Union humor,
Mark warned that the contributions would probably be diverted
to a "Miscegenation Society somewhere in the East." The storm
against Mark immediately broke, and the outraged ladies even
ostracized Orion and Mollie, who had recently suffered the
loss of an only child. Although Twain sent an apology which
modified their wrath, the affair had become so involved through
exchanges in print between the *Enterprise* and the *Union* that it
could not be terminated gently. Personal insult and charges
of cowardice led to preparations for a duel with James L.
Laird, the *Union* editor, but the duel actually never took
place. It is too bad that the versions later told by Twain
and his second, Steve Gillis, have been rejected by scholarship,
for if too good to be true, they are, nevertheless, a contribution to Western mythology. The facts seem to be that Twain by
issuing a challenge in print openly violated a newly passed
law which made it a felony to send or accept a challenge. The
authorities could not ignore a printed challenge, one in fact
presenting a test case for their legal innovation. Twain fled,
then, to escape arrest; he ended his career at the Comstock in
May, 1864, when accompanied by faithful Steve Gillis, Clemens
went to San Francisco (Benson 112).

Thus far Mark Twain had been the writer of burlesque and
extravaganza, the creator of humor for miners on the Comstock,
who reveled in the bloody details of his massacre hoax, or the
fantastic idea of a petrified man, thumb to his nose, whose
burial could be accomplished only after blasting. But he was
a professional writer, and even if a journalist, at least one
whose writings had been reprinted in the East and who enjoyed
popularity the length and breadth of the coast. Moreover, he
had previously written Washoe correspondence for the *Golden Era*
and the San Francisco *Morning Call*. Now a resident of San Francisco, Sam Clemens went to work writing dramatic reviews, court
reports, and local news for the *Morning Call*, a job that probably
lasted from early June until about October 11.[13] Clemens and
Steve Gillis, who roomed together, moved a number of times,
living for a while on a bluff in California Street, from which
point of vantage they enjoyed hurling an occasional beer bottle
on the tin can roofs below, a sport that became their favorite
Sunday amusement. San Francisco appealed to Clemens, who found
its climate "mild and singularly equable."[14]

Since several of his Washoe writings had appeared in the
Golden Era, Clemens had no trouble selling that journal two
sketches shortly after his arrival. Indeed, a close affinity
existed between the *Territorial Enterprise* and the *Golden Era*.

Goodman, McCarthy, and Daggett had once been connected with
the latter before going to Virginia City, and Dan DeQuille
still served the *Era* as Virginia City correspondent, in which
capacity Mark may even have substituted. But another publication soon caught his fancy, the *Californian*, generally considered
superior to the *Golden Era*, which though a magazine in content
was still a newspaper in format. An offer of fifty dollars a
month for one article a week brought Twain to the *Californian*,
although it was the same sum paid by the *Golden Era*. As he
wrote to his mother, the *Era* "wasn't high-toned enough" (*Letters* 1: 100). His first sketch for the *Californian*, "A Notable
Conundrum," appeared October 1, 1864, and his contributions
continued regularly until he left San Francisco. Simultaneously
he continued to report for the *Morning Call* for a few more
weeks.[15]

While not allowed by the *Call* to express himself freely on
corruption and vice in San Francisco, Clemens, through his
connections in Virginia City, furnished the *Enterprise* with
blistering attacks, which Joe Goodman printed. Until a file
of the *Enterprise* is located, we can only guess at the nature
of these philippics, but they were strong enough to cause the
San Francisco chief of police to enter a libel suit against
the paper. Twain then repeated the charges in terms so strong
that he doubted Goodman would print them, and the *Enterprise*
promptly carried the letter, word for word. At this crucial
point, when Twain's unpopularity with the San Francisco police
was at its peak, Steve Gillis decided to enjoy a fight, which
ended delightfully for Steve, but left his opponent, a big
bruising bartender, ready for the hospital. The police now
took their revenge for Twain's scathing articles; Steve was
promptly indicted on charges of assault with intent to kill,
and Twain stood his bond. When it became apparent that the
retaliative police intended full criminal prosecution, Steve
skipped out, followed shortly by Twain, whose personal property
was about to be attached. Steve went to Virginia City, and
Twain accepted an invitation from Jim Gillis to take refuge at
his cabin on Jackass Hill in the Mother Lode country of California, arriving there December 4, 1864 (Paine 1: 264-65).[16]

Here on Jackass Hill near Tuttletown, California, Twain
found a restful haven with congenial companions. Many days
(for the rainy season was on) he sat around the fire with Jim,
Bill Gillis, and Dick Stoker--Stoker and his remarkable cat to
be immortalized in *Roughing It* as Dick Baker and Tom Quartz.
Jim Gillis owned many of the standard classics, and in the
pleasant solitude of the Tuolumne hills Sam Clemens read before
the fire or listened to Jim invent wonderful yarns about Dick
Stoker, extravagant adventures told with humor and fancy, but
also with insistence upon their veracity. And it was Jim,

standing back to the fire, who narrated "The Burning Shame"
later to enrich our literature as "The Royal Nonesuch" in
Huckleberry Finn. Some of these yarns were masterpieces to
commit to memory, which Sam stored away, remarking later that
he never could get them to sound so well as when Jim told them
(Paine 1: 267). If Artemus Ward had provided instruction in
platform technique, here was the art of narration taught by a
past master.

When the weather permitted, Jim initiated Twain in the art
of pocket mining, a trade providing Gillis all he needed for
his simple life; for, like Thoreau, Jim in his Tuolumne Walden
required only books, food, and shelter. Always ready to offer
hospitality or lend whatever money he possessed, Gillis found
no necessity for worldly luxuries. The story of how he and
Twain almost made a fortune through a lucky strike, only to
lose it because Twain was too cold and tired to wash one more
pan of dirt, bears the touch of artistic decoration, but both
Steve Gillis and Joe Goodman vouched for it, and perhaps they
did turn their backs on a gold mine.

The cabin on Jackass Hill was not without neighbors, among
them the pretty Carrington girls, whom Bill Gillis and Twain
nicknamed the "Chaparral Quails." When not reading, listening
to Jim spin yarns, or prospecting, Twain, generally accompanied
by Bill, turned his footsteps toward the Carrington cabin,
where the two attractive daughters lived with their parents.
At other times pocket mining led them farther from camp, and
on New Year's night, 1865, Twain then in Calaveras saw a "mag-
nificent lunar rainbow," shortly to prove a good omen (*Notebook* 5-6). Going on to Angel's Camp, Clemens struck literary
gold in the person of old Ben Coon, an endless talker loaded
with a fund of pointless stories, who was looking for an
audience. Clemens listened, and was rewarded by a literary
nugget he jotted down:

> Coleman with his jumping frog--bet a stranger $50.--
> Stranger had no frog and C. got him one:--In the meantime
> stranger filled C's frog full of shot and he couldn't
> jump. The stranger's frog won. (*Notebook* 7)

This old tale, one Clemens probably would not have bothered
to record if he had heard of it before, was not utilized for
several more weeks. Dick Stoker having joined him at Angel's
Camp, Clemens initiated him to the four kinds of soup served
at the Frenchman's on important occasions: "Hellfire," "General
Debility," "Insanity," and "Sudden Death." Then on February 25,
1865, Clemens departed from Angel's for Jackass Hill in company
with Jim and Dick, the three of them walking across the moun-
tain tops in a snowstorm, the first Clemens had seen in California, impressive indeed in its beauty.

Upon arrival back in San Francisco, Clemens found a three-month's accumulation of letters, among them an invitation from Artemus Ward to contribute to a book he was bringing out. Believing that he still had time, Twain wrote the frog story told by Ben Coon and sent it on, only to have it arrive too late for Ward's publisher, G.W. Carleton, to include in the book. The pages had gone to press, and Carleton gave Twain's contribution to Henry Clapp, who printed it in the New York *Saturday Press*, November 18, 1865. With this story Mark Twain may be said to have entered upon his career in American fiction, for in Jim Smiley and Simon Wheeler he first successfully created characters with colorful and distinct personalities. More than an anecdote, "Jim Smiley and His Jumping Frog" (the original title) immediately received popular acceptance as fictional literature. Now Twain was known in the East as well as on the Pacific coast; the New York correspondent of the San Francisco *Alta* wrote that papers were copying the story far and near, and on December 16, 1865, the *Californian* entitled its reprint "The Celebrated Jumping Frog of Calaveras County." But Twain wrote to his mother and sister that he did not relish a compliment for this "villainous backwoods sketch," an attitude possibly occasioned by one of his "black moods," perhaps by chagrin at having been left out of Ward's book, but more probably by the fact that his associates on the *Californian* held the polite Victorian concept of literature, almost ignoring local color, while devoting their efforts chiefly to bringing "culture" to California rather than establishing an authentic California culture. In fact, this idea that literature should conform in subject and style to the accepted tradition of New England and Europe Twain held all his life, causing him to overvalue *Joan of Arc* and *The Prince and the Pauper* to the discredit of his masterpieces created out of native material and American idiom. Thus Twain in conforming to the literary definitions of the *Californian* writers, momentarily undervalued his effort. But it brought him fame, and Clemens had the good sense to capitalize on it.[17] Now that the name of Mark Twain had leaped across the nation on the Calaveras frog he received an invitation to visit the Sandwich Islands (as Hawaii was then called) on the new steamer *Ajax*, carrying a select party for its maiden voyage. At first he refused, but immediately regretted his choice and hastily persuaded the publishers of the Sacramento *Union* to commission him special correspondent reporting on trade, agriculture, and general topics of interest (Paine 1: 282).

Sailing on the *Ajax*, Twain arrived at Honolulu on March 18, saw its beauty and was conquered. In his letters home *beautiful* became a key word. And his enjoyment in the islands was enhanced by finding himself a celebrity, sought by the United

States Minister to China and the Minister to Japan. From the
Sandwich Islands Twain again wrote travel letters, something
in which he was to excel; and here he began to reach a more
sophisticated audience, embarking upon a course which led to
The Innocents Abroad. Immediately upon arrival he sent his
first letter to the *Union*, following it with twenty-four others,
twenty-one being travel descriptions and anecdotes of human
interest, three being serious statistical reports on trade,
and one a sensational scoop of the *Hornet* disaster, not actually a part of the *Union* correspondence (*Sandwich Islands*
xi-xii). During the four months and a day of his sojourn in
Hawaii, Twain was captivated. From Honolulu, June 25, 1866,
he scored one of the biggest scoops in newspaper history,
assisted by the United States Minister to China, Anson Burlingame. The clipper ship *Hornet* had burned at sea, the survivors had suffered terribly for forty-three days in an open
boat, and only the third mate and ten of the seamen arrived at
Honolulu. Twain had just returned from a horseback trip and
was in bed with saddle boils, but Burlingame had the cot carried
to the hospital, where he helpfully questioned survivors while
Twain took notes. Then Twain, without stopping for food or
sleep, wrote all night to complete a story which was thrown
at nine the next morning onto the deck of the *Milton Badger*
as she pulled away for California. It was a scoop, given front
page prominence by the *Union* in a spread of three and a half
columns (Frear 110). Recovering shortly from his illness,
Twain continued to enjoy pleasant association with Burlingame's
party until they departed; then he himself left July 19, 1866,
for San Francisco on a slow-going vessel requiring twenty-five
days for the voyage.

Back in San Francisco, however, he felt himself "in prison,"
surrounded once again with toil and care. Actually Clemens
had increased his fame with the letters for the *Union*, whose
publishers had paid him $300 extra for the *Hornet* scoop, but
the daily task of returning to a newspaper did not appeal.
Rather he sought some means of earning a living that would
leave him footloose, a desire that led just seven weeks after
his return to his lecture on the Sandwich Islands from the
stage of Maguire's Academy of Music.

The story of this first lecture seems to have been faithfully recorded in *Roughing It* (2: 291-96). Now he was a personality on the platform; "Mark Twain" had come alive from a
newspaper by-line as the trademark of Samuel Clemens, and he
was to proceed on his career as writer and lecturer, the immediate result of his visit to the islands. But one disappointment was to mar his pleasure; a full account of the *Hornet*
catastrophe which he had sent to *Harper's*, seeking recognition
in an Eastern magazine, appeared unsigned in the December,

1866, number and was credited to Mark Swain in the annual magazine index (Johnson 215). One can hear Twain's profanity!

But his lecture led to a successful tour, Denis McCarthy,
his old friend on the *Enterprise*, serving as manager. Traveling through Nevada, Twain was greeted by enthusiastic audiences, who packed the houses at Virginia City and Carson City.
Everywhere during his swing through California and Nevada, old
friends greeted him joyfully while receptive houses vocally
acclaimed his humor. Returning to San Francisco, he lectured
to the enthusiastic delight of the audiences and reviewers.

Only too happy at following Anson Burlingame's advice on
travel, Twain next proposed a trip around the world to be
financed by a series of travel letters. And the *Alta California*
was so enthusiastic over Clemens' success that he secured a
commission from that paper. But first he would go home, then
around the world, leaving San Francisco December 15, 1866.

When Mark Twain left California he was well known as a
journalist, lecturer, and personality, in contrast to the
inconspicuous young secretary who had journeyed west with
Orion. At Virginia City and in San Francisco he had developed
gifts of caricature, humorous exaggeration, and satire which
would appear more artistically in his later work; in the Sandwich Islands he successfully wrote travel letters; the *Jumping
Frog* was the harbinger of a multitude of portraitures to come;
and Mark Twain the personality stood complete upon the lecture
platform.

Newspaper apprenticeship had been his secondary schooling,
the Mississippi River with its expansive curriculum of human
nature had been his college, but it was in the Western school
of journalism and humor that his graduate course was taken.
In the West and through Western humor Samuel Langhorne Clemens
became Mark Twain, professional author, public lecturer and
personality. Back in Hannibal Sam Clemens at seventeen had
contributed his bit to the native literature that filled the
journals on the Southwestern frontier, such as the characteristic humorous yarn and the tall tale, which derived their
form and style from the oral anecdote. Many tendencies of
his Washoe period were prevalent during his cub apprenticeship,
notably a predilection for humor and satire, the preference
for travel letters, and the seeming aptitude for controversy.
But in the masculine world of the big bonanza the humorous
tradition of the Old Southwest grew into literary productions
carrying their author onward to the Eastern seaboard.

This anecdotal literature of the South from which Western
humor grew was the product of men engaged in their professions
who wrote only to amuse. The rough life around them afforded
colorful characters to catch the eye of a conscientious observer; there were extremes of emotion and vivid action--

excellent material for humor. This frontier was uniquely American, an important force in our history which, as Franklin J. Meine explains, has no authentic expression in our literature save through the pens of its humorists. When Mark Twain went West he carried this tradition along, as did the other humorists of the Pacific slope, and he was not "opening up a new vein of American humor with his first famous story, *Jim Smiley and His Jumping Frog*," as Professor Meine demonstrates, but rather continuing a "kind of story-telling that had its home and earlier vogue in the genial South before the War" (*Tall Tales* xv).

In Nevada, however, Twain succeeding as reporter for the *Territorial Enterprise* eventually discarded all previous pseudonyms to associate his personality with his trade name. The carefree, vigorous, and entirely masculine school of journalism left its imprint on his style. No more did he indulge in the forced misspellings of Snodgrass; under the easy guidance of Joe Goodman, Twain turned to getting the facts for informed, interesting writing. From Dan DeQuille, then showing more promise of success than Twain, he learned how to convey serious information while perpetrating hoaxes and filling ironical sketches with droll humor. From the other members of the *Enterprise* staff, Rollin M. Daggett, and Steve Gillis the printer, Twain absorbed the fighting courage that animated both. Freedom, facts, courage, principle, justice, and humor, the latter boisterous with exaggeration and keen with satire--they were the ingredients of Joe Goodman's journalistic wares, as they were those of all his staff; and Mark Twain, these qualities inherent in him, naturally developed.

Ivan Benson says of Twain's associates on the *Enterprise*, "They could jest on occasion, but when principles were at stake their satire and irony invariably worked in the cause of justice, tolerance, loyalty to ideals" (71). In the same way Mark Twain used his pen throughout the remainder of his life. The humor of the Comstock was that of working men intent upon digging their fortunes out of the ground. Their labor was manual, their taste was strong; for in a world lacking refinement, humor was naturally vigorous, robust, and coarse. The miners liked exaggeration, and were not without imagination; the petrified man thumbing his nose across the centuries delighted Washoe (175).

On the *Enterprise* Twain felt no inhibitions; he said what he had to say, enjoying it enthusiastically as his popularity increased. With the transition to the *Golden Era*, the robust, often coarse burlesques, and extravaganzas old as frontier journalism, accompanied him. Social occasions, so minutely depicted by the fashion editors, became fair game for his broad satire.

Twain gradually introduced more thought into his Carson City reporting, leaning less heavily upon the elemental humor of the Comstock, though never indeed substantially forsaking it. From San Francisco as his *Enterprise* correspondence assumed more and more the form of serious satire, "The Wild Humorist of the Pacific Slope" annexed another title through his campaign against municipal corruption, notably among the police--"The Moralist of the Main" (*Washoe Giant* 14).[18]

When Twain turned from the *Golden Era* to the *Californian* and association with Bret Harte, who understood the value of form, his sketches were still breezy and strong. Although years later he credited Harte's refining influence, actually Twain learned little except something of form and aptness of phrasing. He still wrote in Washoe fashion. Old habits of frontier humor were not brushed away so easily as the dust of Washoe. Probably beginning to feel coarseness unbecoming in San Francisco, Twain still enjoyed an occasional outburst, and he seems to have invented Mr. Brown, through whom all vulgarities could be uttered with impunity. Going East from Washoe, this character who had appeared as alter ego in the Sandwich Islands letters continued his irreverent, coarse, down-to-earth comments, while his creator, gradually adapting to another audience, prepared his demise.

Breaking with the West

In a series of twenty-six letters for the San Francisco *Alta California*, Twain described his sailing from the Golden Gate to Nicaragua, the crossing of the isthmus, and subsequent grim voyage to New York, the ship invaded by cholera, and nobody knowing who would be stricken next. Skipper of the *America* was Captain Ned Wakeman. Ned Wakeman, it appears, was in every way a remarkable character; when a runaway couple pleaded loss of their marriage license, the Captain promptly remedied matters by giving them a wedding with witnesses, and when rumors started that the groom had used an assumed name, the old man hauled them in immediately to repeat the ceremony. To Twain he was a delight, a source of inspiration never to be forgotten.

After his arrival in New York, and a brief visit to his boyhood home in the Middle West, Mark settled down to report on the metropolis for his California readers, while also making plans for the trip abroad. At first he is full of criticism: he doesn't like the crowds, he is annoyed by omni-

buses, prices are too high, but gradually as he becomes accustomed to New York City the complaints become fewer, finally
to be replaced by praise.

He liked the chic, New York look of the women, whom he
found, "Charming, fascinating, seductive, bewitching!" He
visited clubs like the Century, where one met distinguished
authors and artists, and was delighted to find an exclusiveness
that insisted upon brains as well as bank accounts and pedi-
grees. Always interested in the clergy, Twain arose one freez-
ing day, "earlier than any Christian ought to be out of his
bed on such a morning," to crowd into the church of Henry Ward
Beecher, whom he confessed he was in a "pious frenzy" to hear.
Listening to the "poetry, pathos, humor, satire" blended into
an "earnest exposition of the great truths," Twain writes that
he felt like applauding (*Travels with Mr. Brown* 94). He was
so pleased that he then went to hear Bishop Southgate, whose
sermon he liked, finding it enhanced by the beautiful music of
the choir.

Twain was attracted by the theater, one of his perpetual
delights, although he was shocked, or pretended to be, by
displays of feminine nudity. Ever in the role of moralist,
Twain warned against exposing on the stage "beautiful clipper-
built girls," who wore barely enough clothes "to be tantalizing."
It was the *Black Crook* specifically, so he said, that touched
his "missionary sensibilities," for its scenic effects, ballets,
and tableaux rivaled the *Arabian Nights*. Indeed, the "Moralist
of the Main" declared, "... the scenery and the legs are everything," and nobody noticed the absence of an adequate plot.
The way things were going, he told his California readers, the
popular taste demanded feminine beauty and nudity, and although
Edwin Booth and the legitimate drama still played to full
houses, Twain prophesied that "... he will have to make a
little change by-and-by and peel some women" (*Travels with
Mr. Brown* 87).

These letters, written over a period of six months after
leaving San Francisco, are the prologue to *The Innocents
Abroad*. They ended on the eve of the *Quaker City*'s sailing
from New York and link the *Letters from the Sandwich Islands*
with the *Alta California* correspondence, which was to be rearranged into Clemens' first travel book. As biography they
record Twain's perceptions of beauty in the Nicaraguan jungle,
his initial depression in the great Eastern metropolis, followed by visits to St. Louis, where Civil War animosity blurred
memories of pilot days on the river, and to Hannibal, now enduring hard times, almost finished by competition and war.
Yet he enjoyed it all, for old friends recalled the past, and
he lectured twice in St. Louis in the Mercantile Library Hall
before large and appreciative audiences.

However "ups and downs" may have affected Hannibal and
Keokuk, Quincy still impressed him as a "wonderful place,"
and indeed his entire journey back to New York left him with
an impression of progress and prosperity. Civil strife and
its aftermath, together with the decline of steamboating, may
have left the Mississippi Valley in depression, but "Such
wonderful cities as we saw, all the way through Ohio, New York
and New Jersey" (*Travels with Mr. Brown* 155). Back in our
greatest city once more, Twain, now free of prejudice, turned
his pen to praise.

"Make your mark in New York," he advised, "and you are a
made man" (*Travels with Mr. Brown* 176). Established with the
public, Twain then lectured in Brooklyn and again in New York,
coming off handsomely. Scant time remained before his boat
sailed, but he was asked to lecture in other nearby towns.
This was in May, the month his first book was published, *The
Celebrated Jumping Frog of Calaveras County and Other Sketches*.
May also marked the date of his arrest and overnight confine-
ment in jail. Yet even this could not turn him against New
York now; later on he praised the weather for its variety and
contrast of four distinct seasons, each one a delight. And
the best New York hotels received his acclaim, especially for
their dining rooms.

Twain frequently exhibited the best of taste, long before
meeting Mrs. Fairbanks or Livy, something often forgotten by
critics who remember only his lapses, as in art or music.
These he never hid: "I am glad the old masters are all dead,
and I only wish they had died sooner," he exclaimed frankly
after seeing a picture of a "naked infant that was not built
like any infant that ever I saw, nor colored like it, either"
(*Travels with Mr. Brown* 239). Soon he was to face the old
masters in Europe with equal candor, which if brash or ignorant,
was at least honest.

The proprietors of the *Alta California* having paid $1,250
for his passage, Mark Twain sailed June 8, 1867, on the *Quaker
City*, a pleasant, satisfactory vessel capable of making ten
knots an hour under steam with the help of her auxiliary sails.
Although most of the excursionists were ministers or middle-
aged people--the Holy Land vists had been extensively advertised and the expenses were high--Twain found a number of congenial associates, among them Dan Slote, his "splendid, immoral, tobacco-smoking, wine-drinking, godless room-mate";
Dr. A. Reeves Jackson, nemesis of guides in *Innocents Abroad*;
Jack Van Nostrand (Jack); and Julius Moulton (Moult). It was
sinful Jack credited by Twain with the remark to the deacons
on the exorbitant boat fares at the Sea of Galilee: "Well,
Denny, do you wonder now that Christ walked?" (qtd. in Paine
1: 337). And there was Emeline Beach, destined to remain a

friend for more than forty years, and especially "Mother"
Fairbanks, herself an able correspondent for her husband's
Cleveland *Herald*, who understood and encouraged him. While
exercising critical judgment over his correspondence, Mrs.
Fairbanks exerted a refining influence Twain had the good
sense to accept.   Another was Bloodgood H. Cutter ("Poet
Lariat" of *The Innocents*), an old-fashioned farmer with an
obsession for rhymes, who generally found Twain writing, partly, no doubt, to escape hearing Cutter's jingles. But then,
it was not all play for the *Alta* correspondent, who had plenty
of work ahead; fifty-three letters to the *Alta* within five
months and six to the *Tribune*.[19]

The more pious travelers were often shocked by Twain's
irreverence, for he doubted the authenticity of relics, joked
about biblical characters. Yet the most important incident of
the journey occurred quietly one day in the stateroom of a
young man, Charles Langdon, Mark's junior and admirer, who
exhibited an ivory miniature of his sister. There in the Bay
of Smyrna Samuel Clemens fell in love with the likeness of
Olivia Langdon; each time he visited her brother afterward,
he asked to see it, even begged for it. And there he resolved
to meet the girl whose face was so delicately tinted on the
dainty ivory, who so evoked his admiration and reverence.

When the *Quaker City* docked in New York, November 19,
1867, Clemens found himself a celebrity. His final letter,
written for the New York *Herald*, was uproariously funny but
personally satirical, causing offense to the stodgy ones who
had almost turned the pleasure excursion into a funeral procession. But Twain did not wait for retributive wrath; the
next day found him in Washington, secretary to a senator, an
arrangement concluded from Naples, unhappily not destined to
last.

Clemens was already established as a Washington correspondent, receiving contracts from the New York *Tribune* and the
Herald, while numerous others sought his services. Then came
a letter from Elisha Bliss, Jr., inquiring if he would be interested in writing a book for the American Publishing Company; Mark replied that he would like to rewrite his *Alta*
correspondence into a travel volume. Since the *Alta* had few
exchanges in the East, Clemens doubted if many readers there
had seen the originals. As Paine observed, then began "one of
the most notable publishing connections in American literary
history" (Paine 1: 351). But the book was not immediately
forthcoming; Bliss became ill and there was further delay in
discussion over the percentage of royalty.

Meanwhile, Dan Slote invited his *Quaker City* friend to
spend Christmas in New York, an invitation which led to a
meeting with the lovely girl of the ivory miniature. The

Langdons, it so happened, were visiting New York, where Mark
was introduced to them two days after Christmas at their
hotel, the St. Nicholas. Years later Mark said of this meeting with Olivia: "It is forty years ago. From that day to
this she has never been out of my mind" (qtd. in Paine 1: 353).
On January 2 or 3, Charles Dickens, wearing a black velvet
coat decorated with a red flower in his buttonhole, read the
death scene of Steerforth from *David Copperfield* in Steinway
Hall, but impressive as he was, Mark Twain remembered better
the twenty-two-year-old Olivia Langdon, with whose family he
had attended the lecture. On New Year's Day he had seen her
also, paying a call as was the fashion, where Olivia was receiving with a niece of Henry Ward Beecher. Soon he was to
dine with Beecher himself at a dinner party including Harriet
Beecher Stowe and his steamship friends, Moses S. Beach and
his daughter Emeline.

Returning to Washington, where a lecture was arranged by
a friend--one "not entirely sober at the time"--Twain confronted with all the details, hardly knowing what he was going
to talk about, managed to improvise something called "The
Frozen Truth." He trusted to luck to carry him through and
it did; the lecture was subsequently given in several other
places. At the same time correspondence with Bliss brought
him to Hartford for an interview, which left the publisher
dissatisfied with Twain's traveling suit and fragrant pipe,
but highly impressed with his personality. Turning down an
outright offer of ten thousand dollars cash for his copyright,
Twain accepted a proposition paying instead five percent
royalty. Now he turned to the job of preparing the *Alta* correspondence, revising, editing, and supplementing, a task
which engaged his attention for six months.[20] In the meantime, he returned to Washington, where he produced newspaper
correspondence and sketches, intent upon earning something
while finishing the book. With that inexhaustible energy
Clemens could at times exhibit he also agreed to a syndicate
arrangement with John Swinton to furnish several other newspapers with letters.

Suddenly came bad news from Joe Goodman; the *Alta* publishers, holding copyright to the letters, were thinking of
bringing them out as a book. It was a bombshell, and Twain
poured out his wrath to Orion upon the thieves who sought to
swindle him. Immediately he telegraphed, then wrote, and receiving no satisfactory answer he left for San Francisco in
March to meet "those Alta thieves face to face" (qtd. in Paine
1: 361). Financed with an advance royalty from Bliss, Twain
again crossed the isthmus and arrived by steamer in San Francisco, where all problems about the letters were quickly
settled to everyone's satisfaction. But before returning,

Twain decided to increase his funds with a lecture tour around
the old circuit of two years earlier, where he was received in
triumph by old friends of Virginia City, Carson City, and elsewhere. Again in San Francisco for his last California lecture,
he advertised it in the form of a purported protest from leading citizens against further infliction.

It was a great success, and Twain sailed July 6, his financial status considerably improved and the manuscript of his
book ready for delivery to the publishers at Hartford. Yet
the last hurdle was still to come; the directors of the American Publishing Company, suddenly discovering the nature of the
venture, decided against publication. As Twain later remembered
it, the contract date for the issue of the book arrived with
no book or any explanation. Going to Hartford, he had talked
with the "staid old fogies" who feared the taint of humor, and
we might add the wrath of stodgy piety. After talking with
the "remains" of one of the "old relics" on the board of
directors, Twain warned Bliss to go ahead or expect trouble.
This warning produced page proof, followed by yet another delay
without explanation. A threat of suit for damages if the book
were not on sale within twenty-four hours broke the logjam,
with the resulting popular reception by the public. That was
how Twain recalled it, but Paine adds that Bliss, who believed
in the book, forced the directors to publish it by a threat of
resignation (Paine 1: 365).

While awaiting publication of *The Innocents Abroad*, Twain
visited the Langdons in Elmira--of course, to pay court to
Olivia. It was a gay and happy week. The home of Jervis
Langdon, a prosperous businessman whose mines produced the
coal sold by his firm, was handsome and hospitable. When
Samuel Clemens discovered how deeply he was in love with
Olivia, he confided his feelings to her brother, at the same
time declaring that he ought to leave. The alarmed Charley
Langdon, who thought nobody good enough for Livy, hastened the
departure, but as the light two-seated carriage started quickly
from the gate, the rear seat, left unbolted, fell backward
carrying Twain with it. Unhurt, he did not recover too quickly, but allowed himself to be carried into the house, where
his presence was now enforced for a day or two.

After a Cleveland trip to confide his courtship to "Mother"
Fairbanks, Clemens returned to Hartford for a conference with
his publishers. There he met the Rev. Joseph H. Twichell,
pastor of a wealthy and fashionable Congregational church,
who became his fast friend. Twichell was a man--physically,
mentally, and spiritually; he had been chaplain for General
Sickles during the Civil War, and he was so generous that his
charitable nature proved his financial undoing. Strong and
athletic, he loved life with an understanding of human nature

and a keen sense of humor. One of many ministers who admired
Mark Twain, Twichell met him on the common grounds of humanity
and manhood. Twichell's house became his home whenever he
was in Hartford.

But once again Twain was away on a lecture tour, this
time directed by James Redpath of the Boston Lyceum Bureau,
with a new and immensely popular lecture on "The Vandal
Abroad." The newspapers, and his audiences, were enthusiastic
over the subject and manner of delivery (Paine 1: 374). Popular and successful, earning more than a hundred dollars an
evening on many a successive night, Twain returned to Elmira
whenever possible to persist in his suit, until finally he
broke down all resistance and the engagement was announced
February 4, 1869. Closing his lecture tour in March with a
profit of around $8,000 Clemens returned to Elmira, where his
fiancee assisted him with proofreading. The book finally appeared July 20, 1869, in an edition of twenty thousand copies.

Now author of a best seller, Twain began to prospect for a
lucrative newspaper connection; a third interest in the Buffalo
Express could be purchased for $25,000. To secure the money,
he launched plans for an extensive tour of the Pacific coast,
when Mr. Langdon, having completely accepted his future son-
in-law, insisted upon advancing the needed funds. All in-
quiries about repayment of the loan remained unanswered by
Jervis Langdon, but Clemens determined to give a note to the
firm's business agent, and paid the interest as it fell due.
Clemens' assumption of editorial duties did not prevent his
leaving in October on a lecture tour through New England,
where the reception was quite as enthusiastic as in the West.
Clemens made his tour headquarters in Boston; there he met
William Dean Howells, assistant editor of the *Atlantic Monthly*,
and James T. Fields, its editor. So anxious was he to earn
all he might to pay off his debts that the wedding was post-
poned from Christmas; and Twain continued on the lecture platform until February, recalling jokes about stewed plums and
that night at Angel's Camp with the story of the frog. A few
days before the wedding he wrote his old friend Jim Gillis
how he wished that Jim and Dick Stoker could be there to see
his bride--"lovelier than the peerless 'Chapparal [sic]
Quails'" (*Letters* 1: 171).

On February 2, 1870, Joe Twichell arrived in Elmira to
help the Rev. Thomas K. Beecher perform the ceremony. Pamela
with her daughter Annie came from St. Louis, and Mrs. Fairbanks
from Cleveland. The wedding took place in the Langdon home
before a few guests, followed by a wedding supper and dancing
during which the bride's father danced with her. On the next
afternoon the gay party set out for Buffalo, where Clemens
expected to carry his bride to a boardinghouse, unaware that

his father-in-law had bought and furnished a fine place on
Delaware Avenue as a gift. Arriving to be met by servants
who ushered them into the newly decorated rooms, Clemens recovered from his amazement to say to his benefactor, "Mr. Langdon, whenever you are in Buffalo, if it's twice a year, come
right here. Bring your bag and stay overnight if you want to.
It sha'n't cost you a cent" (qtd. in Paine 1: 396).

NOTES

1. For further information on Twain's ancestry and inheritance see A.V. Goodpasture, "Mark Twain, Southerner," *Tennessee
Historical Magazine* 1 (1931): 253-60, and C.O. Paullin, "Mark
Twain's Virginia Kin," *William and Mary Quarterly* 15 (1935):
294-98.

2. Twain used this story and Uncle Ned's method as an example in "How To Tell a Story" (*The $30,000 Bequest* 263-70).

3. Dixon Wecter could find no trace of such a person in
Hannibal, but many other characters mentioned are traceable.
It is of vital interest to the student of realism that Mark
Twain saw and recorded the introversion and decay along with
the vigor and health of Tom and Huck. It is also good to keep
in mind that the Mark Twain Papers were bequeathed to the University of California at Berkeley in 1950 by Mark Twain's
daughter Clara. Since that time the University of California
Press has been engaged in an effort to make all of the previously unpublished papers available to the general reader in
a uniform edition.

4. Paine, Wecter, DeVoto, and others have discussed the
details of Mark Twain's apprenticeship, and the facts are that
nobody apparently knows when the apprenticeship began and
ended. However, all agree approximately.

5. These letters were collected in a limited edition
called *The Adventures of Thomas Jefferson Snodgrass*, ed.
Charles Honce (Chicago: Covici, 1928).

6. Paul Baender seems to be the only dissenting voice concerning the Macfarlane influence. In his "Alias Macfarlane: A
Revision of Mark Twain Biography" (187-97), Baender finds it
surprising that the Macfarlane influence has never been challenged. He contends that only two notions for such an influence exist: Paine's discussion of the Clemens-Macfarlane relationship in his biography (1912) and a brief manuscript Paine
included in his edition of Twain's autobiography (1924). The

philosophy attributed to Macfarlane was Twain's, argues Baender, and as for the manuscript it "... belongs to a group of works which have in common Twain's use of the outsiders as a voice for his own opinions" (192). Twain created Macfarlane, suggests Baender, to do best what he did with the other outsiders he created, to state his position without endangering his career.

7. George H. Brownell has revealed that Twain could not possibly have borrowed his name from Captain Sellers as he claimed, for Mark first used the pseudonym in the *Territorial Enterprise*, February 2, 1863, and Sellers did not die until March 6, 1864. Thus the whole story of how Mark adopted his name upon Sellers' death becomes another bit of fiction. See "A Question as to the Origin of the Name 'Mark Twain,'" *Twainian* ns 1.2 (1942): 4-7.

8. Edited by Ernest E. Leisy, *The Letters of Quintus Curtius Snodgrass* were published by Southern Methodist University Press in 1946. A series of ten letters appearing in the New Orleans *Daily Crescent* between January and March of 1861 were attributed to Twain by Leisy. In 1963, however, Claude S. Brinegar published an article bringing into question the claim by Leisy, Brashear, and others that Mark Twain authored the Quintus Curtius Snodgrass letters. Brinegar employed an old but little-used statistical method, a word-length frequency test, to discredit the idea that Twain authored the letters. The word-length statistical method used by Brinegar was developed by T.C. Mendenhall and set forth in "The Characteristic Curve of Composition," *Science* 9 (1887): 237-49, and "A Mechanical Solution of a Literary Problem," *The Popular Science Monthly* 60 (1901): 97-105. Once he has applied Mendenhall's method of statistical analysis, Brinegar observes, "From the standpoint of visual inspection of the results of this literary blood test, we conclude that Mark Twain could not have fathered the QCS letters" (91). At the end of his article Brinegar quotes a letter he received from Frederick Anderson in response to a letter Brinegar had written to Henry Nash Smith. In the letter Anderson writes, "Professor Henry Nash Smith has asked me to write to tell you that we are quite sure that Mark Twain did not write the Quintus Curtius Snodgrass letters" (96). Thus Brinegar concludes that those who have attributed authorship of the Quintus Curtius Snodgrass letters to Mark Twain have done so on the basis of evidence which is anything but conclusive. For Brinegar's article "Mark Twain and the Quintus Curtius Snodgrass Letters," see *Journal of the American Statistical Association* 58 (1963): 85-96.

9. Important to undergraduate research pertaining to Mark Twain in the West, *Mark Twain's Frontier* (1963), edited by

James E. Camp and X.J. Kennedy, focuses attention on the
writings of Twain during the Nevada-California years. The
object is to allow the student to examine the Brooks-DeVoto
controversy concerning the effect of the frontier on Mark
Twain as a writer. The book, however, has little or no value
for the Mark Twain scholar.

10. *The Pattern for Mark Twain's Roughing It* (1961), edited by Franklin R. Rogers, contains letters of 1861-62 from
Nevada by Sam and Orion to the Keokuk *Gate City* and the St.
Louis *Missouri Democrat*. Rogers has collected and edited
four letters by Twain to the *Democrat* and two by Orion to the
Democrat as well as one to the *Gate City*. Here are suggestions
and indications for what would be expanded in *Roughing It*.

11. Edited by Henry Nash Smith and Frederick Anderson,
Mark Twain of the Enterprise (1957) presents for the first
time thirty newspaper articles, letters, dispatches, and other
documents. Some are serious reporting, some are gossipy letters from Carson City and San Francisco, while others are
purely imaginative humor. All throw light on Twain's life
from 1862-64. Smith questions February 2, 1863, as the date
Clemens first used the pen name of Mark Twain; he suggests it
was February 3.

12. Paul Fatout's *Mark Twain in Virginia City* (1964)
supersedes previous studies. It is a full account of Clemens'
lively days in Washoe depicting events such as the visit of
Artemus Ward and that of the actress Adah Isaacs Menken, celebrated for her nudity. Through careful research in contemporary newspapers Fatout has recovered lost articles and items
from Twain's journalistic career before the departure for
California.

13. Clemens was a reporter for the *Call* from June to October, 1864. Edgar Branch has edited *Clemens of the Call* (1969),
in which two hundred contributions are reprinted. Here we see
Clemens as a daily journalist writing about everyday occur-
rences. The collection reveals something of the development
in Clemens' style as well as his interest in exposing abuses.

14. *Mark Twain's San Francisco* (1963), edited by Bernard
Taper, conveniently provides material previously published in
Sketches of the Sixties and *The Washoe Giant in San Francisco*,
both of which were printed in limited editions and are hard to
find.

15. The account of his leaving the *Call* in *Roughing It*
(2: 143-44) is pure fiction.

16. Franklin Walker discounts the trouble with the police,
believing that Twain's *Enterprise* letters were written later

than the incident, and that Jim, a good talker, intrigued
Twain with his yarns, an offer of Western hospitality, and
the chance for a strike in pocket mining (*San Francisco's
Literary Frontier* 192). The validity of Paine's account,
however, is accepted by such as Benson, Ferguson, and Wecter.

17. Benson reminds us that if Mark Twain had been ashamed
of the "Jumping Frog" he would hardly have used it as the
title of his first book and placed it first in that volume
(*Mark Twain's Western Years* 131).

18. From November of 1865 to February of 1866 Twain wrote
dispatches from San Francisco to the *Enterprise*. Henry Nash
Smith and Frederick Anderson have edited these in *Mark Twain:
San Francisco Correspondent* (1957). Based on clippings from
a scrapbook, probably kept by Orion, the writings take Twain
up to the time he left for the Sandwich Islands. There are
suggestions here of passages later to appear in *The Innocents
Abroad*, and the moralist in Clemens emerges through his criticism of the San Francisco police.

19. Dewey Ganzel reconstructs the voyage of the *Quaker
City* in his *Mark Twain Abroad: The Cruise of the Quaker City*
(1968). Each chapter title is merely a list of the names of
places visited, and although the cruise has been much written
about some things which might prove of interest to the reader
are Clemens' need to entertain rather than merely to record a
journey, his debt to Porter's *Guide Book*, and his "padding"
of the Holy Land letters. The real value of Ganzel's book,
as indicated on the dust jacket, is that it shows how Clemens
"transformed his experiences aboard the *Quaker City* into the
art of *The Innocents Abroad*."

20. Daniel Morley McKeithan discusses this in his introduction to *Traveling with the Innocents Abroad* (1958), which he
edited. Based on Twain's letters and his notebook, *The Innocents Abroad* became one of the most popular travel books ever
written by an American (xi), but Twain revised and reworked
his material extensively. Writes McKeithan, "Mark Twain did
not reprint a single letter verbatim" (xii). McKeithan discusses the letters one at a time explaining how Twain made
changes for the sake of decorum as well as to improve "his expression."

WORKS CITED

Armstrong, C.J. "Mark Twain's Earliest Writings Discovered."
    Missouri Historical Review 24 (1930): 485-501.

Baender, Paul. "Alias Macfarlane: A Revision of Mark Twain
    Biography." *American Literature* 38 (1966): 187-97.

Bellamy, Gladys C. "Mark Twain's Indebtedness to John Phoenix."
    American Literature 13 (1941): 29-43.

Benson, Ivan. *Mark Twain's Western Years*. Stanford: Stanford
    U. Press, 1938. A standard work on this period.

Branch, Edgar M. "The Two Providences: Thematic Form in
    Huckleberry Finn." *College English* 11 (1950): 188-95.

Brashear, Minnie M. *Mark Twain, Son of Missouri*. Chapel
    Hill: U. of North Carolina Press, 1934. Invaluable for
    formative influence.

Brinegar, Claude S. "Mark Twain and the Quintus Curtius Snod-
    grass Letters: A Statistical Test of Authorship." *Journal
    of the American Statistical Association* 58 (1963): 85-96.

Brownell, George H. "Mark Twain's Pilot License." *Twainian*
    os 1.8 (1939): 1-3.

————. "A Question as to the Origin of the Name 'Mark Twain.'"
    Twainian ns 1.2 (1942): 4-7.

Camp, James E. and X.J. Kennedy, eds. *Mark Twain's Frontier*.
    New York: Holt, Rinehart and Winston, 1963.

DeQuille, Dan [William Wright]. *The Big Bonanza*. New York:
    Knopf, 1947. An important book on Virginia City and the
    Comstock Lode, written by Twain's old friend on the
    Territorial Enterprise. Splendid for Western background.

Fatout, Paul. *Mark Twain in Virginia City*. Bloomington: In-
    diana U. Press, 1964. Supersedes previous studies.

Ferguson, DeLancey. *Mark Twain: Man and Legend*. Indianapolis:
    Bobbs-Merrill, 1943. Good account of the formative influ-
    ences.

Frear, Walter Francis. *Mark Twain and Hawaii*. Chicago: Lake-
    side, 1947. Definitive for the visit to Hawaii.

Ganzel, Dewey. *Mark Twain Abroad: The Cruise of the Quaker
    City*. Chicago: U. of Chicago Press, 1968.

Goodpasture, A.V. "Mark Twain, Southerner." *Tennessee His-
    torical Magazine* 2nd ser. 1 (1931): 253-60.

Hutcherson, Dudley R. "Mark Twain as a Pilot." *American*

Literature 12 (1940): 353-55. Cites opinion that Twain was unsuccessful as a pilot.

Johnson, Merle. *A Bibliography of the Works of Mark Twain, Samuel Langhorne Clemens. A List of First Editions in Book Form and of First Printings in Periodicals and Occasional Publications of His Varied Literary Activities.* New York: Harper & Brothers, 1935. Indispensable. The most thorough book at the present. Contains descriptions of first editions.

Lillard, Richard G. "Contemporary Reactions to 'The Empire City Massacre.'" *American Literature* 16 (1944): 198-203.

Lorch, Fred W. "Mark Twain and the 'Campaign That Failed.'" *American Literature* 12 (1941): 454-70. A comprehensive examination of the facts and sound evaluation.

————. "Mark Twain in Iowa." *Iowa Journal of History and Politics* 27 (1929): 408-56.

Meine, Franklin J. *Tall Tales of the Southwest.* New York: Knopf, 1930.

Mendenhall, T.C. "The Characteristic Curve of Composition." *Science* os 9 (1887): 237-49.

————. "A Mechanical Solution to a Literary Problem." *The Popular Science Monthly* 60 (1901): 97-105.

Paine, Albert Bigelow. *Mark Twain: A Biography.* 4 vols. New York: Harper & Brothers, 1912. Still a useful source.

Paullin, C.O. "Mark Twain's Virginia Kin." *William and Mary Quarterly* 15 (1935): 294-98.

Twain, Mark [Samuel Langhorne Clemens]. *The Adventures of Thomas Jefferson Snodgrass.* Ed. Charles Honce. Chicago: Covici, 1928.

————. *Clemens of the Call: Mark Twain in San Francisco.* Ed. Edgar M. Branch. Berkeley: U. of California Press, 1969.

————. "How to Tell a Story." *The $30,000 Bequest.* New York: Harper & Brothers, 1917. 263-70.

————. *The Letters of Quintus Curtius Snodgrass.* Ed. Ernest E. Leisy. Dallas: Southern Methodist U. Press, 1946.

————. *Mark Twain of the Enterprise: Newspaper Articles & Other Documents 1862-1864.* Eds. Henry Nash Smith and Frederick Anderson. Berkeley: U. of California Press, 1957.

————. *Mark Twain: San Francisco Correspondent*. Eds. Henry
Nash Smith and Frederick Anderson. San Francisco: Book
Club of California, 1957.

————. *Mark Twain's Autobiography*. Ed. Albert Bigelow Paine.
2 vols. New York: Harper & Brothers, 1924.

————. *Mark Twain's Letters*. Ed. Albert Bigelow Paine.
2 vols. New York: Harper, 1917.

————. *Mark Twain's Letters from the Sandwich Islands*. Ed.
G. Ezra Dane. Stanford: Stanford U. Press, 1938.

————. *Mark Twain's Letters in the Muscatine Journal*. Ed.
Edgar M. Branch. Chicago: Mark Twain Assn. of America, 1942.

————. *Mark Twain's Notebook*. New York: Harper & Brothers,
1935. Selections from Twain's journals.

————. *Mark Twain's San Francisco*. Ed. Bernard Taper. New
York: McGraw-Hill, 1963.

————. *Mark Twain's Travels with Mr. Brown*. Eds. Franklin
Walker and G. Ezra Dane. New York: Knopf, 1940. A very
important link in Twain's development.

————. "A Memory." *Curious Republic of Gondour and Other
Whimsical Sketches*. New York: Boni and Liveright, 1919.
12-19.

————. *The Pattern for Mark Twain's Roughing It*. Ed. Franklin
R. Rogers. Berkeley: U. of California Press, 1961.

————. *Roughing It*. 2 vols. New York: Harper & Brothers, 1913.

————. *Traveling with the Innocents Abroad: Mark Twain's
Original Reports from Europe and the Holy Land*. Ed. Daniel
Morley McKeithan. Norman: U. of Oklahoma Press, 1958.

————. *The Washoe Giant in San Francisco*. Ed. Franklin Walker.
San Francisco: Fields, 1938.

Twain, Mark and Bret Harte. *Sketches of the Sixties*. Ed. John
Howell. San Francisco: Howell, 1926. Rev. 1927.

Walker, Franklin. *San Francisco's Literary Frontier*. New
York: Knopf, 1939. Twain in San Francisco.

Webster, Samuel Charles. *Mark Twain, Business Man*. Boston:
Little, Brown, 1946. Adds biographical information about
the early years of Twain, as well as the business transactions. An important contribution.

Wecter, Dixon. *Samuel Clemens of Hannibal*. Boston: Houghton
Mifflin, 1952. Definitive study of Clemens' youth. Invaluable for the Hannibal influence on Twain's mature art.

Chapter 3

THE MAN OF LETTERS

The East: Buffalo

Once married and settled in his home, Twain turned dili-
gently to his newspaper work; somehow despite the success of
The Innocents he did not yet regard himself as an author.
Meantime he would advance in his journalistic profession,
not only writing editorials and satires for the Buffalo *Express*, but accepting an offer from a magazine, the *Galaxy*,
to supply monthly contributions called "Memoranda" at a stipend
of $2,400 per annum.[1] His working hours, though irregular,
were long and hard (often from eight in the morning until
eleven at night) while he sat at his desk, gradually removing
coat, vest, collar, and finally shoes--anything to insure comfort. Editorials from his pen--he always defended the op-
pressed--were scathing, fearless, and sincere in his attacks
upon injustice and violations of liberty. And he also produced humorous sketches, among them "Journalism in Tennessee"
and "A Curious Dream," the latter a satire directed at cities
allowing graveyards to fall into decay and ruin. Yet the
Galaxy contributions appealed to him more; soon he was sending
in his better sketches, some of them courageous attacks upon
prominent persons, selected as targets because of their
injustices. Two of these were about the renowned minister
DeWitt Talmage, then at the peak of popularity, and another
fashionable churchman named Sabine, but Twain was not concerned
over alienating readers or making enemies--not with a principle
involved. But some of his efforts were just pure fun, devoid
of seriousness, such as "How I Edited an Agricultural Paper,"
or the plain fooling of a "Burlesque Map of Paris" reprinted
from the *Express*.

And his home life was happy; from the beginning Twain
adored Olivia, so much so that he accepted for a time, at
least, such customs as family worship, grace before meals,
and Bible readings. Joe Goodman visited Buffalo shortly after
the wedding and was astounded to hear Twain ask the blessing
and read from the Bible (Paine 2: 411). But Livy's Victorian

crusade in favor of piety and against tobacco soon came to
naught; the Bible readings went first, to be followed by a
resumption of smoking and eventually swearing. Indeed, as
DeLancey Ferguson invites our attention, the household was run
to suit Twain's desires rather than Livy's; he smoked in the
presence of ladies, lounged before the fire in slippers, and
did and said whatever he pleased (152). At first, however,
he strove his best to conform with Victorian standards of propriety, and even after this conformity ceased, he allowed his
wife to lecture him and admitted his shortcomings, only to
continue the practices.

The auspicious beginnings of life in Buffalo unfortunately
were short: first came the serious illness of Mr. Langdon, who
was so stricken with cancer early in the spring that in June
Clemens and his wife went to Elmira to aid in the task of day
and night nursing demanded by the patient's critical condition.
On August 6, Jervis Langdon died. To Olivia, physically exhausted, it was a crushing blow emotionally. Plans for a summer in England or joining the Twichells in the Adirondacks
were forgotten, as it seemed best to remain quietly at home.
Actually, it was the worst thing they could have done, for
fate, as if ironically stacking the cards, ordained that an
old school chum of Livy's, Emma Nye, should become dangerously
ill with typhoid fever while visiting them. Another long
siege of nursing ensued, ending tragically September 29 with
the death of Miss Nye. Olivia was now ill herself from anxiety
and nursing; the death of her friend in the new home, following
so closely upon that of her father, had been too much. Yet
fate still had more ironic trumps concealed: when another
friend, invited to cheer her, departed hurriedly to catch a
train, Olivia, accompanying her guest to the station, was so
prostrated by the jolting of the cab that her first child,
Langdon, was prematurely born, November 7, 1870. Both mother
and child passed through a crisis of five days before Twain
felt they were safe enough for him to write friends of his
son's arrival. With so much disaster Twain and Livy naturally
found Buffalo uncongenial and gloomy; somehow they had never
really managed to feel themselves a part of the community,
Twain's venture with the *Express* had not worked out as anticipated, and they were both ready to move elsewhere.

Meanwhile, however, his career had brought fortunate
changes in the lives of his relatives; not far from Buffalo
was a little city, Fredonia, where Jane Clemens and Pamela
moved at Twain's request. Now that they were settled, all
that remained was to take care of Orion, which was done in
time by securing him a position originally offered to Sam himself, the editorship of a new paper, *The Publisher*, just established by Bliss, who was prevailed upon to give Orion the
job.

His relations provided for, and anxious to follow up the
success of *The Innocents* with another book, Twain logically
caught upon the idea of writing up his Western journey to
Nevada and California, places about as strange to Eastern
readers as Constantinople--if not more so. To facilitate sales
of *The Innocents Abroad*, which within a year passed the 67,000
mark and continued at a rate of several thousand copies each
month, he reverted to his sagebrush days with a hoax. Twain
"reproduced" in the *Galaxy* a purported article on *The Innocents
Abroad* from the English *Saturday Review*, which was actually a
delightful burlesque pretending to treat the humorous situations
with deadly seriousness. But the hoax backfired, readers accepting it as a genuine English criticism, but regarding it as
humor which Twain had failed to perceive. This was too much;
and he rushed into print with an explanation, one many failed
to accept, the Cincinnati *Enquirer* being particularly objec-
tionable about it (Paine 2: 430).

April, 1871, found Clemens giving up his work for the
Galaxy entirely and with no regrets, the same month in which
he disposed of his interest in the *Express* at a loss of $10,000
under the purchase price. As soon as Livy and little Langdon
were able to travel they moved to Elmira, going at once to
Quarry Farm, the home of Mrs. Clemens' sister, where they remained through the summer. With the health of his wife and
baby improving Clemens found that his work on the book was
going well. At first it had progressed slowly, but a visit
from Joe Goodman provided the needed enthusiasm, Joe carefully
reading the manuscript and declaring that it was a great book.
In February, 1871, while still in Buffalo, Twain had his third
book published, but it was an unpretentious little volume,
which he later regretted and tried to suppress by buying up
the plates.[2] Working steadily on what he hoped would be a
fitting companion to *The Innocents Abroad*, Twain's spirits
rose as manuscript accumulated and family health improved; he
would produce a readable, "starchy" book. Truly his stock was
looking up; with the book proceeding well, offers were flood-
ing in for articles, almanacs, other books, and lecture tours.
Twain did find time from his major project to write several
sketches,[3] sending three to Bliss during June, while he also
contrived an automatically adjusting vest strap, one of the
many inventions he was always perfecting. Reconsidering the
decision to forsake the platform, Twain agreed finally with
James Redpath for another season. Then he went to Hartford,
where he and Livy had both decided they wished to live, largely
because of the Twichells, although his publishers were also
located there. Arrangements were completed for a house on
Forest Street on the first of October, where his neighbors
would be Charles Dudley Warner and Harriet Beecher Stowe.

After the disposal of his Buffalo property, Clemens shipped
the furnishings away from the bridal home that had seen so
much sorrow.

The question has been raised concerning the effect of
Mark Twain's residence in the East upon his art. Stephen Leacock, for instance, believed that Howells, Twichell, and Mrs.
Clemens imposed a censorship that was damaging (69). According
to Van Wyck Brooks Olivia Langdon killed whatever artistry in
Mark Twain the frontier had not obliterated. "There is something for the gods to bewail," he charged, "in the sight of
that shorn Samson led about by a little child who, in the profound somnolence of her spirit, was merely going through the
motions of an inherited domestic piety" (147). Actually, however, the record proves the opposite; Twain's influence on Livy
far outweighed hers upon him. As Dixon Wecter emphasizes,
Twain's apparent submission during his courtship and early marriage soon evaporated, with the old habits of smoking, drinking, and excursions into profanity returning, never more to
depart. In fact, the whole Clemens household was adapted to
suit the husband, for Livy "surrounded him with a gracious
social life in which he was always cast as the prima donna"
(*Love Letters* 11). So far as Twain was concerned Livy was perfection, nothing about her needed change; and as for Livy's
desires to "reform" him, the result was that she gradually
ended by making concessions until Twain had his way. He
dressed as he pleased, smoked when he wished, lounged with
his leg over the chair arm, and comported himself generally
after his own fashion. To all of which Livy quietly assented.
Samuel C. Webster tells us that Twain liked to complain about
Livy's tyranny "but only in Livy's presence"--a joke some
theory-ridden biographers have failed to perceive (113).

Of course the major charge against Livy--with Brooks the
chief prosecutor--is that of emasculating Twain's style, an
indictment no longer taken very seriously by Twain scholars.
Wagenknecht observes that Mrs. Clemens used her influence
"against burlesque, against extravagance, against blasphemy and
irreverence of all kinds" (174). Yet he adds, "After all, he
did attack the missionaries, he did write *Huckleberry Finn*, he
did formulate his philosophy of determinism" (185). It is
Wagenknecht's conviction that Twain had too much virility to
be "pushed very far from his native bent"; moreover, his obvious
faults do arise from too much burlesque and extravagance--ex-
actly the major targets of Mrs. Clemens' criticism. DeLancey
Ferguson goes even further in rebuttal: "Detailed study of the
manuscript of his greatest books, in short, reveals no evidence
of blighting censorship" (227). And Ferguson credits Livy with
saving Mark's readers from "boresome minutiae" in many of his
books, at the same time averring that the few "strong" words

she deleted have been magnified in the minds of her critics
(273). Bernard DeVoto, who finds "considerably less bowdlerization" in Twain's writings than frequently inferred, believes
"... the greater part of it was Twain's voluntary act, in
obedience to his own judgment and his own conception of propriety and public taste" (*Mark Twain at Work* 85). Pattee's
blunt answer to the charge that Livy, abetted by neighbors,
kept Mark from writing as he wished, is simply, "Nonsense!
Twaddle!" (*Representative Selections* xxvii). Dixon Wecter,
while freely admitting the censorship of Livy and Howells over
"certain vivid words and phrases," believes that Twain proved
to be "his own most attentive censor," because he realized the
curtailed expression of Victorian print, a curb to which "...
in the main he gave unstinting consent" ("Mark Twain" 2: 925).
In a word, those who have studied the Twain papers and manuscripts find that Livy did change words or phrases, but that
in the main her alterations more often saved Twain from bad
judgment rather than weakened his style; there is no evidence
of anything more.

Hartford

After the new home had been opened in Hartford during the
fall of 1871, Clemens left almost immediately upon an extended
lecture tour to finish paying his debts incurred through the
family illnesses and the unfortunate sacrifice sale of his
Buffalo interests. Nothing was more to his distaste than the
inconvenience of a tour, but he could not afford to overlook a
means of quick and ready income, even though he was hustled
about, here and there, from Boston to Chicago. Yet there were
some compensations not monetary, for Twain did enjoy the triumph
of an enthusiastic reception, and congenial company awaited him
at the Lyceum headquarters in Boston, where Petroleum V. Nasby
(D.R. Locke) and Josh Billings (H.W. Shaw), fellow humorists
and good friends, met to exchange pleasantries. They along
with Twain were pioneers in reverse, bringing the humor of the
Old Southwest and the frontier into the Atlantic States.
    Boston offered other pleasant associations as well, for
there were William Dean Howells, and Thomas Bailey Aldrich,
and Twain's old associate on the *Californian*, Bret Harte, who
had won his literary way across a continent to become a contributing editor of the *Atlantic* at a salary of $10,000 a year
for whatever he might choose to write (Pattee, *Development*
220). There were pleasant, informal occasions when Clemens
met with Aldrich, Fields, Harte, and Howells, dinners made enjoyable by good stories, wit, and aimless fun.

Yet Twain was never quite accepted in Boston as Bret Harte was, the reason being, as explained by Albert Bigelow Paine, that Harte was understood, a part of the convention, while Twain was not. The creator of "The Outcasts of Poker Flat," despite his Western humor, spoke their language through his pathos and his Victorian sentimentality, his art being essentially close to that of Charles Dickens, while the "Wild Humorist of the Pacific Slope," on the other hand, was something yet to be classified (Paine 2: 451). Among the traditionalists of the Brahmin caste only Charles Eliot Norton and Francis J. Child welcomed Mark Twain with unqualified approval.

By the end of February Clemens was completing the lecture tour, made more difficult by the task of reading proof for the new book as he jumped from place to place. But now he was out of debt, the advanced sales of *Roughing It* (1872) were large enough to rival his earnings from *The Innocents Abroad*, and Twain's mind was made up to follow authorship alone as his profession. Yet the new book, despite the fact that it dealt with one of the most picturesque phases of American history, failed to attain the popularity of *The Innocents Abroad*, its sale gradually diminishing after the first three months until ten years were required to reach the mark of one hundred thousand copies attained by the former book in three. This disappointment was not great, but again as in Buffalo, fate prepared to deal another blow.

With the birth of their first daughter, Susan Olivia, at Elmira, March 19, 1872, the Clemens family appeared to be happily progressing, but on June 2, in the new home at Hartford, occurred the death of little Langdon, for which Mark Twain reproached himself as the sole cause. Actually the child was so delicate that his life had often been uncertain, but because he was entrusted to his father at a time when the carriage robes slipped, exposing him to the chilling air and causing a cold which developed into diphtheria, Twain felt the blame, a remorse that dwelt with him to the end. This second loss coming so soon after the death of her father made Mrs. Clemens feel as if death were pursuing them. Thinking that the air of the seashore would be good for the baby, they spent the summer at Saybrook, Connecticut, while Orion, to whom Twain had generously sent $1,000 for aiding him with *Roughing It*, took charge of the house at Hartford. Naturally Clemens did very little writing that summer, yet possibly to forget his grief he turned to the invention of the "Mark Twain Scrapbook." Its pages were covered with strips of dry glue to be moistened when used, a device which was successfully marketed by Dan Slote of the *Quaker City* party, whose stationery firm paid royalties on it of around $2,000 a year (Webster 160). Although this profit continued through 1881, Twain felt that it should have been three times as much, and as the returns grew smaller after that, his friendship with Dan was eventually disrupted.

As creative energy returned Twain decided to write another travel book, this time about England, and he began to make plans. Ostensibly, however, the reason for his trip would be to protect his copyright against English book pirates. No international copyright law then existed, and the legal vacuum encouraged publishers to have more respect for profits than morality, but British law did grant copyright to any book first published there. Consequently *Roughing It* had been brought out by Routledge in London prior to the American publication, and although Twain had not been a British resident at the same time, nobody challenged the legality by pirating an edition.

Having sailed alone on the *Scotia*, August 21, 1872, Mark Twain arrived in Liverpool and took the train to London; his first glimpse of the English countryside filled him with "rapture and ecstasy," words he admitted too poor to convey his actual delight, but the best he could find at the moment (Paine 2: 458-59). The first meeting with his publishers, occurring just as they were about to sit down to lunch, lasted until after dinner that evening as Twain talked on and on to their cordial enjoyment. Finally leaving the establishment, all went to the Savage Club, where Stanley the explorer, Sir Henry Irving, Harry Lee, and the younger Tom Hood, joined enthusiastically in the welcome. Indeed literary London subsequently followed suit, with the White Friars' Club and others honoring Clemens with banquets, while his jokes circulated everywhere. London had not forgotten Artemus Ward, nor Bret Harte, while Joaquin Miller had put on an act in professional Western garb that was as dramatic in its way as Buffalo Bill's Wild West Show. Yet here was something entirely different; most of our American writers had their English counterparts, but Twain was completely and distinctly American. When he returned to his own country in November, loaded with Christmas presents for friends and relatives, Clemens realized for the first time that he was a literary figure. Boston might not accept him as the equal of Holmes and Lowell, but London acclaimed him their superior, whom he transcended as Lincoln did an academic Seward.

The book about England, however, never was written; perhaps, as Paine says, because he enjoyed England too much to write humorously about a "country so beautiful that you will be obliged to believe in fairy-land," where he had "a jolly good time," and where he declared, "I would a good deal rather live here if I could get the rest of you over" (qtd. in Paine 2: 470). Ferguson, however, seems more penetrating with the explanation that since his focus was London there was no framework of narrative, no pattern of movement upon which to construct a narrative as in *The Innocents Abroad* or *Roughing It* (165). Whatever the reason, the book was never written, though it was not long before Twain found himself involved in another task arising from a boast similar to James Fenimore Cooper's that he could write a better novel than the one he and his wife were reading. During the winter of 1873, when the Clemens household seemed settled happily into its first real home life since their early months in Buffalo, they enjoyed a particularly intimate friendship with the Warners. One evening at the dinner table, Clemens' and Warner's light treatment of certain novels read by their wives provoked the retort to furnish the public with better ones, a challenge mutually accepted on the moment to do a novel in partnership.

For some time Twain had hesitated to undertake an extended work of fiction, although he had in mind a tale about James Lampton, his mother's visionary cousin. Now when Warner approved the idea and agreed to help, he immediately set to work. The first eleven chapters of the book, written by Twain in a burst of enthusiasm, were then read to Warner, who continued the story through the next twelve chapters. The book was to be evenly divided; however, the work was not entirely separated into sections, for a number of passages written by one were rewritten by the other, portions were alternately added, and as the manuscript accumulated the separate contributions became more intimately interwoven. As Mark Twain's own annotated copy of *The Gilded Age* reveals, the task was evenly but not clearly divided: a chapter mapped out by him was actually written by Warner, each made paragraph interpolations throughout, and although labors of both are evident, they also become inextricable (Leisy 445-47). The separate division of chapters recorded by Paine, while originally intended, did not work out in practice (Paine 2: 477). Whenever Twain saw a chance to enliven the dialogue or expose abuse he did so, while Warner, on occasion, modified some of Twain's wrath, or even set down an incident told him by his collaborator.

The Gilded Age, begun in February, was rapidly completed during April; and though only partly by Clemens, stood as a *fait accompli* of fiction writing; he was now a novelist, a creator of characters and deviser of plot. If today its melodrama seems to damn it, yet it has successfully characterized and accurately named an era of graft, greed, and corruption, a period of exploitation in our national life when a policy of "anything goes" was producing personal fortunes on the one hand at the expense of public welfare and natural resources on the other. There was another co-worker on *The Gilded Age*, J. Hammond Trumbull, who prepared the chapter headings in many and diverse languages, a humorous contrivance that misfired. Trumbull was a learned linguist, who "according to Clemens could swear in twenty-seven languages" (Paine 2: 477-78).

That same winter Twain and Livy purchased a lot on Farmington Avenue, preparatory to building a new home, but in May while it was still under construction, Twain and his family, accompanied by Livy's girlhood chum, Clara Spaulding, went to England. This second visit, like the first, turned into a round of enthusiastic receptions, entertainments so numerous that Livy begged Twain to cancel further engagements and slip away quietly to Scotland. Unfortunately they did not go before the effects of social stress left her ill in Edinburgh; there they formed a warm friendship with the well-known author and physician, Dr. John Brown, who became a devoted playmate for Susy. The entire family, as a result, remembered Edinburgh with pleasure. They left for a brief stop in Glasgow and a short trip to Ireland, then returned to England, where they visited the beautiful Cholmondeley estate, Condover Hall, near Shrewsbury. Before the end of the six-month vacation in England, a trip to Paris with sightseeing and shopping added zest, but even so, Livy was becoming homesick.

Not wishing to endanger copyrights by returning to the States before his next book appeared, Twain on October 13 lectured on "Our Fellow Savages of the Sandwich Islands" to a large audience in Queen's Concert Rooms, Hanover Square. He was greeted on five successive nights and a matinee with delighted roars of laughter. Yet lingering only long enough to repeat the lecture once in Liverpool, Clemens sailed home with his family on October 21 to be met by Orion, November 2. The older brother was just then characteristically engaged inventing a flying machine, writing a Jules Verne-type novel, reading newspaper proof, and contemplating a lecture tour. Twain was received with acclaim, so surrounded by admirers that the president of the Mercantile Library Association tried vainly four times to reach him with offers of a lecture tour. Going to see Booth in *Hamlet* that evening, Twain was invited behind the scenes; when he proposed to add a new character to the play, a bystander who makes humorous comments, Booth was not shocked but "laughed immoderately."[4]

Within a month, Twain was once more in England, lecturing again, this time with "Roughing It on the Silver Frontier." Again he rode the crest of popularity: the Athenaeum Club made him a visiting member, he was feted everywhere, callers besieged him, and--the humorist's accolade--he was quoted by *Punch* (Paine 2: 496). The poet Charles Warren Stoddard then in London acted as Clemens' secretary, even patiently collecting the daily news reports of a now-forgotten legal farce, the Tichborne trial. To Twain, however, this case recalled the claimant in the Lampton family, who continued to supplicate

for aid in a futile effort to establish himself as Earl of
Durham, a character later utilized in *The American Claimant*.

The *Gilded Age* appeared a few days before Christmas, and on
January 13, 1874, Clemens sailed home on the *Parthia*. By the
end of January, 26,000 copies of the new book had been sold,
sales later increasing to 40,000 a month; with the new home
nearing completion and the family in good health, prospects
for the coming year seemed bright. Though at first refusing,
Twain later agreed to lecture for Redpath--"a persistent devil"
--who arranged dates here and there during February and March.
Then in April the family moved to Quarry Farm, where Twain
worked in a separate study, a small room filled with windows
like a pilot house. Here he began another autobiographical
book, but not of travel this time; he would convert actual experiences into fiction. More than four years earlier Clemens
had written an old friend about their boyhood pranks, schoolday episodes, and childhood games in the woods on Holliday's
Hill; now old days and old faces began once more forming in
his memory (*Letters to Will Bowen* 18-20). And as happy recollections bodied forth into the idyll of youth in preindustrial
America, Twain turned to the writing of *Tom Sawyer*. Immersed
in the subject, oblivious to everything else, Twain accumulated
manuscript at the rate of fifty pages a day.

That June, Clara was born, and the family enjoyed occasional
holidays, mostly Sundays, when Clemens ceased work for relaxa-
tion with the children or reading with Livy. Yet with prodigious creative power, in addition to *Tom Sawyer*, he also produced a play based on *The Gilded Age*, written for the actor
John Raymond, who performed the part of Colonel Sellers, though
not to the author's satisfaction.

Despite Twain's disapproval of Raymond, who debased Colonel
Sellers into low comedy, it appears to have been his acting and
knowledge of theater audiences which turned a rather poor play
into a profitable venture. The play was founded upon a plot
constructed by Gilbert Densmore, a script Twain not only frankly
admitted using, but paid for accordingly, causing Densmore himself to refer to the "very handsome manner in which you have
acted in this matter" (qtd. in Paine 2: 518). Meanwhile Clemens
achieved the distinction of joining the contributors to the
Atlantic Monthly, which accepted for publication in November,
1874, "A True Story, Repeated Word for Word as I Heard It."
As Twain stated when submitting the manuscript to Howells, the
story was written just as he heard an old black servant, "Auntie
Cord," tell it, only starting with the beginning rather than
the middle as she did.

Upon Twain's return to Hartford, the new home though pro-
nounced "ready" was still filled with workmen, causing Charles
Dudley Warner, then visiting in Egypt, to send humorous condo-

lences on Mark's discomfort. Finally the place was finished,
everything in order, and a charming, happy home life began.
Filled with Oriental rugs, handsome draperies, fine paintings
and statuary, the home was worthy of its frequent visitors,
among them Twichell, Howells, and Aldrich, who took their ease
before the English fireplace beneath a window, where they could
watch at once the cheerful fire and falling snow. Or if it
were autumn, guests visited the upper balconies to enjoy the
hazy tints so beautiful in that section of Connecticut.

Shortly, when Howells requested something for the January
number of the *Atlantic Monthly*, Twain at first declined. Then
during a walk with Twichell, conversing about old days on the
Mississippi as seen from the pilothouse, Mark received an enthusiastic response, "What a virgin subject to hurl into a
magazine!" (qtd. in Paine 2: 531). So it was--its very newness
pleased Twain. Immediately he wrote Howells, "I am the only
man alive that can scribble about the piloting of that day--
and no man ever has tried to scribble about it yet" (*Letters*
1: 236). Then Clemens at once produced seven installments,
the first appearing in January and the last in August under the
heading "Old Times on the Mississippi." Twain grew so enthusiastic that he proposed taking Howells on a trip to refresh his
memory and add to his material. But Howells, unable to leave
his desk at the *Atlantic*, declined; Osgood was invited, then
John Hay. When none could go, it finally proved seven years
before the trip materialized. Now, however, the piloting
chapters surging forth from memory appeared in the *Atlantic
Monthly*, the best writing he had achieved up to that time,
destined to take their place among the classic pages of American letters. Successful at once, they were reprinted everywhere by the newspapers, even pirated into book form in Canada.
Here was the raw material from which *Huckleberry Finn* later
grew, and with it Twain began for the first time to work that
source of inspiration for his greatest books--Sam Clemens' boyhood in the great Mississippi Valley during preindustrial days.
Indeed, the first half of *Life on the Mississippi* is devoted
to the boy serving an apprenticeship, for it is the cub rather
than the pilot who is pictured there. The contributions to the
Atlantic from which the book grew were retained as chapters
four through seventeen. They are not a factual history of the
times, rather the pure gold of actual experience lifted into
the realm of art by the creative force of gifted imagination.
If crime is ignored and sex unmentioned, it is done with deliber-
ation; Mark was uninterested in the sordid side of river traffic.
What absorbed him were his boyhood ambitions arising from environment, his efforts as a cub to master a difficult profession,
the customs of piloting, and varied aspects of human nature
ranging from the kindly George Ealer to the venomous, inverse
class hatred of the tyrant Brown.

In January, 1875, the Sellers play was performed in the Hartford Opera House with every seat sold. Raymond by now acted his role to perfection, Kate Field played Laura Hawkins, while a young man from Hartford, William Gillette, was also in the cast. The play was successful wherever it went; all in all a hundred thousand dollars was divided between actor and author.[5]

Accepted now by Hartford socially and intellectually, Samuel Clemens was received into the Monday Evening Club, composed of the best minds of the community; among them were Warner, Twichell, Professor Calvin E. Stowe, Dr. Horace Bushnell, and J. Hammond Trumbull. Elected just after his first trip to England, Twain made his debut with a paper on the "License of the Press." Another paper prepared for club reading was "The Facts Concerning the Recent Carnival of Crime in Connecticut," one of Twain's delvings into the problem of man versus conscience, something of a self-chiding allegory. Later he talked on "What Is Happiness?," which presented the theory he was to develop into his gospel, the basic idea of "What Is Man?" Yet the club came eventually to bore him, because except for his own contributions there appears to have been little life or exhiliration. And Twain finally suggested that "... these tiresome damned prayer-meetings might better be adjourned to the garret of some church, where they belonged" (*Autobiography* 1: 305).

Psychic theories and "mental telegraphy" (his own phrase) fascinated Twain. One morning while lying in bed, as he recalled, "... suddenly a red-hot new idea came whistling down into my camp" (qtd. in Paine 2: 543). It was to get his old friend Dan DeQuille to write a book about the Comstock Lode; the time was ripe and Dan was the man. Promptly Twain prepared a detailed plan, holding it only until he could talk with his publishers, but within a week a letter arrived addressed by Dan's hand, bearing a Nevada postmark. Twain turned to a visitor saying he would perform the miracle of revealing the date, contents, and signature of the letter without opening it, which he did. The incident, along with others, is recorded in "Mental Telegraphy." Of more interest to posterity, however, is that Dan accepted Twain's invitation to be his guest and write the book. *The Big Bonanza*, though not the best seller Twain or Dan expected, was successfully published by Bliss and remains a valuable and entertaining book on the shelf of Americana.

Meanwhile the "inspiration tank," as Twain liked to call it, having filled up again, the story of Tom and Huck progressed steadily. The family did not visit Elmira that summer, going instead to Bateman's Point, Rhode Island. Then during the fall (1875) appeared the book contracted for five years

before, *Sketches New and Old*. Mostly made up of sketches
originally published with the *Jumping Frog*, selections of
"Memoranda," and contributions to the Buffalo *Express*, it contained a few new items, one being "Some Fables for Good Old
Boys and Girls," a satiric account of a scientific investigation into the ways of men conducted by wood creatures. Although
given a laudatory review by Howells, *Sketches*, after an initial
sale of twenty thousand copies, made a rather poor showing.
The public seemed to sense that it was not in the same class
with *The Innocents Abroad* or *Roughing It*, for the original
sales presumably were based more on the author's reputation
than the contents. And the public was right; indeed Twain
himself declared most of it should never have been collected.

In the above-mentioned review Howells had commented on the
more serious side of Twain exhibited in "A True Story," and in
the October (1875) *Atlantic* Twain contributed "The Curious Republic of Gondour," his own version of a Utopia secured through
intellectual qualifications for voting. It was unsigned--
Clemens sometimes felt that his nom de plume might suggest a
hoax--but it delighted Howells, who wished continued reports
from the model republic. By now, however, Twain's fancy had
been caught with a jingle composed by Noah Brooks and Isaac
Bromley, who had seen a placard posted in the streetcars for
the information of passengers and conductor. The chorus, so
Twain pretended, kept running through his brain to the exclusion
of everything else; all he could think of was:

> Punch, brothers! Punch with care!
> Punch in the presence of the passenjare!

The result, "A Literary Nightmare," published in the February
(1876) *Atlantic*, started an epidemic of horsecar poetry.
Howells' children recited it in chorus, and going out to
dinner, he found the Longfellow ladies knew it by heart. From
Boston it swept across the nation, even carrying its nonsense
jingles into Europe (Paine 2: 557).

Yet *Tom Sawyer* remained unpublished, despite Howells' ad-
monition to hurry--"That boy is going to make a prodigious
hit" (qtd. in Paine 2: 570), he wrote Twain. But Tom's creator
was first anxious to find a means of outwitting the book
pirates, especially in Canada, who grabbed everything in the
Atlantic or elsewhere. He therefore gave the manuscript to
Moncure D. Conway, who carried it to London, where arrangements
were made for publication with Chatto & Windus. Thus began a
friendly business relation between Twain and his English publishers, which lasted throughout his life. Although *Tom Sawyer*
was not to appear on the American market until the end of the
year, it came out in England on June 9, 1876.

During that centennial summer the Clemens family sought
refuge at Elmira, where the children could romp on the shady
lawn of Quarry Farm, while Twain returned to his study. But
far more important, he had begun work on a manuscript destined
to become an American classic and one of the great volumes in
world literature--*The Adventures of Huckleberry Finn.* For a
time he was enthusiastic over this sequel to *Tom Sawyer,* especially about narrating the story in the first person, but
gradually his interest flagged. Declaring that he liked it
"only tolerably well," he pigeonholed the half-completed manuscript and let it lie unfinished for years. Now his imagination, stimulated by reading Pepys' *Diary,* turned to the court
manners and conversations of olden times. He would try his
hand at the days of Queen Elizabeth, recording conversation
with outspoken frankness and coarseness. Written in a letter
to good old Joe Twichell, whose reverend profession had not
weakened his robust sense of humor, this sketch of manners and
talk among a group of courtiers and ladies in the presence of
Queen Elizabeth was called at first *Fireside Conversation in
the Time of Queen Elizabeth*; later *1601.* Before mailing, it
was shown to David Gray, who urged Twain to sign it and print
it, declaring, "You have never done a greater piece of work
than that" (qtd. in Paine 2: 580). In due time *1601* reached
John Hay, who hailed it as a classic. Four years later Hay,
also, allowed proofs to be made of it, from which a very private circulation followed. Eventually it escaped into the
public domain, and a number of editions have since been printed.
Too much has been made of this bit of ribaldry, both by en-
thusiasts who claim literary qualities it does not possess and
the Freudians who see it as the way Twain would have always
written if unhampered. Neither is correct, yet it remains an
amusing story for the smoking room. Moreover, it is funny and
illustrates the coarse strain of Twain's nature, but its literary importance is minor.

Eighteen seventy-six, besides being the centennial of
American independence, marked the presidential campaign between
Hayes and Tilden. Clemens, like his friends Twichell and
Howells, voted for the Republicans. Howells wrote a campaign
biography for Hayes, and Clemens spoke at a rally over which
he also presided. Yet later in life Clemens declared this
election "one of the Republican party's most cold-blooded
swindles of the American people" (*Eruption* 287).

The Adventures of Tom Sawyer appeared on the market probably about the second week in December (1876) in an edition of
about five thousand copies. With it Twain added his first
volume to the classic shelf of American fiction, as well as
contributing in Tom and Huck two immortals to the portrait gallery of permanent literature. Though destined to be overshadowed

by its sequel, *Tom Sawyer* is a masterpiece; here is the idyll
of boyhood, the charm of a past era--all portrayed through
vivid, lifelike characterization and a plot at times reaching
dramatic intensity.

Destined to reach the highest sales to date of all Twain's
books, *Tom Sawyer* was issued by subscription, the same form of
door-to-door sale which had so successfully launched *The Innocents Abroad*. When this method was finally abandoned in 1904,
its grand total, including many moderately priced editions,
rose to more than two million. The book retains to this
moment its wide appeal for all ages; popular as a "children's
classic," its magnetism is equally great to those adults who
still remember childhood. In fact, when Twain finished the
manuscript he wrote to Howells: "It is *not* a boy's book, at
all. It will only be read by adults. It is only written for
adults" (*Letters* 1: 258). And Howells, while designating it a
boy's story, declared adults would enjoy it no less, admitting
he had sat up fascinated until one a.m. to finish it.

While waiting for *Tom Sawyer* to make its debut, Twain confided to Howells: "... Bret Harte came up here the other day
and asked me to help him write a play and divide the swag,
and I agreed" (*Letters* 1: 287). Twain was to put in Scotty
Bridges (of the Buck Fanshaw funeral episode in *Roughing It*),
and Bret was to develop a wonderfully funny Chinese man. The
two authors wrote separate plots, so they could "gouge from
both and build a third." Wishing to keep the whole transaction
secret Twain requested Howells to get the title "Ah Sin, a
Drama" printed on a page for him, the rest of the application
for copyright being allowable in longhand.[6] Both Mark and
Bret worked hard on the play until it was finished. However,
when *Ah Sin* opened at the National Theatre in Washington,
May 7, 1877, Twain was unable to attend because of bronchitis,
and Charles T. Parsloe, who played the Chinese laundryman, found
Harte unbearably annoying. *Ah Sin* was not a success; when produced in New York by Augustin Daly at the Fifth Avenue Theatre,
July 31, 1877, it enjoyed only a short run, followed by a career
equally brief on the road. Indeed the curtain speech by Twain
was the best thing connected with the whole performance. Perhaps this tended to increase the friction, arising between the
authors during its composition, a mutual antagonism destroying
their former friendship and making future association impossible. While writing the play Harte made sarcastic remarks
about the Clemens home, finally uttering a disparagement which
Twain thought aimed at Livy. This was too much; Harte was
ordered from the house, never to return. Twain henceforth had
nothing but contempt for the man, a hearty dislike he did not
fail to express publicly and in strong language.

Soon, however, Twain was off on a delightful holiday to
Bermuda, accompanied by Joe Twichell, a real pleasure trip
marred only because Howells could not be with them. The *Note-*
book records the sensitivity with which Twain reacted to the
beauty of the spot with its houses like marble, only "whiter,
daintier, richer--white sugar is the nearest to it" (124).
On returning to Hartford, undaunted by *Ah Sin*, he finished
another play, *Simon Wheeler, the Amateur Detective*, which he
submitted to Dion Boucicault. Others read the play, too, and
while all agreed that the dialogue was entertaining and the
situations well constructed, somehow or other it just would
not act. Like many another novelist, Twain was unable to
transfer the dramatic incident from the printed page to actual
sound and motion before the footlights. Fortunately he did
not pursue theatrical activities further at this point, but
probably realizing that playwriting was not his forte turned
to a more profitable venture in fiction. While reading Charlotte M. Yonge's *The Prince and the Page*, Clemens suddenly
received a parallel idea from her plot of a prince who disguised himself as a blind beggar. Why not add also a beggar
disguised as a prince, giving a double plot and a new twist to
the situation? Thus began the composition of *The Prince and*
the Pauper, about four hundred pages of manuscript being
finished that summer, before faltering inspiration caused him
to lay aside the task, not to be touched again for more than
three years.

During that winter occurred perhaps the greatest faux pas
in Mark Twain's entire life. The *Atlantic Monthly* staff proposed to honor John Greenleaf Whittier on his seventieth birthday with a banquet; it was to be a great occasion, the literary elite would be there, and Clemens, among others, was invited to speak. With the distinguished guest list headed by
Emerson, Longfellow, and Holmes, Twain, happy to be included,
determined to give them one of the funniest speeches of his
career. Anywhere else it would have been funny, but the unfortunate subject matter was as out of place as would be making
fun of Robert E. Lee at a Confederate reunion. Boston and Cambridge had gathered to honor not only Whittier but New England
literature. It was a tribute to their cultural heritage, embodied in the venerable figures of the poets who graced the
banquet on this auspicious evening. Each speaker in turn paid
his respects to the poets present and the environment that had
nurtured them; then to quote Howells "... the amazing mistake,
the bewildering blunder, the cruel catastrophe was upon us"
(*My Mark Twain* 60). Mark began a story about a miner whose
lonely cabin had been invaded by three literary men, "Mr. Longfellow, Mr. Emerson, and Mr. Oliver Wendell Holmes--confound
the lot." At those words the audience froze, and as the story

proceeded with a description of the supposed Emerson as "a
seedy little bit of a chap, red-headed," the pretended Holmes
as "fat as a balloon; he weighed as much as three hundred,
and had double chins all the way down to his stomach," and
the bogus Longfellow "built like a prize-fighter," the atmosphere grew colder with every word.[7] The next day, abject with
apology, the unhappy speaker sent letters to Emerson, Longfellow, and Holmes, beseeching pardon, which the three, being
gracious gentlemen, quickly granted. This did not ease his
mind, however, for Clemens, still mortified, feared lest Howells
exclude his future writings from the pages of the *Atlantic*.
Though he finally got over feeling disgraced, in later years
even declaring it a funny speech, at the time he was overcome
by chagrin and shame.[8]

Perhaps this unhappy occurrence had something to do with
Twain's decision to revisit Europe, where he resolved to spend
a year or two, but there were other reasons, one being the demand for another travel book. About this time, also, Clemens
had given way to a tendency to invest money in numerous enter-
prises, most of which involved him in vexatious patent rights,
but yielded no profits. All this consumed time and prevented
completion of a half dozen manuscripts already started. Social
events were frequent, and now since he had determined to live
awhile in Germany, he began to study the language. Though he
had no chance to write, he characteristically found time to
read a manuscript for Orion and offer suggestions about its
publication. Their correspondence reveals that Twain had
probably already written part of *Captain Stormfield's Visit
to Heaven*, which he had been revising from time to time for
about five years.

The Clemens family accompanied by Clara Spaulding sailed
for Hamburg on the *Holsatia*, April 11, 1878, a miserable voyage
with screaming children, crashing crockery, lurching ship, and
a "special hell" added--a piano! From Hamburg, where they
rested a few days, the party proceeded through Hanover and
Frankfurt to Heidelberg: there Clemens took accommodations at
the Schloss Hotel, which afforded the visitor one of the most
beautiful views to be found in Germany. Twain wrote enthusiastically to Howells how the view by day changed from "one en-
chanting aspect to another" and how Heidelberg by night became
"a cobweb, beaded thick with lights" (*Letters* 1: 330). Select-
ing a house across the river, Twain rented a room in which to
write: all seemed perfect. Yet the beauty of the landscape
did not ease the struggles with the awful German language,
though one suspects an exaggeration of the difficulties. There
are many amusing incidents and comments, enough to indicate
that Twain was having a battle with cases and genders.

Twichell joined Clemens for a walking tour through the
Black Forest into Switzerland, where they escaped from public
attention. As the holiday ended they joined Mrs. Clemens at
Lausanne, Twichell set out for home by way of England, and
the Clemens party wandered down into Italy. At Rome and
Florence they visited art galleries, and occasionally made
purchases for their home. In Venice they bought a massive
carved bed with serpentine columns surmounted with rosewood
cupids, a bed perhaps three hundred years old, abandoned from
a Venetian palace. It became a custom in their family for the
children, when ill, to enjoy the privilege of occupying this
bed and having one of the cupids removed to play with.

Although Twain did not dislike the old masters so intensely
as when he viewed them as an Innocent, he still could not approach them with the same reverence as Livy and Miss Spaulding.
Once accompanied by Sarah Orne Jewett, Twain declared that if
the old masters had labeled their fruit, one "wouldn't be so
likely to mistake pears for turnips," a witticism quickly re-
proved by Livy, to which Miss Jewett added, "Now, you've been
spoken to" (qtd. in Paine 2: 634). Leaving Italy and the old
masters, Clemens, acting as his own courier, finally arrived
at Munich after suffering bad connections and weary delay.

That winter in Munich work progressed well, while the
children enjoyed the German Christmas with its decorations,
trees, and toys. The family decided to spend the spring in
Paris and unhappily encountered the longest spell of winter
ever to curse a visitor there. When they could stand the cold
and rain no longer, Clemens moved to Brussels, then to Antwerp,
followed by rapid visits to Rotterdam, Dresden, and Amsterdam.
They arrived in London on July 29 (1879) amid more rain and
cold, which seemed to characterize the weather throughout all
Europe that summer.

To Twain London always meant a series of brilliant functions with notable associates. Now he met Whistler and Henry
James, and before leaving took a trip up to Windermere Lake
to see the "great Darwin." Sailing from Liverpool August 23,
homeward bound, Clemens again saw a lunar rainbow, a brilliant,
complete arch. Back in New York, September 3, 1879, they went
directly to Quarry Farm, ever a delight, now after long absence
a "foretaste of Heaven." But by November Twain was in Chicago,
delivering a speech at the reception for General Grant by the
Army of the Tennessee, an occasion memorable with historic names,
and one at which Clemens delivered an address that shook the
crowd, brought praise from Sherman, and acknowledgment from
Grant himself (*Letters* 1: 371-72). Never had the boy from
Hannibal dreamed of greater success, and soon thereafter came
an opportunity to redeem his one public humiliation, the
fiasco of the Whittier birthday speech. The *Atlantic Monthly*

honored Holmes with a breakfast, another notable gathering at
which Emerson, Longfellow, Whittier, and Parkman were present;
Clemens, who accepted at the insistence of Warner and Howells,
this time made a very careful tribute, gracious with praise and
salted with just the proper touch of humor. And so the year
closed happily for him.

Once again at home a chief pleasure became the acting of
charades invented by Clemens, who also costumed the performers,
and frequently participated with enthusiasm. Other times
Twain played and sang spiritual and jubilee songs loved from
boyhood, while the children joined in the melody. And, of
course, he liked nothing better than to read aloud; it appears
that this first winter back in the States began the custom of
reading his manuscripts to Mrs. Clemens and the children.
Twain was just then resuming work on *The Prince and the Pauper*,
which he read with pleasure as each chapter was completed. But
his other project, *A Tramp Abroad*, had become a nightmare;
when it was finally finished Mark expressed to Howells "the
unutterable joy of getting that Old Man of the Sea off my back,
where he has been roosting for more than a year and a half"
(*Letters* 1: 376). Delight with *The Prince and the Pauper*,
however, was as great as his boredom with *A Tramp Abroad*;
whereas the travel book had taxed him to fill out the necessary pages, the novel gave him so much pleasure that he worked
enthusiastically.

When *A Tramp Abroad* appeared, March 13, 1880, there was an
advance sale of 25,000 copies. An added satisfaction was a
proposal by Tauchnitz to issue an illustrated edition in Germany, in addition to the regular printing. Though Howells reviewed it favorably and Brander Matthews gave it critical acclaim, it remains today one of Twain's books less likely
to live. It lacks the gusto, the joy, the sheer genius of the
important books.

At Elmira, July, 1880, Jean, a third daughter, was born.
Clemens alternated work that summer, turning first to *The
Prince and the Pauper*, then to the story begun four years
earlier, the saga of Huck Finn, suddenly now of new interest
for him. Yet he did not read the Huck manuscript aloud to his
family; rather it was the lesser novel that he considered his
major task and read for approval as the manuscript accumulated
at the end of each day. It was a pleasant summer.

Later that year Twain was agitating for international copyright, making at least one trip to Washington to see his old
friend, Rollin M. Daggett, now a congressman, who offered to
introduce any bill that the authors agreed upon. During the
year he decided to change publishers; feeling that the American
Publishing Company had not earned all the profits he was entitled to, Twain gave *The Prince and the Pauper* to James R.

Osgood, thereby starting an association which inspired Twain
to devise new publishing methods and ventures. In fact,
Clemens had actually, without realizing it, become his own
publisher; for he advanced the money to meet publication costs
and paid Osgood a royalty for selling the book, a reversal of
the usual procedure. When he decided to go further with the
publishing business by having Osgood bring out a *Library of
Humor*, to be edited by Howells and Charles Hopkins Clark,
Clemens actually became a businessman.

   Next summer, June 8, 1881, Twain emerged more prominently
into public life by speaking at a dinner in Hartford for General Sherman and Secretary of War Robert Lincoln, traveling in
their private car to address the military students at West
Point. That summer President Garfield was assassinated
(July 2, 1881) and was succeeded in office by Chester A. Arthur,
a change which caused Howells to worry over his father's being
continued as consul at Toronto. An appeal to Twain, who took
the matter to Grant, had the desired results; not only was
Twain active in public affairs--he also had influence.

   Meanwhile *The Prince and the Pauper* was published in England, December 1, 1881, and to insure Canadian copyright Clemens
resided in Montreal for two weeks, only to find that he still
had to rely upon the previous publication in England to secure
his rights (Johnson 41). Paine states that the book also appeared in Germany early in December, 1881 (2: 716). Perhaps
Mark Twain's best constructed plot, *The Prince and the Pauper*,
remains as its subtitle explained, "A Tale for Young People
of All Ages." It is a charming romance and historical novel,
both dramatic and humorous, having as its deeper current the
underlying theme of democracy.

   About this time Twain became involved in a multiplicity of
interests other than literature. A patent steam generator
absorbed part of his bank account, to be followed by a steam
pulley which cost him $32,000, and a watch company which did
not exist long enough to pay dividends. Ironically, when a
young inventor, Alexander Graham Bell, tried to interest him
in a telephone, Twain, momentarily fed up with wildcat speculation, declined. He continued to write, giving Osgood a collection of sketches called *The Stolen White Elephant*, but a far
more important project was in mind--the completion of a book
on the Mississippi River. Osgood agreed to a trip to renew
inspiration and get the river atmosphere once more; starting
down stream on the steamer *Gold Dust* they concealed their
identity, but Twain was quickly recognized both on boat and
ashore. At New Orleans Clemens met Bixby, now captain of the
City of Baton Rouge, one of the last imposing steamboats on the
river, and he arranged to make the up-river trip on Bixby's
boat. In New Orleans Clemens delighted in exploring the old

French Quarter with George W. Cable and Joel Chandler Harris.

After a trip of copious note taking back up the river to St. Paul, during which he enjoyed three days in Hannibal, Twain started to write, a task made difficult by a time limit, something which always seemed to shackle his creative force. Finally the book was completed and handed to Osgood, although the real work of publishing descended upon the shoulders of Charles L. Webster, newly added to the firm; Webster was also the husband of Twain's niece. Osgood spent most of his time with Clemens playing billiards, a business method much to Twain's taste, while Webster put the book through the press, and it appeared about the middle of May (1883). Although *Life on the Mississippi* had a good sale at first, it has been the steady sale throughout the years, including numerous recent editions, which has put it in the best-seller category. And as time goes on, its importance increases; though a collection of facts, regional sketches, and humorous anecdotes, it preserves the story of an era and the flavor of a profession.

To insure copyright Clemens made another trip to Canada, where he was entertained by the Marquis of Lorne, the son-in-law of Queen Victoria, then Governor-General. That summer, back on Quarry Farm, Twain toyed with a number of ideas for books, among them "Captain Stormfield's Visit to Heaven," but the only immediate result was a play with Howells as collaborator. The plot concerned Colonel Sellers in his comic aspect with all of his marvelous schemes and his impractical inventions. Howells says that he and Twain wrote scenes in turn until the final play emerged (*My Mark Twain* 24). No producer would take it, however, and no actor would play it; yet Clemens, and Howells too, for that matter, refused to give up, finally resorting to having an elocutionist put it on as a burlesque of Raymond in the role of Sellers. Although they talked Daniel Frohman into promoting this double burlesque, when Howells saw the actuality his enthusiasm turned to suffering, and Twain, summoned from Hartford, readily agreed to pay for the theater, release the actors, and call it quits (Paine 2: 762).

Yet the footlights continued to fascinate him, for Twain sought next to dramatize both *The Prince and the Pauper* and *Tom Sawyer*. He made extensive plans for writing about the Sandwich Islands, another project to be turned into a play, this last again with the help of Howells. Though his dramatic efforts failed because Clemens possessed no practical knowledge of stagecraft, this particular winter of 1883-84 proved, nevertheless, one of entertainment and gaiety.

By spring, 1884, Clemens had his publishing business definitely under way with Charles L. Webster and Company located at 658 Broadway. But he was suffering trouble with the proof sheets of *Huckleberry Finn*, from which Howells offered

to help extricate him. *Huckleberry Finn* received ample notice
from time to time in the press; selections appeared in the
Century, and in January and February, 1885, Twain read passages
during his lecture trip with George W. Cable in Iowa. The book
was illustrated by E.W. Kemble, later a foremost cartoonist,
whose successful drawings for the portions appearing in the
Century promised well for the book.[9]

   The Adventures of Huckleberry Finn, though officially
published in England and America, December, 1884, was not in
the hands of the salesmen until February, 1885. Delays arose
from a last minute decision of Twain's to use as frontispiece
a picture of his bust executed by Gerhardt, and from an unfortunate incident of a damaged plate which gave one illustration
such an off-color meaning that it had to be withdrawn for cor-
rection. Despite the advance buildup, at the time of *Huck
Finn*'s appearance only one reviewer noticed it, T.S. Perry
writing a favorable review in the *Century*. More helpful, however, was the banning of the book by the Concord, Massachusetts, Public Library, which led the New York *Tribune* to pre-
dict an immediate rise in sales (Vogelback 265). With an advance order for 40,000 copies, and interest stimulated by the
Concord ban, *Huckleberry Finn* was off to a good start; yet in
total sales it did not surpass *Tom Sawyer*, still the best
seller of all Mark Twain's books. Indeed, critical as well
as general readers, with slight exception, seemed unaware that
a masterpiece had appeared.

   A masterpiece of great character painting, filled with
sensitive passages of rare poetic quality, *Huckleberry Finn*
recounts in vigorous style the social history of an era and
the atmosphere of a region. However much the reading public
at large failed to see this at the time, the humor and the adventure appealed enough to insure financial success. Then
came another publishing venture, this time the memoirs of
General Grant, for which the contract was closed, February 27,
1885. Clemens inadvertently learned from Richard Watson Gilder,
editor of the *Century*, that Grant, who had written three war
articles for that magazine, was preparing a fourth. When Gilder, innocent of true value, mentioned that he paid five hundred dollars for each article, Clemens was amazed; but when he
stated further that the General was in need and happy to make
some "trifle of bread-and-butter money," Clemens sought to
rectify a grave mistake (*Autobiography* 1: 32). Since neither
Grant nor Gilder sensed the immediate sales value of the articles, Clemens offered the amazed General $25,000 in advance
on the manuscript of each volume of his personal memoirs.
Realizing that he had a best seller, Clemens through the Webster Company employed sixteen general agents and ten thousand
canvassers on the advance sales; by May sixty thousand sets

were sold.   Clemens himself records the subscription to
320,000 sets by October 26, 1885 (*Notebook* 189).   The venture
was a great success: the time was ripe for such a book, Grant's
courageous fight against illness and poverty created a sympathetic reception, and the business details were handled admirably by the Webster Company.

Publishing Ventures: The Typesetter

Now at the age of fifty, Twain was not only a popular
writer; he appeared also to be a successful businessman.   His
birthday, one of the happiest, brought a number of greetings
and poems from such notables as Oliver Wendell Holmes, Frank R.
Stockton, Charles Dudley Warner, Joel Chandler Harris, and
Andrew Lang.   Though his hair was now iron gray, Twain still
looked young, for he was youthful in both spirit and vigor.
Loved by his family, liked by the public, Mark Twain at fifty
stood upon a pinnacle of success with the vista of boundless
others ahead.
    Yet the turning point to a down grade was close at hand.
It started with an unfortunate publishing venture, one that
Twain with Sellers-like optimism thought would be a greater
success than the Grant *Memoirs*--a life of the Pope, to be
written with the blessings of his Holiness himself.   The contract was made in Rome, April, 1886, Webster being granted
the special honor of a private audience; plans were made to
launch the book simultaneously in six languages, each purchaser
to receive a volume blessed by the sovereign pontiff (Paine 3:
855).   Also, as early as 1880 the villain in Mark Twain's life
had appeared, the destroyer of his happiness, and the drainer
of his resources--the Paige typesetting machine.   On December 1,
1885, Clemens enthusiastically listed in his notebook an account of this machine's assets (*Notebook* 181).   From then on
his belief in its future caused him to sink even more money
into what might well have proved a profitable venture, but
which unfortunately led to disaster.
    In his enthusiasm over the Grant book, Clemens seems to
have forgotten his own; the only writing project which appeared
to attract him was *Captain Stormfield*, the manuscript of it
remaining locked away in a safe.   But there was another book
he expected to write, one that he may have begun as early as November, 1884, and upon which he worked now and then for about
five years--*A Connecticut Yankee*.   About this time the Browning
readings began, lasting through the winter of 1886-87, during
which Twain conducted a sort of class, among which were members

from the Saturday Morning Club as well as the family. Finally
the Browning readings tapered off into a German class; out of
this grew Clemens' three-act play *Meisterschaft*, a humorous
and picturesque mixture of German and English. The class twice
performed it successfully; it appeared in the *Century* (January,
1888), and subsequently found its way into the collected works.

The publishing business still continued to be a major interest. The *Library of Humor*, edited by Howells and Clark,
with which Twain had little to do save write a "Compiler's
Apology," sold fairly well--not so well as hoped--but well
enough to insure a profit and a subsequent printing by Harper
in 1906 (Blodgett 78-80). And a book by General Sheridan sold
profitably, as did the ten volume *Library of American Literature*; but unfortunately *The Life of Pope Leo XIII* was not a
best seller, not even popular, though it did earn something.
Not so fortunate, however, were the books by Rollin M. Daggett
and General Hancock, neither of which managed to get out of
the red (Paine 3: 856). What the publishing house really
needed was another book by Twain himself.

For several reasons Twain wished *A Connecticut Yankee* to
appear in the best possible format: the publishing house needed
a book badly--it was Mark's first in five years--and finally
here were his mature opinions upon democracy and humanity at
large. Dan Beard was selected as illustrator, a most happy
choice, for the pictures in the *Yankee* not only catch the eye
but illuminate the text. As Paine said, "Beard realized the
last shade of the author's allegorical intent and portrayed it
with a hundred accents which the average reader would otherwise
be likely to miss" (3: 889). In England where one pays homage
to the king, the irreverent aspects of Twain's satire upon
monarchy seemed vulgar, just as his bitter attacks upon an established church were likely to give offense to a devout
Catholic. It is unfortunate, for the author told a delightful
fantasy of a Connecticut Yankee suddenly swept back into the
days of chivalry, a fine comic situation that has proved popular on both stage and screen. Moreover, it is a great declaration of democratic principles, and in the final analysis it is
not just the court of King Arthur that is exposed to the light
of the truth, but the "damned human race."

Following publication of the *Yankee* Clemens suffered an
attack of rheumatism in his arm, making writing difficult.
For relief he wished for some German baths, especially as Livy
also suffered occasionally with the same trouble. Yet business
affairs would not permit; instead the family went up to the
Onteora Club at Tannersville in the Catskills, where they took
a cottage for the season. At evening, often before the fire,
Mark told wonderful stories, once favoring them with the
thrilling climax of the Golden Arm. Each day pantomimes and

charades, and burlesque races with Twain as starter added light-
hearted amusement.

Yet the gay season ended sadly; Mark was summoned to his
mother's bedside in Keokuk, and on October 27 Jane Clemens
died. Then shortly afterward Livy's own mother died in Elmira,
and at the same time Jean became suddenly ill. The typesetter
continued to cost money, while the publishing company made
little or none. No wonder that Twain, exasperated by the end
of the year (1890), wrote to Hall, his publishing manager,
"Merry Christmas to you, and I wish to God I could have one
myself before I die" (qtd. in Paine 3: 901).

Financial strain and worry were aggravated by recurrent
attacks of rheumatism; then came news from the publishing company that the *Library of American Literature*, sold on the in-
stallment plan, required cash to meet costs of production until
the monthly driblets should accrue. But one dependable source
for revenue was left, and Twain seized his pen, turning the
old play about Colonel Sellers and the claimant to a dukedom
into a novel. He even ransacked his desk for anything that
might sell immediately; the old article "Mental Telegraphy"
was expanded and sent to *Harper's*, as was another old sketch
titled "Luck." To counteract the impediment of rheumatism
Twain tried dictating into a phonograph, finally compromising
on writing by hand until forced from pain to turn to dictation.
Yet the claimant story went on, with the McClure syndicate
eventually paying twelve thousand dollars for the serial
rights. McClure also agreed to join W.M. Laffan of the *Sun*
in paying a thousand dollars each for six travel letters to
be written on a trip which Clemens was then planning (Paine
3: 919).

Since both Twain and Livy continued to suffer from rheumatism, Livy also being bothered by a heart disturbance, the
European baths seemed necessary. On June 6, 1891, the *Gascogne*
bore them toward Le Havre, whence they proceeded immediately
to Paris. Soon in Geneva, then quietly resting awhile at Aix,
afterwards visiting Bayreuth with its Wagner festival, they
finally came to Marienbad in Bohemia. At Aix, Clemens recovered
the use of his arm and at once began his first travel letter.
From Bayreuth he wrote "At the Shrine of St. Wagner" (*What Is
Man?* 209-27). But believing it easier to write a book than independent and complete articles he determined to write no more
for serial publication than the six promised letters.

Leaving the family behind, Clemens engaged Joseph Very,
courier of earlier travels recorded in *A Tramp Abroad*, and
embarked upon a journey during which they spent the night in
the old castle of Chatillon before reaching the Rhone, where he
indeed found it "too delicious, floating with the swift current
under the awning these superb, sunshiny days in deep peace and

quietness" (qtd. in Paine 3: 924). After his return from
Switzerland and France, the family spent the winter in Berlin,
enjoying an eventful social season, the high point being a
dinner with Emperor William II, at which Twain was the guest
of honor--pomp and circumstance enough to delight even Tom
Sawyer. Yet Twain was just as pleased with a compliment on
Old Times on the Mississippi from the *portier* at his hotel as
he had been with praise for the same volume from the emperor.
As a Christmas gift for the children, Mark Twain translated
Der Struwwelpeter, reading aloud to his daughters the rhymes
of Slovenly Peter, from a manuscript, wrapped in a huge red
ribbon, he had placed under the tree.

When Twain's health failed to improve satisfactorily, he
set out for Mentone in the south of France accompanied only by
Livy. After a month of second honeymoon there, as it were,
they went to Pisa, then to Rome to join the rest of the family.
Sightseeing in Venice for a fortnight, they traveled by way of
Lake Como to Lucerne, finally through Berlin to Bad Nauheim,
where the family spent the summer. But Twain now felt business
affairs demanded his presence in America; though the publishing
company remained in straitened circumstances, at long last it
seemed the typesetter was about to reach the stage of manufacture. Hurrying to Chicago, where a factory really did exist
capable of manufacturing fifty machines, Twain then returned
to Nauheim for a summer of rather steady writing. As his arm
improved he completed several short articles while beginning
work on *Tom Sawyer Abroad*, and upon what became *Those Extraordinary Twins*, then finally a part of *Pudd'nhead Wilson*.
And there he met the Prince of Wales, later Edward VII, who
enjoyed Twain so much that he invited him to supper, followed
by a pleasant evening of conversation.

The American Claimant was published in May (1892), following
a little volume called *Merry Tales*, issued shortly before; yet
neither was up to Twain's earlier successes. Naturally the
returns on both were slight; and Twain, still losing money on
the typesetter and making no progress in the publishing business, had to work even harder at his writing. Soon Twain
ferried back across the Atlantic, for the country descended into
one of its worst depressions, further deteriorating the publishing business. To the typesetter he looked for financial
help; once again fifty machines were about to be manufactured,
and Twain's spirits rose. In May, however, at the Villa Viviani
Twain found that he could do little save figure up his indebtedness. Again the family moved, settling in Munich for a while
until Twain, finding he could stand it no longer, once more
sailed for New York (August 29, 1893).

The first of March (1894) Clemens hurried across the ocean
for a three weeks' visit with his family in France, then arrived

back in New York the middle of April, only to find the publishing business backed against the wall. On April 18, 1894, the
firm of Charles L. Webster and Company closed its doors, and a
meeting of creditors was called with Henry H. Rogers serving
as Clemens' representative. And wisely so, for Clemens would
have been picked clean but for Rogers' acumen in pointing out
that Livy, who had lent the firm sixty thousand dollars, was
now preferred creditor and thereby entitled to the assignment
of copyrights until her claim should be paid in full. Other
claims amounted to a hundred thousand dollars to be settled at
the rate of fifty cents on the dollar; Clemens declared that
he would work until he had fully paid his entire debt, but
this only he and Livy believed possible. The creditors, according to Rogers, were "bent on devouring every pound of flesh
in sight and picking the bones afterward" (qtd. in Paine 3:
984), but by saving the copyrights (which then did not appear
so valuable) as well as the Hartford home, Twain was not left
penniless.

On the very day of the failure, *Tom Sawyer Abroad*, the
last book issued by Webster, was filed for copyright in Washington. Now seeking a publisher for *Pudd'nhead Wilson*,
Clemens, fortunately through the offices of Frank Bliss, again
secured the American Publishing Company to bring forth his
books after a lapse of twelve years. The failure of Webster
and Company demonstrated to Clemens how many sincere friends
he possessed, for several immediately offered financial aid,
Poultney Bigelow and Douglas Taylor each sending him a check
for one thousand dollars, while a number of creditors urged
him to forget their claims until such time as he might be able
to take them up unburdened. Although Livy wrote her husband
encouraging letters, actually she was horrified at the "hideous
news," for she said to her sister, "... business failure means
disgrace" (qtd. in Paine 3: 987). Clemens hastened back to
Paris, soon taking the family to a quiet watering place in the
south of France, finally settling down in Étretat. In July
(1894) "In Defense of Harriet Shelley" appeared in the *North
American Review*, one of the finest pieces of critical analysis
Twain ever wrote, delightful with wit, and illuminating with
penetrating insight.

At Étretat in Normandy work progressed on *Joan of Arc*,
interrupted momentarily by news of the failure of the typesetting machine, a disaster Clemens could scarcely believe;
yet he soon recovered to commence writing again. Not only
Joan, but *Tom Sawyer, Detective* poured forth from the inspiration tank, now rapidly filling since entirely released as a
literary reservoir. Settled down in Paris for the winter,
Twain finished *Joan of Arc* there and sent it to *Harper's*.
Accepted promptly for serialization, *Joan*, however, was pub-

lished anonymously; the author feared if it appeared over his
name that people would expect a humorous story. Disappointed
readers he wished to avoid, but as he avowed to Rogers sales
did not interest him: "... it was written for love" (*Letters*
2: 624).

Yet, just then he needed a best seller, or something more,
for debts continued heavy. Then suddenly a better idea evolved:
why not lecture his way around the world, at the same time
acquiring material for a new book? Back in the states at
Quarry Farm, Mark planned the trip around the world; Susy was
to remain at home with her aunt and Jean, while Clara was to
go with her parents. When they left Elmira on July 14, 1895,
they did not dream that the sight of Susy waving good-bye would
be the last they should ever have of her.

Lecturing Around the World

Faced with either touring India during the hot season or
beginning his lectures in America during July, Clemens chose
the latter as the lesser evil. For thirty-three days they
traveled through blistering heat from Elmira to Vancouver,
with readings in Cleveland, Duluth, Minneapolis, St. Paul,
Winnipeg, and Butte. Before sailing, August 23, Twain announced to the press that the profits of his tour should go
to his creditors, for honor demanded one hundred percent settlement of all debts. Then began the long tour to Australia,
New Zealand, India, and South Africa.

Though the first month of lecturing returned a net profit
of five thousand dollars, which was applied to the indebtedness,
this was partially offset for Clemens by keen disappointment at
not being able again to visit the Sandwich Islands, where his
scheduled lecture at Honolulu was prevented by an outbreak of
cholera. Yet they could gaze at the shoreline, which seemed
to him "just as I had seen it long before, with nothing of its
beauty lost, nothing of its charm wanting" (qtd. in Paine 3:
1008). Indeed Clemens declared that he would like to "go ashore
and never leave." But it was not to be; soon they sailed away
crossing the equator on September 5. "Clara kodaked it" (*Notebook* 251), said her father.

In Australia, they were royally received with crowded
houses, ovations, and lavish entertainment, which delighted
Twain and served the more practical purpose of clearing another
two thousand dollars to apply on his debts. At Melbourne even
lancing a carbuncle could not dampen Clemens' enthusiasm, which
continued as he lectured his way across Australia and New

Zealand. With the New Year they were off to Ceylon, thence
across India from Bombay to Calcutta, with Twain delighting
in all the romantic atmosphere of Lahore, Delhi, and Lucknow.
Nor could the discomforts of travel change his happy mood;
of a thirty-five-mile descent in a handcar down the Himalayas
he acclaimed, "... the most enjoyable time I have spent in
the earth" (qtd. in Paine 3: 1012). He saw all of India from
the vantage point of a tour for which government officials and
native potentates outdid themselves to make it worth remember-
ing for a lifetime. The Clemens family were entertained in
Arabian Nights fashion by Prince Kumar, whose servants piled
bales of rich goods before them for the selection of whatever
presents they desired. They lunched at the Governor's House,
and Twain delivered a lecture in the great hall of the palace
where the Durbars were held. Yet this did not shut his eyes
to the abject position of the Indian subjects, for Twain commented upon the Hindu servant squatting barefooted on the cold
tiles outside his master's door, and the parched earth with
mud villages crumbling into decay impressed him as "a sorrowful
land--a land of unimaginable poverty and hardship" (*Notebook*
276).

Twain next visited South Africa, just after the Transvaal
invasion had been repulsed and the Jameson raid had ended
disastrously with fifty or more prisoners in jail at Pretoria.
Clemens gave a number of readings, paid a visit to the Kimberley
diamond mines, and had an audience with President Kruger. Here
as elsewhere Twain's poetic perception of natural beauty is
revealed: "I think the Veldt in its sober winter garb is as
beautiful as paradise" (*Notebook* 296). Finally just one year
exactly after leaving home (July 14, 1896) Clemens sailed with
his family for England, where they arrived in Southampton,
having actually circumnavigated the globe.

It had been arranged for Katy Leary to bring Jean and Susy
to England; instead a letter came announcing Susy's illness.
Mrs. Clemens and Clara immediately decided to return home,
leaving Twain alone to write the book based on his recent
travels. Just three days after they sailed on August 15, the
solitary father received the saddest message that could have
reached him: "Susy was peacefully released to-day" (Paine 3:
1021). She was his favorite, the one most nearly like himself;
with her he had so much in common, and now she was gone.
Other hard blows Twain had taken in stride, but this shattered
his defenses. Susy's final illness had been one of raging
fever, turning into delirium, until blind from brain infection,
she had groped for Katy Leary's face and said "Mamma." The
death of Susy brought to the surface all the latent pessimism
in his nature; whereas before it had been confined chiefly to
private utterance, henceforth it was to appear more openly,

though the most bitter expressions were not to be published
until after his death.

Seeking seclusion, the Clemens family hid away that winter
at 23 Tedworth Square in London. Clemens tried to escape his
sorrow in work; it was the best way out, and besides debts
still remained to be liquidated. Yet his own troubles did not
prevent his helping Helen Keller, the little girl who though
totally deaf and blind managed partially to overcome her mute-
ness.

With passage of time Clemens once more appeared socially;
the Savage Club elected him to honorary life membership, and
by summer he was in the mood to write for the American papers
about the Queen's Jubilee, June 22, 1897, being the day the
sixty-year reign was celebrated.

Finally after careful manuscript reading by Livy, with more
profit from deletion of boring details than suffering from
prudery, *Following the Equator* was finished. There is neither
the freshness of *The Innocents Abroad* nor the gay burlesque of
A Tramp Abroad, for Twain put more padding into this book than
he had ever used before, no doubt because of his weary desire
to bring the task to a close. The chapter mottoes from
Pudd'nhead Wilson's calendar, however, are both amusing and
bitter, for he had looked upon much exploitation during his
course around the earth, seeing social and political injustices to make a Christian blush. *Following the Equator* is of
more interest as a storehouse of Twain's mature judgments than
anything else, but when it appeared, November, 1897, it enjoyed an early sale comparable to *Roughing It*. People were
anxious to aid a man who had the honor to pay his debts, especially when that author was Mark Twain, a name synonymous
with good reading.

All royalties went to Rogers for liquidating debts, which
were cleared by the end of January, 1898. Clemens was a free
man again, and he now took his family to Vienna, where they
enjoyed, as usual, a series of brilliant social gatherings.
More than once, however, politics intruded, for it was the eve
of the Spanish-American War and most Austrians were in sympathy with their fellow Europeans. Though he would change
his mind later, at the outset Twain thought the American cause
righteous.

Twain never worked harder than he did during this period
following his freedom from debt. There were many false starts,
but not all, for two of his finest pieces were produced that
winter: *The Man That Corrupted Hadleyburg* and *The Mysterious
Stranger*. The former represents Twain's pessimistic attitude
toward the human race, an attitude which included himself, and
which if the reader is honest and objective is seen to embrace
him, too; for it is the corruption and downfall of an entire

town that is depicted, the yielding to temptation of once
honest people who succumb through weakness to the lure of
wealth.

Yet as Twain's pessimism increased, material prosperity
returned. Now the family actually had $107,000 on deposit in
the bank, the house in Hartford with all its furnishings was
clear of debt, while income from English and American copyrights was equal to the returns upon a $200,000 capital in-
vestment (Paine 3: 1073). But mental repose did not accompany
material wealth. Jean's epilepsy took a turn for the worse,
forcing Clemens to take her to Sweden for treatment at Dr.
Kellgren's sanitarium at Sanna, where she remained from July
until October (1899). Hoping that osteopathy might succeed
where medical science had failed Clemens even tried the treatment himself. In order to allow his afflicted daughter to
continue the cure Clemens settled his family in London, where
Kellgren maintained another institution; and there they spent
the winter of 1899-1900, seeing the new century appear as hope
for Jean's recovery vanished.

Twain finished an essay, "St. Joan of Arc," which Douglas
Hyde took the liberty of editing, thereby drawing upon his
head the full wrath of a temper risen to "104 in the shade."
At this "long-eared animal--this literary kangaroo--this illiterate hostler with his skull full of axle-grease" (qtd. in
Paine 3: 1091), Twain stormed as he withdrew the piece, which
several years later appeared in *Harper's*. A few unimportant
articles constituted the rest of his output that winter.

At this time S.S. McClure tried to interest Twain in the
editorship of a magazine and was almost successful, but when
he realized that he would be harnessed with all managerial
details, and that it was not a matter of having a magazine to
write for as the spirit moved him, Twain lost interest. Still
clinging to any faint hope that Jean's condition might be improved by Kellgren, Twain remained in England during the summer, taking a beautiful residence surrounded by trees just
outside of London, Dollis Hill House, which had once been a
vacation spot for Gladstone. The entire family found it a
paradise, but toward the end of summer their anticipation of
returning home became more compelling than their attachment
to the old English manor.

                    Home Once·More

America received Mark Twain like a returning conqueror.
If there were any doubts about his permanent hold upon the

public, they were now dispelled. But though again home, the
family was still homeless, for they could not bear to look
upon the house at Hartford; it held memories too sad, suddenly
made more so by the death of an old neighbor, Charles Dudley
Warner, only five days after their landing. On his way to
serve as pallbearer, Twain looked into the old home, coming
away with the feeling that "... if we ever enter the house
again to live our hearts will break" (Paine 3: 1112). Through
Frank N. Doubleday a house was secured at 14 West Tenth Street
in New York, where Twain immediately moved without the formal-
ity of signing a lease.

Twain thought his reasons for not returning to Hartford
were only the ghosts haunting him with memories of happy associations, yet it is doubtful if he could have remained long
away from a metropolis; he had become so accustomed to being
in the centers of world activity that he would probably have
gravitated to New York anyway. Here the many dinners and
speechmakings forced Twain to adopt a habit of arriving too
late for food but in time to talk. One club after another
plied Twain with honors, one of the most lavish being a dinner
at the Lotos Club, where he with characteristic generosity
told his audience how considerately he had been treated by
his creditors.

One of the most interesting speeches Twain ever made was
an introduction for Colonel Henry Watterson at a Lincoln
birthday celebration in Carnegie Hall, during which Twain referred openly to his own service for the Confederacy and spoke
of "you of the North and we of the South," as he paid his respects to Lincoln -and expressed his faith in the future of a
united country (Paine 3: 1124). He continued to call public
attention to evils and abuses. "To the Person Sitting in
Darkness," which appeared in the *North American Review*, February, 1901, was a scorching indictment of injustice and hypo-
crisy, cleverly achieved by placing against the complacent
Christmas Eve editorial of the New York *Tribune* several clippings from the *Sun* which juxtaposed the "contentment and happiness" of the former with the human degradation appearing in the
latter.

At Saranac Lake in June the Clemens family lived in a log
cabin, which Mark called "The Lair," swimming, boating, and
taking long walks through the woods. It was a happy summer
free from visitors and newspapers, during which Twain did no
writing except *A Double Barrelled Detective Story*, written in
six days and dispatched immediately to *Harper's*. For this
burlesque of Sherlock Holmes, Jean acted as her father's
secretary; it contained one of Twain's most fortunate parodies,
a takeoff on the fine writing so popular with the Victorians,
in which a "solitary esophagus" was introduced into a paragraph
of lilacs and laburnums.

When summer ended, the family, after a week in Elmira, settled at Riverdale-on-the-Hudson, within easy access to New York. Fall and winter were filled with activities leaving scant time for writing. In October Yale conferred upon Clemens the degree of Doctor of Letters, an honor also shared by his old friend Howells. Then with characteristic desire to help the human race--however much he might protest that it was irrevocably damned--Twain threw himself into a fight for municipal reform.

Twain then turned from serious matters to seek recreation with Henry Rogers on the latter's yacht, sailing to Nova Scotia, August, 1901. Joe Twichell, who was invited but unable to go, received a joking note from Twain, "We had a noble good time in the yacht, and caught a Chinese missionary and drowned him" (*Letters* 2: 712). Another voyage to the West Indies followed in April, a delightful trip for Twain, devoted mostly to draw poker, at which Tom Reed, Speaker of the House of Representatives, succeeded in winning twenty-three pots in a row (*Paine* 3: 1163).

Finally, at long last, the University of Missouri, following in the wake of Yale, honored Clemens with an LL.D. Arriving in St. Louis at the end of May, Twain met his old pilot friend, Horace Bixby, who escorted him to the Pilots Association rooms, where several old companions were still on hand to greet him. Then came five days in Hannibal, a triumphant return to meet the survivors of his youth, during which he visited the old home on Hill Street, met Buck Brown, his rival in spelling bees, walked over Holliday's Hill with John Briggs from Tom Sawyer's band, shook hands with Jimmy McDaniel, to whom he had first told the story of Jim Wolfe and the cats, talked with Laura Hawkins, and was escorted to the churches and Sunday schools by John Robards.

At every station along the line from Hannibal to Columbia crowds acclaimed him, a dramatic recognition climaxed on June 4, 1902, with the bestowal of the honorary degree by the University of Missouri. When Clemens returned home, the family moved for the summer to York Harbor, Maine, with Howells nearby at Kittery Point. But the season was blighted by Livy's becoming seriously ill, an illness so alarmingly persisting that it was not until December 30 that Clemens was allowed to see her, and then only for five minutes.

Shortly before Christmas Jean developed pneumonia, sinking so dangerously as to require constant attendance. It was imperative to keep her condition secret from Livy, a circumstance which eventually developed its amusing side. Clara, the only member of the family permitted to see Mrs. Clemens daily, had to prevaricate--something she enjoyed a reputation for never doing. Amused by his veracious daughter's predicament, Clemens

questioned Clara after each visit so that he might corroborate
her deceptions in the little notes he sent his wife. As spring
approached, Livy gradually improved until the physicians held
out hopes for recovery in a milder climate. Memories of Villa
Viviani turned their thoughts toward Florence, where Clemens
was willing to spend the rest of his days if it would only pro-
long Livy's life. After selling the house purchased the previous summer at Tarrytown, they reached Quarry Farm by the
first of June; here Livy spent three peaceful months recupera-
ting, and Twain again occupied the old octagonal study, the
birthplace of Tom and Huck. But little writing came forth,
only "A Dog's Tale" being completed, and that written to
please Jean, who abhorred vivisection of animals.

It was October 22, 1903 when Henry Rogers completed nego-
tiations with Harper to publish all of Twain's books and
guarantee the author at least $25,000 each year (Paine 3: 1207).
Actually the books sometimes earned twice that much, freeing
Clemens of financial worry and leaving him more time to devote
to Livy, with whom he promptly sailed for Genoa on the *Princess
Irene*.

Abroad Again

Taking residence in the Villa Quarto, located in a picturesque garden of ancient trees and crumbling walls, looking
toward Florence and the Chianti Hills, they immediately suffered disappointment from the weather which brought more fog
than sunlight. Moreover, Livy's seeming improvement revealed
itself to be a false hope; as she alternately appeared better
one day and retrogressed the next, the spirits of the family
rose and fell. On June 5, 1904, Clemens found her looking
"bright and young and pretty," so much so that on that very
day he and Jean enthusiastically selected a new villa for
their home and found her animated over the prospects. That
evening, because she seemed improved, Clemens remained with
her longer than usual, talking over old times; then blowing a
kiss until his return to say goodnight, he went to the piano
and softly sang the spirituals Susy had so loved. Hearing the
distant music Livy said, "He is singing a good-night carol to
me" (qtd. in Paine 3: 1218). A moment after the music ceased
she died, though her husband did not discover it until he came
to say goodnight and found Clara and Jean standing dazed by
the bed. Clemens and the children sailed for home to bury
her beside Susy and Langdon, taking passage on the *Prince
Oscar*, June 29, for although the *Princess Irene* sailed earlier

they could not bear to return on the boat that brought them over. The funeral was held on July 14 at the old home in El-mira, where Joe Twichell, who had performed the marriage ceremony thirty-four years earlier, now rendered the last service. At the grave Clemens placed a simple marker which gave only her name and the dates of birth and death, followed by this expressive line in German: *Gott sei dir gnadig, O meine Wonne.*[10]

As if the loss of Livy were not enough to bear, fate promptly dealt a series of disasters. Clara, who had borne the brunt of her mother's long illness, now that the strain was past, suffered a nervous collapse, which necessitated her being taken to a sanitarium, where she remained for a year of rest. Jean, out for a moonlight ride with a group of friends, suffered bruises and a broken tendon in her ankle when her horse collided with a trolley car, an accident which killed the animal and knocked Jean unconscious. She was taken to a hospital, and when the news reached Clemens he was completely prostrated. Only a short time before he had put out a fire because he remembered the birds had built a nest in the chimney, but now memory failed and he rushed to Clara with news of the ac-cident when his actual intentions were to hide it from her. Then on September 1, Pamela, his sister, died at age seventy-three. It was a disastrous year because of illness and death.

New York

But Clemens managed to move to New York in the fall, where he took a house at 21 Fifth Avenue on the corner of 9th Street, and there the furniture, stored at Hartford for thir-teen years, was placed in its new surroundings by faithful Katy Leary, who with Jean constituted the household. For once Clemens wished seclusion. Restless and disturbed he wrote but little, though he did furnish the *North American Review* one of his best papers on the copyright problem. And Paine believed that he now began, or at least contemplated, *Eve's Diary*, which closes with Adam speaking the sentiments of Sam Clemens for Livy: "Wheresoever she was, *there* was Eden" (*The $30,000 Bequest* 381).

Feeling the need for solace, Twain purchased an Aeolian Orchestrelle, for however much he derided his own taste in music, the stately and harmonious did appeal to him.[11] To Mrs. Crane Twain confided his feelings that "Tannhaüser" was "solemn and impressive and so divinely beautiful," while to Jean he said that his favorite piece of music was Beethoven's

Fifth Symphony (Paine 3: 1227). Consolation came through
these majestic melodies, and though he went out but little
that winter, Clemens gradually assumed something of his former
habits, attending an intimate dinner of friends at the Metro-
politan Club, and turning his attention once more to world
affairs. A massacre of Jews in Moscow brought forth "The
Tsar's Soliloquy," a withering satire on Russian despotism,
and the atrocities perpetrated by King Leopold in the Belgian
Congo produced "King Leopold's Soliloquy," so blistering that
it was not thought suitable for magazine publication but was
issued as a pamphlet by the Congo Reform Association. The
policies of our own government aroused Twain's anger to the
point of his denouncing President Roosevelt in a letter to
Twichell, in which he expressed admiration for Theodore Roosevelt the man but stated his intense dislike of him as the
politician. Most scathing of all, however, was the "War
Prayer," which he read to Dan Beard and to Jean, but which
he felt was too contrary to the illusions and traditions of
mankind to be published.

With the coming of summer Twain took a house at Dublin,
New Hampshire, where he turned his attention to a lengthy
satire, "3,000 Years Among the Microbes," the fantastic autobiography of a microbe living on the person of a tramp, Blitz-
owski, upon which human continent all the seething problems
of life occur in a Lilliputian satire upon social and political
problems.

Returning to New York in the fall, Mark entered naturally
again into public life. When his seventieth birthday arrived,
Colonel Harvey arranged a celebration at Delmonico's to be
held December 5, 1905, so as not to conflict with the Thanks-
giving holidays. Most of the leading authors of the day
gathered to honor Clemens, and when he rose before an audience
including such old friends as Joe Twichell and Brander Matthews,
he recapitulated the story of his own life.

It was January 3, 1906, at a Players Club dinner with
Brander Matthews presiding, that Albert Bigelow Paine, then
unknown to Clemens, gathered courage to ask permission to call
upon him. A friend suggested that Paine approach Clemens
about a biography, and the interview at Twain's home ended
with Clemens saying, "When would you like to begin?" (qtd. in
Paine 4: 1264). Thus the authorized biography started. Soon
Paine engaged a stenographer to take dictation, and Clemens
plunged into his autobiography, though actually he revealed
little of his inner thought while unhappily dwelling on much
of only transitory interest. Paine soon discovered, also,
that many of Twain's self-dramatizations "were not safe to
include in a record that must bear a certain semblance to
history" (Paine 4: 1269), for he adorned and improved with

magical imagination and the great gift for the dramatic which he had exercised too long to cast aside in the interest of mere facts.

It was April 19, 1906, that Twain gave his farewell lecture at Carnegie Hall for the benefit of the Robert Fulton Memorial Association. As Mark entered, the band played "America," while the audience, including General Frederick D. Grant and his uniformed staff, rose to greet him. Thus Samuel Clemens, relating the old tales that had proved so popular in his long trip around the world, closed a chapter in his career, first opened in San Francisco forty years before.

This same year Clemens determined upon a private printing of his "Gospel" for distribution among a few intimate friends. Frank Doubleday, who took charge of the matter, arranged with the De Vinne Press for two hundred and fifty numbered copies printed on handmade paper and published anonymously under the title *What Is Man?* In this form it appeared August 20, 1906. That same summer Twain yielded to Colonel Harvey's persuasions to publish some selections from the *Autobiography* in the *North American Review*, in return for which he was paid thirty thousand dollars. Promptly thereafter he began plans to build a house at Redding, located on a beautiful hilltop, affording so delightful a view that Twain wrote Howells begging him to build nearby and make the situation perfect (Paine 4: 1323).

Though at the peak of a long life's achievement, Clemens at this time confided to intimates that not a month passed without his having a recurring dream of being in reduced circumstances and forced again into piloting to earn a living. Usually in this unpleasant dream he was just about to go into a black shadow without being able to distinguish between a solid bluff and the darkness of night. But another persistent dream, even more nightmarish, was that he had been compelled to return to the lecture platform, where he tried to say funny things without success until the audience walked out leaving him alone in semidarkness. And a third dream equally persistent carried Twain to a brilliant gathering in his nightclothes, where people looking suspiciously in his direction refuse to believe he is Twain, finally leaving him standing alone ashamed.

Yet fortune and acclaim continued for Clemens despite the nightmares; he lived extravagantly, his household expenses now amounting to more than fifty dollars a day. But though he lived on a lavish scale, enjoying the best and giving his money away liberally, Clemens was never wasteful, for his Boswell records that he was careful to turn down the gas jets, objected violently to any overcharge, and abhorred any visible waste (Paine 4: 1371). For an old friend, however, generosity was never lacking, as shown by his sending an expensive set of his books, each volume autographed, to Steve Gillis in

California when Steve wrote that he was now an invalid with
plenty of time to read Sam's books if he only had them.

   Christian Science appeared February 7, 1907. Parts of the
book were originally published in *Cosmopolitan* and the *North
American Review*, but everything following the first hundred
pages was entirely new.[12] In fact, there is evidence that
Twain changed his mind during its course of preparation, for
though the earlier portions are in a comic vein, the later
portions are a serious estimate of Mrs. Eddy and her influence.
The healing principle of Christian Science, or the importance
of mind over matter, Twain never undervalued, but for the
"ignorant village-born peasant woman" whose shrewdness had
enabled her to capitalize on its principle by making it into
a religion and a well-paying source of income he had only
contempt; she was "a tramp stealing a ride on the lightning
express" (DeVoto, "Letters" 786).

   During the winter of 1907 Clemens went with Joe Twichell
on a brief trip to Bermuda, their first since thirty years
earlier when they had been so charmed by the fresh greenness
and full bloom of the island. Now they walked and drove about,
happy as before. In March of the same year Albert Bigelow
Paine made a journey to Hannibal which took him along the
Mississippi to the cave and Holliday's Hill, and then following
the trail of Twain lore to the Far West, he went in company
with Joe Goodman to Jackass Hill for an unforgettable visit
with Steve and Jim Gillis. Steve, now a hopeless invalid,
sent Clemens this message: "Tell Sam I'm going to die pretty
soon, but that I love him; that I've loved him all my life,
and I'll love him till I die. This is the last word I'll ever
send to him" (qtd. in Paine 4: 1377). On his return from this
trip, while coming up the river on one of the old steamers,
Paine read in the paper that Mark Twain was to receive an
Oxford degree.

   On arrival in England Twain was again acclaimed everywhere,
the climax being reached on June 26, 1907, when at the Shel-
donian Theatre, to the strains of "God Save the King" he
marched in the procession headed by Lord Curzon to "receive
the highest academic honors which the world has to give"
(Paine 4: 1393). During this visit Twain was honored by the
Athenaeum and Garrick clubs in London, and elaborately entertained at the Dorchester House by the American ambassador.
Clemens attended the King's garden party at Windsor Castle;
he was also honored guest at a luncheon given by the Pilgrims
at the Savoy. After reviewing the Oxford pageant from a box
with Rudyard Kipling and Lord Curzon, Twain went to a dinner
given by the Lord Mayor of London at the Mansion House. So
many social functions were held in his honor that it was not
until July 13 that he finally sailed for home.

The following winter *Captain Stormfield's Visit to Heaven* appeared in *Harper's Magazine* for December, 1907, and January, 1908, without causing any furor. Originally intended as a burlesque of Elizabeth Stuart Phelps' *The Gates Ajar*, this extravaganza built upon Captain Ned Wakeman's dream was no longer blasphemous or irreverent to readers whose ideas about Christian orthodoxy had molified greatly since Clemens' youth.

With the death of Edmund Clarence Stedman on January 18, Twain was again reminded that he and Howells were the last lingering leaves from the literary tree of the past century. And as a bronchial cough threatened, Twain sailed that same month for Bermuda, where his cold disappeared the same day, leaving him free to enjoy the sunlight in the company of a delightful child, Margaret Blackmer, whom he adopted as a granddaughter after meeting her in the hotel dining room.

Shortly thereafter the new house at Redding was completed and ready to receive him on June 18. Actually Clemens had taken small part in planning the establishment beyond stipulating a large living room for the orchestrelle, a large billiard room which was to be in red, and ample accommodations for guests. Otherwise he declared he did not even wish to see the place until the cat was purring on the hearth.

In August Clemens was shocked to receive news of Samuel E. Moffett's death by drowning, for this was his nearest male relative, Pamela's son, and a favorite nephew. Twain returned from the funeral greatly depressed; a day or so later he suffered an attack of illness which he thought biliousness, but which was perhaps the heart ailment that eventually caused his death. By now Clemens had determined to live the year round at "Stormfield," the name given to the house because a wing was constructed with money received from the captain's adventure, and the house on Fifth Avenue was vacated. He spent most of his time playing billiards, reading, and entertaining guests, living a tranquil existence, bothered little by interest in public affairs or politics. Life at "Stormfield" was one of individual convenience, with guests eating when or where they pleased, while the afternoons were devoted to games--hearts or billiards. And Clemens usually spent the forenoon in bed, reading or looking over his mail. As summer turned to autumn he delighted in the changing colors of the Connecticut landscape; the red tones in the foliage pleased him so that he referred to the windows in his room as the picture gallery.

When winter arrived with bad weather, Twain amused himself with the Shakespeare-Bacon problem; he had read *The Shakespeare Problem Restated* by George Greenwood, which seemed to him to clinch the argument of authorship in favor of Lord Verulam. Another book then in press, *Some Characteristic Signatures of*

Francis Bacon by William Stone Booth, added the final touch
of conviction, and Twain eventually published a small volume
of his own on the subject, *Is Shakespeare Dead?* Though it
contains no new arguments, it gives an amusing presentation
of the old ones. Like everyone else swept away by the desire
to attribute authorship of the plays to others than the actor,
Twain was not a profound student of Elizabethan drama as a
whole; Shakespeare he knew, but not Dekker, Middleton, Webster,
and the rest.

On a trip to Norfolk, Virginia, to speak at the opening
ceremonies of the Virginia Railway, Clemens used the occasion
to pay his personal respects to Henry H. Rogers, telling of
Rogers' aid to Helen Keller, the deaf and dumb child who had
learned to communicate her thoughts. Later in the same month
H.H. Rogers died while Twain was on his way to meet his good
friend and benefactor in New York, the news reaching him as
he alighted from the train. Twain, who served as pallbearer
at the funeral, felt the loss too deeply to talk about it.

That summer at Stormfield, which was to be his last,
passed quietly, for Clemens seemed uninterested in company.
Clara was preparing a concert tour, and Twain, eager for her
success, urged her to spend her time in study. Jean, who now
suffered from recurring attacks of epilepsy, spent most of her
time collecting poultry and caring for animals. Though enduring
attacks of angina which crumpled him with pain, Twain continued
to walk about a good deal and to play billiards, never com-
plaining of his ailment. Once he remarked, "I came in with
Halley's comet in 1835. It is coming again next year, and I
expect to go out with it" (qtd. in Paine 4: 1511). Though he
actually stated it would be a great disappointment not to depart from the earth with the comet, he discussed with Paine
plans for finishing *The Mysterious Stranger*, which existed in
several forms, one of which his biographer advised working to
a conclusion. And he continued to devise moral ideas, as he
called them, a series of stories about Little Bessie, who
plagued her mother with unorthodox questions about the scheme
of things.

The marriage of Clara to Ossip Gabrilowitsch, the concert
pianist, took place October 6, 1909, a perfect day of peaceful
autumn. Only a few friends and relatives were invited, and
Joe Twichell performed the ceremony. By request Twain wore
his brilliant Oxford gown over his white clothes, and it was
a happy occasion, one he declared Livy would have enjoyed.

Now with Clara away and Jean unable to look after affairs
Clemens suffered the misfortune of a betrayal of trust from
his private secretary. The young woman in question went on a
three-day drunk, and it then came to light that she had been
robbing him of money all along. Clemens, however, refused to

prosecute a woman, and simply turned all settlements over to Paine, who took charge as secretary and reduced monthly expenses to less than a third of what they had been. The humiliation of a betrayed trust, another example of human perfidy, influenced Twain no doubt to write for his own satisfaction a book he felt could never stand publication, *Letters from the Earth*. Most of the ideas were ones he had long ago exhausted, but here with no restrictions of print he let his fancy free and exuberantly reveled in irreverence.

In the middle of November, 1909, Twain again visited Bermuda. Just the day before sailing, word came that Richard Watson Gilder was dead, and the next morning brought news of the death of another friend, William M. Laffan. The leaves were now falling fast, but though he experienced an occasional paroxysm, none was severe and Twain enjoyed driving about the island, discussing philosophy or history and talking of a book which fascinated him, *The Pith of Astronomy*. Here he spent his seventy-fourth birthday, playing hearts by the fireside with no visitors save Helen Allen, one of the "Angel-fish" to whom he read several favorite passages from *Tom Sawyer*. Of course, there was a cake, but no celebration, as cigars and fireside conversation quietly closed the evening. In Bermuda Twain completed his last article for publication, "The Turning-Point of My Life," valuable as a final summation of his general philosophy, though as autobiography it was more entertaining than accurate.

Ironically, the last secretarial act of Jean for her father was telephoning his message to the associated press, for on Christmas Eve she was found dead in her bathtub, a victim of epileptic convulsion. On Christmas day Jean's body was carried away amid a snowstorm such as had always delighted her, while Twain, too feeble in health himself to attend the funeral, stood sadly at the window of his empty house.[13] Next day as the snowstorm turned bitterly into a blizzard Twain composed a tribute to Jean, tenderly and sadly. It was, he said, the last of his autobiography.

Twain remained at Stormfield for ten days after Jean's death, the extremely cold weather persisting; then with Claude, his butler, Twain sailed again for Bermuda. There he was contented, and though he suffered occasional spasms of pain, his health seemed to improve in the mild climate. When in April Paine learned that Twain's bronchial trouble had become serious, he proceeded straightway to Bermuda, at the same time advising Clara and her husband to sail at once from Europe. Twain suffered several sinking spells during the journey home, which Paine feared they might not complete. Though Twain himself thought death near, he was calm and undismayed, showing consideration for his companion and regret at being such a

care. Finally, the trip over, he was carried back to Stormfield, where upon arrival he insisted upon stepping from the
carriage unaided, although he was then carried to his room by
Paine and his manservant.

Halley's Comet appeared in the sky, April 20, and next
morning though clear in mind Twain had trouble speaking. He
tried to write requests for his spectacles and a glass pitcher.
Just after midday he reached to take Clara's hand. "Goodbye
dear, if we meet" (qtd. in Clemens 291), he said, and then
passed into a doze lasting until about sunset, and at that
time on April 21, 1910, Mark Twain peacefully died.

From every corner of the earth condolences reached his
daughter; newspapers round the world paid him tribute. Dressed
in the white he had enjoyed, Twain was carried to the Brick
Church in New York, where Dr. Henry van Dyke spoke briefly
and Joseph Twichell delivered a prayer, broken with grief.
As he lay in state thousands filed by the flower-covered bier,
people from all walks of life, wishing to show their devotion
to a great author, a lovable personality, and a noble gentleman.
Sunday afternoon, April 24, Clemens was quietly buried at Elmira, New York, by the side of his loved ones, while a slow,
steady rain fell.

NOTES

1. *Contributions to the Galaxy 1868-1871 by Mark Twain*
(1961) is reproduced in facsimile with introduction and notes
by Bruce R. McElderry, Jr. Most of Clemens' contributions to
the *Galaxy*, the "Memoranda," were pure clowning on his part,
but some serious satire and social criticism were included.

2. This volume, *Mark Twain's (Burlesque) Autobiography
and First Romance*, is described by Merle Johnson (*A Bibliography of the Works of Mark Twain* 12-13); it is also described
by Paine (*Mark Twain: A Biography* 2: 433).

3. Much scholarly attention is finally being paid to
Twain's sketches. Edited by Edgar Marquess Branch and Robert
H. Hirst, *The Works of Mark Twain: Early Tales & Sketches*,
presently in two volumes with more to come, brings together
more than 360 of Twain's early works--including some pieces of
imaginative journalism, a few speeches, and a few poems--
written between 1851 and 1871. With a narrative account of
the history of circumstances surrounding composition and first
publication of the 360 works included, the reader is also
given a running account of the conditions of Clemens' employ-

ment and the growth of his reputation. The first section in
volume one is titled "Hannibal and the River (1851-1861),"
and the second section is titled "Nevada Territory (1862-
1864)." The second volume consists of part of section three,
"California, Part 1 (1864-1865)," of four sections which have
been projected. As projected, section three calls for "California (1864-1866)," and the fourth section calls for "The
Midwest and the East Coast (1866-1871)." Completion of the
project appears not to be near.

4. Mark did write such a play, adding the character of a
book salesman. The manuscript is in the papers of the Mark
Twain Estate.

5. Arthur Hobson Quinn writes of "the tradition of the
remarkable performance of John T. Raymond as Colonel Mulberry
Sellers" in *A History of the American Drama from the Civil War
to the Present Day* (114). And in *The American Dramatist* (185),
Montrose J. Moses writes, "Raymond, in the public eye, was
Mulberry Sellers."

6. In 1961 Frederick Anderson edited a text of *Ah Sin*
based on an amanuensis copy apparently written for rehearsals
of the play. The central character is Bret Harte's, but it
is the Plunkett women depicted by Clemens that emerge as the
strongest characters. Nothing, however, could keep the play
alive.

7. This speech is available in Paine (4: 1643-47).

8. The best account of this incident is given by Bernard
DeVoto (*Mark Twain's America* 196-204).

9. Selections from *Huckleberry Finn* appeared in the
Century during December of 1884 and January and February of
1885, according to Vogelback ("The Publication and Reception
of *Huckleberry Finn* in America" 261).

10. Translated into English, the line reads, "God be mer-
ciful to thee, Oh, my rapture" (Paine, *Mark Twain: A Biography*
3: 1223).

11. Frank M. Flack says that Mark, unlike most of his
countrymen, who had no liking for operatic or symphonic
music, "gradually obtained a more intimate knowledge of higher
musical art" ("Mark Twain and Music" 3). Twain found pleasure
in the works of Beethoven, Brahms, Chopin, and Schubert in his
last years.

12. The articles appeared in *Cosmopolitan*, October 1899,
and in the *North American Review* for December, 1902, and January, February, and April, 1903.

13. Mark wrote in the guest book: "Night--at 6 p.m. the hearse and carriages moved to the station. Jervis and Katy will take Jean to Elmira, where her mother, Susy and Langdon lie buried. A snow storm is raging. Clara is in Germany."

WORKS CITED

Blodgett, Harold. "A Note on Mark Twain's *Library of Humor*."
     American Literature 10 (1938): 78-80.

Brooks, Van Wyck. *The Ordeal of Mark Twain*. New York: Dutton,
     1933. More perceptive of Twain's feelings than of his
     thoughts or actions.

Clemens, Clara. *My Father, Mark Twain*. New York: Harper &
     Brothers, 1931. A valuable and intimate picture by Clemens'
     daughter.

Cohen, Morton N. "Mark Twain and the Philippines." *Mid-
     continent American Studies Journal* 1 (1960): 25-31.

DeQuille, Dan [William Wright]. *The Big Bonanza*. New York:
     Knopf, 1946.

DeVoto, Bernard. *Mark Twain at Work*. Cambridge: Harvard U.
     Press, 1942. Not biography, but an interesting account of how
     Clemens wrote, and a penetrating analysis of his pessimism.

————. *Mark Twain's America*. Boston: Little, Brown, 1935.

————, ed. "Letters." *The Portable Mark Twain*. By Mark
     Twain. New York: Viking, 1946. 745-86.

Ferguson, DeLancey. *Mark Twain: Man and Legend*. Indianapolis:
     Bobbs-Merrill, 1943. Good narrative. Based on facts.

Flack, Frank M. "Mark Twain and Music." *Twainian* ns 2.1
     (1942): 1-4.

Gribben, Alan. "The Master Hand of Old Malory: Mark Twain's
     Acquaintance with *Le Morte D'Arthur*." *English Language
     Notes* 16 (1978): 32-40.

Howells, William Dean. *My Mark Twain*. New York: Harper &
     Brothers, 1910. Twain's mind as revealed by an intimate
     friend.

Johnson, Merle. *A Bibliography of the Works of Mark Twain,
     Samuel Langhorne Clemens. A List of First Editions in
     Book Form and of First Printings in Periodicals and Oc-
     casional Publications of His Varied Literary Activities*.
     New York: Harper & Brothers, 1935.

Leacock, Stephen. *Mark Twain.* New York: Appleton, 1933.

Leisy, Ernest E. "Mark Twain's Part in *The Gilded Age.*" *American Literature* 8 (1937): 445-47.

McKeithan, Daniel M. "The Morgan Manuscript of 'The Man That Corrupted Hadleyburg.'" *Texas Studies in Language and Literature* 2 (1961): 476-80.

Moses, Montrose J. *The American Dramatist.* Boston, 1911. Rpt. New York: Blom, 1964.

Paine, Albert Bigelow. *Mark Twain: A Biography.* 4 vols. New York: Harper & Brothers, 1912. Invaluable. Intimate and full account by Clemens' personal secretary.

Parsons, Coleman O. "Mark Twain in Australia." *Antioch Review* 21 (1961): 455-68.

―――. "Mark Twain in New Zealand." *South Atlantic Quarterly* 61 (1962): 51-76.

―――. "Mark Twain: Traveler in South Africa." *Mississippi Quarterly* 29 (1976): 3-41.

Pattee, Fred Lewis. *The Development of the American Short Story.* New York: Harper & Brothers, 1923.

Quinn, Arthur Hobson. *A History of the American Drama from the Civil War to the Present Day.* New York: Crofts, 1936.

Twain, Mark [Samuel Langhorne Clemens]. *The Adventures of Huckleberry Finn.* New York: Harper & Brothers, 1918.

―――. *The Adventures of Tom Sawyer.* New York: Harper & Brothers, 1922.

―――. *Ah Sin.* Ed. Frederick Anderson. San Francisco: Book Club of California, 1961.

―――. *The American Claimant.* New York: Harper & Brothers, 1924.

―――. *Christian Science.* New York: Harper & Brothers, 1907.

―――. *A Connecticut Yankee in King Arthur's Court.* New York: Harper & Brothers, 1917.

―――. *Contributions to the Galaxy 1868-1871 by Mark Twain (Samuel Langhorne Clemens). Facsimile Reproductions.* Ed. Bruce McElderry, Jr. Gainesville: Scholars' Facsimiles & Reprints, 1961.

―――. "The Curious Republic of Gondour." *Atlantic Monthly* 36 (1875): 461-63.

————. *The Curious Republic of Gondour and Other Whimsical Sketches*. New York: Boni and Liveright, 1919.

————. *A Double Barrelled Detective Story*. New York: Harper & Brothers, 1902.

————. *Eve's Diary*. New York: Harper & Brothers, 1906.

————. *Extract from Captain Stormfield's Visit to Heaven*. New York: Harper & Brothers, 1909.

————. *Following the Equator*. 2 vols. New York: Harper & Brothers, 1925.

————. *The Innocents Abroad*. 2 vols. New York: Harper & Brothers, 1911.

————. *In Defense of Harriet Shelley*. New York: Harper & Brothers, 1925.

————. "In Defense of Harriet Shelley." *North American Review* 159 (1894): 108-19, 240-51, 353-68.

————. *Is Shakespeare Dead?* New York: Harper & Brothers, 1909.

————. *Joan of Arc*. 2 vols. New York: Harper & Brothers, 1924.

————. *King Leopold's Soliloquy: A Defense of His Congo Rule*. Boston: Warner, 1905.

————. *Letters from the Earth*. Ed Bernard DeVoto. New York: Harper & Row, 1962.

————. *Life on the Mississippi*. New York: Harper & Brothers, 1917.

————. "A Literary Nightmare." *Atlantic Monthly* 37 (1876): 167-69.

————. *The Love Letters of Mark Twain*. Ed. Dixon Wecter. New York: Harper & Brothers, 1949. Valuable addition to our knowledge of Twain's ideas, especially religion and politics.

————. *The Man That Corrupted Hadleyburg*. New York: Harper & Brothers, 1928.

————. *Mark Twain in Eruption: Hitherto Unpublished Pages about Men and Events*. Ed. Bernard DeVoto. New York: Harper & Brothers, 1940.

————. *Mark Twain: Representative Selections*. Ed. Fred Lewis Pattee. New York: American, 1935.

————. *Mark Twain's Autobiography*. Ed. Albert Bigelow Paine. 2 vols. New York: Harper & Brothers, 1924.

————. *Mark Twain's (Burlesque) Autobiography and First Romance*. New York: Sheldon, 1871.

————. *Mark Twain's Letters*. Ed. Albert Bigelow Paine. 2 vols. New York: Harper & Brothers, 1917.

————. *Mark Twain's Letters to Will Bowen, "My First, & Oldest & Dearest Friend."* Austin: U. of Texas Press, 1941.

————. *Mark Twain's Notebook*. New York: Harper & Brothers, 1935.

————. *The Mysterious Stranger*. New York: Harper & Brothers, 1922.

————. "Old Times on the Mississippi." *Atlantic Monthly* 35 (1875): 69-73, 217-24, 283-89, 446-52, 567-74, 721-30; 36 (1876): 190-96.

————. *The Prince and the Pauper*. New York: Harper & Brothers, 1909.

————. *Roughing It*. 2 vols. New York: Harper & Brothers, 1913.

————. *Simon Wheeler, the Amateur Detective*. Ed. Franklin R. Rogers. New York: New York Public Library, 1963.

————. *1601, or Conversation as It Was by the Social Fireside in the Time of the Tudors*. n.p., 1880.

————. *Sketches New and Old*. New York: Harper & Brothers, 1917.

————. *The $30,000 Bequest*. New York: Harper & Brothers, 1917.

————. *Tom Sawyer Abroad*. New York: Harper & Brothers, 1917.

————. *Tom Sawyer Abroad, Tom Sawyer, Detective, and Other Stories*. New York: Harper & Brothers, 1896.

————. *Pudd'nhead Wilson*. New York: Harper & Brothers, 1922.

————. *A Tramp Abroad*. 2 vols. New York: Harper & Brothers, 1921.

————. *What Is Man?* New York: De Vinne, 1906.

————. *What Is Man?* New York: Harper & Brothers, 1917.

————. *The Works of Mark Twain: Early Tales & Sketches*. Ed. Edgar Marquess Branch, et al. 2 vols. Berkeley: U. of California Press, 1979-81.

Twain, Mark, and Charles Dudley Warner. *The Gilded Age*. Hartford: American, 1874.

Vogelback, Arthur Lawrence. "The Publication and Reception of *Huckleberry Finn.*" *American Literature* 11 (1939): 260-72.

Wagenknecht, Edward. *Mark Twain: The Man and His Work.* New Haven: Yale U. Press, 1935. Important. Examines Twain's mind and work.

Webster, Samuel Charles. *Mark Twain, Business Man.* Boston: Little, Brown, 1946. Adds to our knowledge of Twain's environment.

Wecter, Dixon. "Mark Twain." *Literary History of the United States.* Ed. Robert E. Spiller, et al. 2 vols. New York: Macmillan, 1948. 2: 917-39. The best single essay on Twain in print.

Chapter 4

MIND AND ART

Sources

Twain, like all other writers, drew source material from
experience, either through actual contact or vicariously from
reading. Perhaps more than any other American author of first
rank his work assumes autobiographical characteristics; yet
evidences of source materials from books are not infrequent.

More than twelve years prior to Twain's "Jumping Frog"
the Sonora *Herald* printed "A Toad Story," probably written by
the editor, Walter Murray. Something over five years later
Samuel Seabough printed a frog yarn in the San Andreas *Independent* (1858). However, the Sonora *Herald* version is the
merest sketch with no characters developed, while Sam Seabough's
tale, though more elaborate, remains a brief sketch of similar
type. It is evident that the frog story was known in California, but only locally, for it awaited the pen of Mark Twain to
give it currency on both coasts (Lewis 19). There is no evidence, by the way, that Clemens ever saw either one of these
sketches. The source for the story, on the other hand, was
really old Ben Coon, garrulous derelict of Jackass Hill, who
spun the yarn for Twain's ears as it had been told around the
campfires of mining camps for decades.

DeLancey Ferguson points out that the realistic, unpoetic
Brown, pervading Twain's humor throughout the Sandwich Islands
journey, even continuing into the trip that produced *The Innocents Abroad*, obviously derived from Oliver Wendell Holmes'
The Autocrat of the Breakfast Table (*Man and Legend* 106). In
fact, Twain later unconsciously borrowed his dedication for
The Innocents Abroad from a volume of Holmes' poems. For like
everyone else Twain read the popular New Englander, who in the
Autocrat created a young character named John to provide humor
through a crude and materialistic interpretation of the older
man's more ideal philosophizing. And Twain saw how such a
creation of his own, Brown, might serve equally as a projected,

though detached, aspect of his nature, through whom bodily
vulgarities and mental crudities could be expressed.

Though *The Innocents Abroad* is obviously based upon Clemens'
journey to Europe and the Holy Land, even it had forerunners,
which may have served as sources, for instance Samuel Fiske's
Mr. Dunne Browne's Experiences in Foreign Parts, published in
Boston, 1857, which presented a traveler who found a great
deal of fault with European art, even as he mistook the Thames
for a creek (Blair, *Native American Humor* 155). Likewise
J. Ross Browne, whose earlier life had been rather similar to
Twain's, had written satires of travel literature in *Yusef*
(1853) (Blair, *Native American Humor* 158). Whether or not
Clemens read these books we do not actually know, for especially in the case of J. Ross Browne, the similarities in
outlook could have arisen from their common background of frontier environment. However, one definite source, at least as
it furnished inspiration for burlesque, was William C. Prime's
Tent Life in the Holy Land.

Even as his *Yusef* had anticipated *The Innocents Abroad*,
J. Ross Browne was in the field of Western writing ahead of
Twain with *Adventures in the Apache Country* (1869), using the
same tricks of humor and employing the same journalistic appeal as may be found in *Roughing It*. And there were other
sketches by Browne--depictions of his fellow travelers, tales
of the great rush to Washoe, incidents found on the Comstock
Lode--all in *Crusoe's Island* (1864). Again we do not actually
know if Twain was indebted to his forerunner, who won slight
recognition and dropped from view, for both covered the same
ground under very similar circumstances.

With *The Gilded Age*, however, there is more definite
evidence. DeVoto believes that J.M. Field's *The Drama in
Pokerville* (1847) furnished most of the details for Chapter IV
of that volume, in which Laura is brought into the story
(*Mark Twain's America* 253-54). And Franklin Walker reminds
us of a notorious trial that took place in San Francisco, certain details of which bear marked similarities to the plot and
characterization in *The Gilded Age* (63-66). In a general manner, however, the character types and contrasts may have derived from Thackeray's *Vanity Fair* (Ferguson 170). Wagenknecht, by the way, sees a similarity to Dickens in Sellers'
description of the clock in Chapter VII, while he believes that
Senator Dilworthy's speech in Volume II, Chapter XXII, might
have been directly modeled on that of the Reverend Chadband
in Chapter XIX of *Bleak House* (270).

Though Twain has told us how he based *The Adventures of
Tom Sawyer* upon his own youth, there is here again evidence
of other sources. Walter Blair points out the similarity of
Aunt Polly to Shillaber's Mrs. Partington (*Native American*

Humor 151). Franklin J. Meine discovered, moreover, that the identical picture of Shillaber's character was used to illustrate Aunt Polly in *Tom Sawyer*; they even look alike (*Native American Humor* 151). Walter Blair in further substantiation parallels a passage from Chapter III of *Tom Sawyer* with a similar conversation in Shillaber's *Knitting-Work* (1859) (*Native American Humor* 152). Chapter XVIII of Twain's story, on the other hand, suggests the inventive boy of Longstreet's "Georgia Theatrics," who triumphantly defeated an imaginary opponent. Another Southwestern humorist, George W. Harris, may also have contributed to the plot with a sketch suggesting the boys in the loft who played jokes on the teacher in Chapter XXI. Then Twain's own sketches written for the *Golden Era*, such as "Those Blasted Children," may have been a reminder to him—not alone in themselves—but to recall humor of a kindred pattern. Yet memories were varied, for Twain read Poe during his days in Keokuk and "The Gold Bug" seems to have lent its influence on Tom Sawyer's treasure hunt.

It was a juvenile volume, an English story concerning the thirteenth century by Charlotte M. Yonge, *The Prince and the Page*, which gave Clemens the idea for *The Prince and the Pauper*. Albert Bigelow Paine, however, declared that all Twain received from the earlier volume was mere suggestion (Paine 2: 597). Actually Clemens made greater use of *The English Rogue* by Richard Head and Francis Kirkman, first published in London, 1665-1680, from which he acquired a general knowledge of the lower social orders. Several passages about beggars in *The Prince and the Pauper* closely parallel similar ones in *The English Rogue*. Twain wished this novel to be considered seriously as social history, and since he believed fiction based on fact superior to that based on imagination, he drew upon *The English Rogue* for atmosphere and specific customs which he incorporated into the pauper backgrounds. He probably used a four-volume reprint, published in 1874.

For many devices in *Life on the Mississippi*, DeVoto believes that Twain went directly to the humorists who preceded him, even though the indebtedness shades into generalizations (*Mark Twain's America* 256). The misquotations, ramblings, and garrulities may be traced to Longstreet and Hooper. The tall talk, such as in the raftsmen passage, has the ring of authentic reporting, yet numerous examples existed in the Davy Crockett books, in the "Polly Peablossom's Wedding" of T.A. Burke, and in the type specimen of them all, *The Big Bear of Arkansaw*. For the rest of his narrative Twain drew his material from his own contributions on piloting, published in the *Atlantic* in 1875.

Life on the Mississippi presents the raw material from which Twain's masterpiece *Huckleberry Finn* was made. For instance,

the feud between the Darnells and the Watsons in Chapter XXVI
of the former improved through artistic transmutation to become the Grangerford-Shepherdson episodes. But there were
outside sources. Blair believes that the passage about Huck's
trip to the circus may have come from one of the frontier
humorists: W.T. Thompson, G.W. Harris, or Richard Malcolm
Johnston, though the evidence indicated strongest probability
of Johnston, whose "The Expensive Treat of Col. Moses Grice"
was well known to Huck's creator (*Native American Humor* 154).
DeVoto, on the other hand, thinks that this same passage "rests
solidly" on William Tappan Thompson's "The Great Attraction"
(*Mark Twain's America* 254). DeVoto believes also that the
playbill produced by the Duke of Bilgewater derived from J.M.
Field's *The Drama in Pokerville*, while the mutilated Shakespeare speech composed for the King to render as Juliet was
perhaps from one of the books by Sol Smith, *Theatrical Apprenticeship* (1845) or *Theatrical Journey Work* (1854) (*Mark Twain's
America* 254). The King's visit to the camp meeting has marked
identity with Chapter X of *The Adventures of Simon Suggs* by
Johnson J. Hooper, the only instance, by the way, in which
DeVoto thinks Twain failed to surpass his original.
     We should not forget Jim Gillis of Jackass Hill, at this
point, for Jim's artistic narration of "The Burning Shame" was
to assume literary permanence in Chapter XXIII of *Huckleberry
Finn*. Then there are the scholarly considerations of Olin H.
Moore, who sees the influence of Cervantes and believes that
Twain made Huck into "a prosaic Sancho Panza, a foil to the
brilliant Tom Sawyer."[1]
     A Connecticut Yankee in King Arthur's Court has, as DeVoto
suggests, affiliations with the Jack Downing letters (*Mark
Twain's America* 272). Here is political and economic satire,
present in Down East humor before it reached amplification
through the authors of the Old Southwest and the literary
comedians, but it is now given expression of genius. Constance
Rourke perceives even more of the native humor tradition in
the sources for this book, believing Twain wrote *A Connecticut
Yankee* in the same spirit as *The Innocents Abroad*, something
of a grotesque naturalism, critical of ancient myth. She sees
the Boss akin to "such creatures of the American fancy as Sam
Slick and Sam Patch" (215). Of course, as both Paine and
Clemens have told us, it was the reading of Malory's *Morte
d'Arthur* which first stimulated his imagination (Paine 2: 790;
Notebook 171).
     Always interested in inventions, Twain as early as 1868
toyed with the idea of a story about a balloon trip, but it
was not completed until *Tom Sawyer Abroad* appeared in 1894.
The title page announced that the book was by Huck Finn,
edited by Mark Twain, and many of the incidents are from the

same sources that furnished the inspiration for Twain's earlier
volumes about Tom and Huck; but D.M. McKeithan has demonstrated
that there is also an indebtedness to Jules Verne's *Five Weeks
in a Balloon* (257-70). An English translation of Verne's romance was published in the United States in 1869, and its
similarities to some of the balloon adventures of Tom, Huck,
and Jim are close enough to indicate that Clemens had read it.
But the most valuable parts of *Tom Sawyer Abroad*, the characters and their conversations, are Twain's own creations.

Of *Tom Sawyer, Detective*, Twain himself stated, "It trans-
fers to the banks of the Mississippi the incidents of a strange
murder which was committed in Sweden in old times" (*Letters* 2:
623). Actually it was in Denmark in the seventeenth century.
In a footnote to this story when published Twain affirmed the
incidents to be facts, "even to the public confession of the
accused" (qtd. in Johnson 63). Taking the strange events recorded in the story of this criminal trial, Twain claimed that
he merely changed the characters and scenes to America.

For *Joan of Arc* Clemens did more research than for any
other book. Mentor L. Williams summarizes the works used in
preparation for the *Personal Recollections*:

> In 1850, J.E.J. Quicherat examined and edited the original
> documents connected with Joan's rehabilitation. Jules
> Michelet's moving and sympathetic story, *Jeanne d'Arc*,
> appeared in 1856; H.A. Wallon's unbiased, objective his-
> tory was published in 1876; and Janet Tuckey's biography
> in 1880. Joseph Fabre reworked Quicherat's materials
> into a masterpiece of historical writing in 1883, and
> Lord Ronald Gower's biography appeared in 1893. (243)

Twain once said that for the first two-thirds of the book he
used "only one French history and one English one," but for the
last third he resorted to "five French stories and five English
ones." Characteristically he adds, "and shoveled in as much
fancy work and invention on both sides of the historical road
as I pleased" (*Letters* 2: 624). Indeed he did; DeVoto finds
examples of the tall tale, as in Chapter VII, where "... the
Paladin is embroidering the narrative with yarns that are in
the strict tradition..." (*Mark Twain's America* 244), while Sut
Lovingood furnished the incident of Uncle Laxart and the bull
(Long 37-39).

The Gates Ajar by Elizabeth Stuart Phelps, which Twain
sought to satirize, suggested the idea of utilizing a dream
recounted by Captain Ned Wakeman, the result of these combined
sources being *Captain Stormfield's Visit to Heaven*. Here,
however, as in all the discovered sources used by Clemens, the
material seen or heard outweighed in importance anything derived from reading. Twain's reading often suggested a plot

or a germinal idea, but the stuff that went into the flesh of
the characters--the things they did, what they thought and
said--more frequently came from memories stored within, recollections of the great valley or of Washoe.

Folklore

Of more importance is the folklore so often present in
Twain's writings, the common beliefs and superstitions of the
Mississippi Valley during the nineteenth century. Reminiscences and survivals from other lands mingled there, adapted
to local conditions and customs. Similarities in folk beliefs
always interested Clemens, who inquired into the customs of
foreign lands with the interest of an anthropologist. In India
he sought the facts of caste, suttee, thuggee, while admitting
that to comprehend such customs truly one must have an understanding of the *how* and *why* lacking to an outside observer.
So it is with the folklore of his own region.

With *The Prince and the Pauper*, as with *A Connecticut
Yankee*, Twain drew upon the deadening effects of superstition
upon intellect. Here many superstitions of early England are
dramatically presented. Again it is human nature rather than
scholarship furnishing materials, for no one can read *A Connecticut Yankee* without feeling the continuity of human fail-
ings reaching into the present.

Joan of Arc, however, as Victor R. West reminds us, turns
to continental folklore (8). Fairies were not common in the
folklore of Missouri, either among blacks or whites, yet Twain
makes use of the traditional fairy tree, showing in his opening
incident the relationship of Joan and her playmates to the
fairies, whose banishment Joan so strongly deplored (*Joan of
Arc* 1: 9-14). In this fictional biography of the Maid of
Orleans channels were already charted by history and tradition,
and it is interesting to note that this alone of all Twain's
writings shows any interest in fairy lore. For it was the
folklore of his youth which he knew of firsthand, acquired unconsciously, and therefore embodied throughout his work with
natural artistry.

Much of this folklore came to him through childhood association with blacks. Some of these stories which impressed him so deeply he was to tell again to audiences as
rapt with interest as that of the children who had squatted
before the cabin fireplace of his youth.

In Hannibal belief was common that a departed person's
spirit took form as a ghost; the night of John Clemens' funeral

when Sam walked in his sleep, both his mother and sister had
at first mistaken the white clad figure for a ghost (Paine 1:
75). Moreover, popular superstition, held by white and black,
assumed that the ghost would look just as it did in life.
Thus the "awful scream" of Jim upon beholding Tom Sawyer's
white face when he thought the boy had plunged to death from
the balloon. And Huck, who holds similar beliefs, understands
at once. In *Life on the Mississippi*, Chapter lII, the raftsmen recount the story of a ghost barrel bringing ill fortune
upon any unlucky vessel it chances to follow. And the pilots
added their tales of the supernatural to those implanted in
youthful breasts by the blacks.

    The Adventures of Tom Sawyer, with its sequel *Huckleberry
Finn*, presents Twain's three chief purveyors of ghost lore,
Tom, Huck, and Jim. All know the intricate ways of ghosts and
how to detect their presence. When Huck suggests leaving the
treasure spot because "Injun Joe's ghost is round about there,
certain," Tom reminds him, "Looky here, Huck, what fools we're
making of ourselves! Injun Joe's ghost ain't a-going to come
around where there's a cross" (*Tom Sawyer* 275). And Huck sees
the point immediately. Yet some problems remain unsettled; in
the graveyard at night Tom asks, "Say, Hucky, do you reckon
Hoss Williams hears us talking?" When Huck replies in the af-
firmative, Tom says, "I wish I'd said *Mister* Williams" (*Tom
Sawyer* 82).

    Haunted houses, also, were believed in and avoided by
people. Tom tells us "mostly because they don't like to go
where a man's been murdered." But in a particular case blue
lights have been seen, which means one thing only to Huck, for
"... where you see one of them blue lights flickering around,
Tom, you can bet there's a ghost mighty close behind it" (*Tom
Sawyer* 208). A haunted house serves as a useful prop in
Pudd'nhead Wilson; once its reputation was established "Nobody
would live in it afterward, or go near it by night, and most
people even gave it a wide berth in the daytime" (*Pudd'nhead
Wilson* 70). Here Roxy's false son based his thieving opera-
tions with impunity.

    As would be suspected, dwarfs, giants and a forest denizen
appear through dreams and superstitions in *The Prince and the
Pauper*, *A Connecticut Yankee*, and *Joan of Arc*. Even Satan is
mentioned in *Tom Sawyer*. When Joe perjures himself with impunity during his murder trial, Tom and Huck "expecting every
moment that the clear sky would deliver God's lightnings upon
his head" become frightened by his immunity, for "... plainly
this miscreant had sold himself to Satan and it would be fatal
to meddle with the property of such a power as that" (*Tom
Sawyer* 100).

Witchcraft also appears in Clemens' writings. When Twain visited the witch's cave at Endor he noted the repellent appearance of the place with "camel dung on the roofs and caked against the houses to dry" (*Notebook* 94). Accusation of witchery naturally was included in *A Connecticut Yankee*; of course, *Joan of Arc* employs a similar belief. The English soldiers think of Joan, "... surely this *is* a witch, this is a child of Satan!" (*Joan of Arc* 1: 251). And at the end of her conviction, the populace hears, "*The witch's time has come!*" (*Joan of Arc* 2: 258). But in humorous vein, there is the belief expressed by Jim when Tom and Huck take his hat off and hang it on a limb: "Afterward Jim said the witches bewildered him and put him in a trance, and rode him all over the state, and then set him under the trees again, and hung his hat on a limb to show who done it" (*Huckleberry Finn* 8). Jim's story was so favorably received by the other blacks that he enlarged the territory covered until the witches "rode him all over the world, and tired him most to death, and his back was all over saddle boils" (*Huckleberry Finn* 8).

Sometimes, so superstitions ran, witches intervened in the course of affairs, and something of this nature happened to Tom Sawyer, who employed a charm to be sure. Roxy, however, in *Pudd'nhead Wilson* employs the familiar device of a horseshoe to guard against dangers of witchcraft through Wilson's hobby of fingerprinting (24). There was superstition enough in general among all classes through the entire region of Sam Clemens' boyhood, and it was not confined to witches or devils. Signs, portents, and omens figure prominently in responses by Huck, Tom, and Jim, whose thinking, we may be sure, is representative. Many of these signs portended bad luck. But many signs had nothing to do with luck, good or bad. Bees, according to Jim, would not sting idiots. Birds flying a yard or two at a time indicated rain; as did young chickens so behaving; and to catch one of them would surely bring death. From Jim, too, Huck learned that it was bad luck to talk about a dead man who might have been murdered. Some taboos carried greater portent than others; Jim bewailed Huck's handling of a snakeskin: "He said he druther see the new moon over his left shoulder as much as a thousand times than take up a snake-skin in his hand" (*Huckleberry Finn* 74).

Victor Royce West in the most comprehensive survey of folklore in Twain's writings tells us that all "crawly things" were supposed to be ill omens, pointing out that Huck upon suffering the misfortune of killing a spider invoked the aid of witchcraft (59). West further reveals that in the folk beliefs of the Southern black it was a sign of death to see a gray mare. Mississippi steamboat captains did not consider the gray mare alone so dire an omen, but if one were combined with a preacher, then calamity was imminent.

Tom and Huck, even as young Sam Clemens, are learned in
the lore of animal omen. When a dog "set up a long, lugubrious
howl" both realize immediately that death is meant for one of
them should the dog prove to be a stray. At first Tom thinks
he recognizes the animal, but when he discovers his mistake,
the boys believe death is meant for them together.

When the boys discover Joe's guilt but decide against
telling, they revert to the ancient covenant of blood. On a
shingle Tom scrawls: "Huck Finn and Tom Sawyer swears they will
keep mum about this and they wish they may drop down dead in
their tracks if they ever tell and Rot" (*Tom Sawyer* 92). Using
the ball of his finger for a pen, each affixes his initials in
blood, and belief is firm that if either tells he will actually
fall dead on the spot. And another ancient superstition that
a corpse will bleed in the presence of its murderer appears
when Joe helps to raise the body of his victim; but so firmly
is suspicion centered on Muff Potter that the sign is mistaken,
people remarking: "It was within three feet of Muff Potter when
it done it" (*Tom Sawyer* 101).

Mark Twain's folklore, like his plots and characterizations,
exhibits the firsthand knowledge of intimate association.
Through companionship with the blacks and through saturation
of boyish beliefs, founded upon slave lore and upon common
grounds of superstition, Samuel Clemens knew that children and
the uneducated believed in ghosts, signs, and portents. These
folk elements he introduced into his fiction with the natural-
ness of art that springs spontaneously from organic truth.
Later, as West tells us, there appeared "the second-hand information gained from wide and intelligent inquiry during his
later travels, and what might be called the third-hand or
literary knowledge gleaned from the many books to which his
lively interest in the subject directed him" (77).[2] Interesting
they are, but far more important is that lore which permeates
the thought of Tom, Huck, and Jim, and which plays so large a
part in the minds of many around them, the firm beliefs found
in the folk thinking of the old-time black in the Mississippi
Valley.

Literary Sources

The influence of books on Mark Twain began with his youthful reading in Hannibal.[3] There through the promptings of his
mother and his sister little Sam began his acquaintance with
the Bible. He had read it through, reluctantly no doubt, before he was fifteen years of age, and Wagenknecht agrees with

Paine that much of the beauty of Twain's style came from that
common inspiration for so much that is great in English literature. Twain simply takes for granted his reader's knowledge
of scriptures; Charles W. Stoddard has described how Twain one
night in London thrilled his listeners with a beautiful reading
from the Book of Ruth (Wagenknecht 44). In all, it appears
that Clemens made more references to the Bible than to any
other work, 124 such allusions appearing in his books (Wagenknecht 43).

     Along with an early reading of the Bible, Sam became con-
versant with his father's copy of *Don Quixote*, an influence
which both Wagenknecht and Moore regard as next in importance
(Wagenknecht 44). DeLancey Ferguson, also, believes that the
boy absorbed Cervantes thoroughly, and he indicates that a
pervasive influence of Poe appears in certain parts of *Tom
Sawyer* (26). There is no doubt that Mark Twain read a great
deal in his youth, and Minnie Brashear has devoted an entire
chapter to a description of the material then available in
Hannibal--journals as well as books--for a boy so inclined
(196-224). Even though Twain said that he could never read
Dickens, both Ferguson and Wagenknecht feel certain that he
did (Ferguson 45; Wagenknecht 270). Writing to Orion in 1860,
Sam tells his brother of reading Tom Hood's letters, confiding
at the same time that his "beau ideals of fine writing" are
Don Quixote and Goldsmith's "Citizen of the World." While on
the river Sam read *Paradise Lost*, remarking upon "the Arch-
Fiend's terrible energy"; there too he read Shakespeare, who
was to furnish him with humor in an early Snodgrass letter,
who was to be burlesqued in the *Californian*, and who was
finally to become the subject of a volume, *Is Shakespeare
Dead?* During cub days on the river Sam read Tom Paine's *Age
of Reason*; after moving East he read Carlyle's *French Revolution*, both exerting a permanent influence upon his thinking.
The latter was one of the few books Twain reread every year,
others being Lecky's *History of European Morals*, Pepys' *Diary*,
and Suetonius' *Lives of the Caesars*. Mark's interest in evolution led him to *The Universal Kinship* by J. Howard Moore, to
whom he wrote an appreciative note saying the book had stated
his own "long-cherished opinions & reflections & resentments"
(qtd. in Paine 4: 1363). Though he could not bear most of
Scott--he found *Rob Roy* and *Guy Mannering* a blight--when he
read *Quentin Durward* Mark confessed delight, qualified by the
query, however, "I wonder who wrote *Quentin Durward*?" (qtd. in
Paine 3: 1198). At the same time Twain was charmed--"enchanted"
was his word--with Helen Keller's *The Story of My Life*, the
wonderful achievements by the blind girl through the help of
her teacher, Anne Sullivan; this book appealed to his sense of
courage and devotion. The *Literary Essays* of Professor William

Lyon Phelps held Clemens' attention until he finished the book
without putting it down (Paine 4: 1562).

During the winter of 1886-87 Twain earnestly turned to the
poetry of Robert Browning, conducting a group who gathered to
hear him read the verses he had so carefully studied until
obscurity disappeared through the clear insight of the reading.
Admitting Browning's many dark intervals, Clemens stated that
these were broken by great passages like a splendor of "stars
& suns" (Paine 3: 847). But for Meredith, Twain could experience no such enthusiasm.

Twain read Macaulay on English history, rereading him again
in old age. Thomas Hardy's *Jude the Obscure* impressed Clemens
so favorably that he urged his biographer to read it, the moral
problems presented in this, his last continuous reading, being
the chief matter of interest. Pepys' *Diary*, always a favorite,
Twain read yearly, once determining to write something similar--
but the result was *1601*. One summer when Howells' *Foregone
Conclusion* was running in the *Atlantic Monthly*, Twain followed
the serial; and though he seldom read fiction, on this exception
he complimented his friend highly. Similar praise went to
Elizabeth Robbins, whose *Open Question* moved Twain to write
her, "I have not been so enriched by a book for many years,
nor so enchanted by one" (qtd. in Paine 3: 1089). When Twichell
lent Twain a copy of Jonathan Edwards' *Freedom of the Will*,
Clemens was led to set down some theology of his own in dialogue form, a colloquy between the Master of the Universe and
a Stranger, for although he heartily approved Edwards' contention that mankind never creates an impulse itself, from there
on Clemens suffered a "haunting sense of having been on a
three days' tear with a drunken lunatic" (qtd. in Paine 3:
1157).

But Lowell's *Letters*, read while smoking, were more congenial matter. Twain also once expressed admiration for
Coventry Patmore's *The Angel in the House*. At the same time
he objected to the obscurity in Elizabeth Barrett Browning's
Aurora Leigh. While the "Recording Angel" passage in Sterne's
Tristram Shandy once drew his praise, on the whole he found
the book too coarse, at least to be read by Livy.

When Edward Everett Hale died, Clemens expressed privately
that he held "the greatest admiration for his work." But for
Jane Austen, he exclaimed that when he read one of her books,
"... such as *Pride and Prejudice*, I feel like a barkeeper entering the kingdom of heaven" (qtd. in Paine 4: 1500). *Gulli-
ver's Travels*, read in boyhood, furnished greater pleasure as
he grew older, despite his dislike of Swift as a man. And
Don Quixote, an influence already noted, Twain early praised
as "one of the most exquisite books that was ever written, &
to lose it from the world's literature would be as the wresting

of a constellation from the symmetry & perfection of the firma-
ment ..." (*Love Letters* 76). Yet Clemens was alert to the work
of new, young writers, discovering a poem by Willa Cather,
"The Palatine," in the *Saturday Times Review*, which brought his
praise and revealed foresight in discovering one who was to
prove an important figure in American letters. Andrew D.
White's *Science and Theology*, a history of the warfare between
science and unenlightened theological beliefs, Twain read and
reread, calling it a "lovely book." Charles Kingsley's *Hy-
patia* Mark found too tiresome to continue; however, *The Cloister
and the Hearth* by Charles Reade he read with all the enchantment that O. Henry found in the same volume.

Interest in contemporary literature led him to Booth
Tarkington, whose *Beasley's Christmas Party* actually brought
tears from Twain; Tarkington's work in general pleased the
older writer. Another book read with great pleasure for its
subtle art, *Chivalry*, by James Branch Cabell, also drew expressions of high praise.

On the table by his bed, as on the billiard room shelves,
Twain kept those books he constantly returned to: the three
volume *Memoirs of Saint-Simon*, Suetonius, and Carlyle's *French
Revolution*. Henry H. Breen's *Modern English Literature--Its
Blemishes and Defects* furnished Mark with enough examples of
slipshod English for a paper on that subject, read before the
Saturday Morning Club.

Twain's copy of Plutarch revealed frequent usage, and his
catholicity of taste appeared in the equally thumbed pages of
the *Life of P.T. Barnum, Written by Himself*. The before-men-
tioned *Letters* of Lowell furnished frequent enjoyment, as did
one of the few novels he ever cherished, Richard Henry Dana's
Two Years Before the Mast. Several books of an introductory
nature on astronomy and geology seem to have held his interest,
and though he came to peruse it less in old age, a much read
book from earlier days, Darwin's *Descent of Man*, furnished
influence through its very presence. Albert Bigelow Paine
tells us that during the days of his association with Clemens
the latter read steadily not much besides Suetonius, Pepys,
and Carlyle, though the *Morte d'Arthur* and Kipling's poems
were kept where he might reach them.

It would appear that to the end of his days Twain's taste
altered scarcely from the earlier sentiments expressed in an
interview with Rudyard Kipling, "Personally I never care for
fiction or story-books. What I like to read about are facts
and statistics of any kind" (Kipling 2: 180). Twain once set
down a literary declaration: "I like history, biography, travels,
curious facts and strange happenings, and science. And I detest novels, poetry, and theology" (qtd. in Paine 2: 512).

Sources from Life

The most vital sources in Clemens' writings came from personal experiences. For his first novel, the collaboration with Warner, Twain depended upon family reminiscences to write about Jamestown, the unmaterialized boom town of dashed hopes from the Tennessee land. But the character of Colonel Sellers, that enthusiastic optimist--"There's millions in it!"--was modeled from life upon a favorite cousin of Clemens' mother, James Lampton. The author further claimed that all the impossible, extravagant incidents of *The Gilded Age*, in both novel and play, merely seemed so, for he had actually seen them, or at least believed he had, even to the turnip-eating episode.[4]

The farm of John A. Quarles, where Sam visited for several months each year until he reached his teens, was generously utilized for *Huckleberry Finn* and *Tom Sawyer, Detective*; in these works Twain moved it from Missouri down to Arkansas. On the farm was an old black, regarded affectionately as good friend and adviser to all the children, "Uncle Dan'l," who was an old-time Southern black like Uncle Remus. Shearing away the years to create physical vigor, Twain turned "Uncle Dan'l" into Jim. From his boyhood, also, came the impressions of Sunday school later expressed in *Tom Sawyer* and *Huck Finn*. Naturally, in spite of later associations with scholarly ministers, Twain continued to associate theology with the dull, long-winded sermons of boyhood.

From youthful memories, too, came the episode of whitewashing the fence in *Tom Sawyer*, Twain recalling that he had once so tried to impose on a little slave named Sandy, upon whom the ruse failed to work. And the villain "Injun" Joe was an actual half-breed, once lost in the cave near Hannibal, where he would have starved if the bats had run short. Twain suggests, though only by implication, that Pap in *Huck Finn* may have been based upon the town drunkard, Jimmy Finn, whose predecessor, "General" Gaines, may also have figured in the characterization. In fact, the "General" like "Injun" Joe became lost in the cave, where he effected escape by pushing his handkerchief through a hole miles from the entrance, the good fates causing somebody to see it and dig him out.

As Ferguson notes, all of *Tom Sawyer* may be autobiographical through its characters, altered or colored for dramatic purposes (29). Twain once flatly stated that Huck Finn was based on Tom Blankenship. Tom's father, moreover, at least in Twain's memory, had been a town drunkard like "General" Gaines and Jimmy Finn, and one gathers that Finn perhaps filled that office with greater competency than the others. And there were

other memories from youth incorporated into the saga of Tom
and Huck, when Twain conveyed the actual description of Dawson's schoolhouse to the pages of *Tom Sawyer*, just as he employed "that distant boy-Paradise, Cardiff Hill" from whence
the "drowsy and inviting summer sounds" floated through the
school windows (*Autobiography* 2: 179). Yet more inviting was
the countryside near his uncle's farm.

And other real people appear in Twain's literary portrait
gallery; the original of Becky Thatcher in *Tom Sawyer* was
Laura Hawkins, the little girl with whom Sam Clemens went to
school in Hannibal. She bears no resemblance, however, to
Laura Hawkins of *The Gilded Age*, beautiful but dangerous ad-
venturess, who committed a murder, for perhaps the original
of that icy brunette was Laura Dake, whom Clemens once found
fascinating and may have been trying to write out of his system.

In some ways, at least, Twain's mother served as the model
for his portrait of Tom's Aunt Polly, while Pamela Clemens in
her gentle fashion became Cousin Mary. Sam's brother, Henry,
was utilized for the Sid of *Tom Sawyer*, though Henry was in
every way a finer lad than Sid. Moreover, many of the incidents of that book--the shirt sewed with colored thread, the
painkiller administered to the cat--actually happened, or
Twain thought they had. To his old friend, Will Bowen, Clemens
once wrote of a conscious effort to recall the old days at
Dawson's school, now fading from his "treacherous memory,"
though one incident vividly protruded, Will's buying a louse
of "poor Arch Fuqua" (*Letters to Will Bowen* 17).

From the verdant solitude of the Tuolumne hills came the
stories of Tom Quartz the cat, the Jaybird and Acorns, and the
cameleopard skit in *Huckleberry Finn*, bowdlerized from "The
Burning Shame" as narrated by Jim Gillis. Angel's Camp, where
the weather was bad as the beans and dishwater served three
times a day, furnished the story of "Coleman with his jumping
frog," while from the same locality came a story which grew
many years later into "The Californian's Tale." Though derived
at second hand from Joe Twichell the biblical explanations of
Captain Ned Wakeman were incorporated into "Some Rambling Notes
of an Idle Excursion." The old seaman, unaware of his passenger's identity, undertook a logical clarification of the miracles, his profanity in full swing.

The incident of the lost sock in *A Tramp Abroad* was another
story derived directly from experience, Twain transferring the
scene from Munich to Heilbronn and substituting Twichell for
Livy as his traveling companion. The whole episode was written
immediately after it happened, as Twain's subsiding anger gave
way to perception of the literary values in the ridiculous
situation of a person fully dressed save for one sock crawling

about in the darkness of a hotel room in a futile search for
the missing article. It is difficult to evaluate Twain's own
statements of his sources for the same reasons that his *Autobiography* must be carefully weighed on the scales of established fact. But when all scholarly returns are in and the
counts of his literary sources are tallied, the essential
truth, if not always the actual fact, of Twain's indebtedness
to his own experiences persists. It is in the world of memory
recorded in the *Autobiography* that the primary sources of his
major contributions may be found, the world of Hannibal, of
John Quarles' farm, of old times on the Mississippi, and of
tumultuous days in Washoe.[5]

Vocabulary

The accuracy with which Twain recorded the speech of boys
reveals patient observation and a keen ear. Like the writers
of the frontier tradition preceding him, Twain followed the
colloquial idiom and colloquial syntax, and it is not only in
the conversation of youngsters, but in that of adults, that
the flow of language in his books follows the stream of life.
Never addicted to bookish speech, Twain had as early as the
Philadelphia travel letters shown a tendency to vigorous
writing, for a comparison with their sources reveals that the
young printer valued simplicity and directness of style.[6]
And Sam Clemens, like Emerson, who listened to the live language of teamsters, and Robert Burton, who listened to the
bargemen, perceived the vitality of common speech, transferring
it to the printed page.

From his early youth Clemens had listened to talk between
untutored men, he had heard the dialect of black slaves, and
he knew how the general person spoke in his everyday conversation. Before him, moreover, was the entire tradition of frontier humor, told in the language of a Sut Lovingood or a Simon
Suggs, a tradition devoted to realism, one quick to laugh at
any affectation. In maturity Twain criticized Professor
Dowden's biography of Shelley as a "literary cake-walk." Here
is insistence on realism of speech, the absence of which aroused
Twain's ire toward James Fenimore Cooper. Clemens' precise ear
is evident in his comments on the differences between our language as spoken in England and as used in the Southern and
Western portions of the United States. And his understanding
of the value of the spoken words of the majority is also clear.
For this latter Twain became the literary spokesman.

If there are fewer dialect variations in *Huckleberry Finn*, for instance, than Twain imagined, and those rendered into print more haphazardly than painstakingly, the very lack of a studied conformity, as Katherine Buxbaum observes, makes for vigor, vividness, and imagination; for Twain's dialect is natural, real, with a "wealth of clear-cut, pointed phrases" (236). Out West he took the strong, racy slang of the miners, contrasting it with accepted, literary usage (236). It is when Twain turns to the colloquial, however, that we are most indebted to him for broadening the scope of dialogue in American letters. "You don't know about me," says Huckleberry Finn, "without you have read a book by the name of *The Adventures of Tom Sawyer*; but that ain't no matter. That book was made by Mr. Mark Twain, and he told the truth, mainly. There was things which he stretched, but mainly he told the truth." And as Huck continues, "Now the way that book winds up is this: Tom and me found the money that the robbers hid in the cave, and it made us rich" (*Huckleberry Finn* 1), we have authentic, native American idiom used for the first time in a masterpiece of world literature.

In his descriptions Clemens was as accurate as in dialogue, making language fit the subject perfectly. Here is Hannibal:

> After all these years I can picture that old time
> to myself now, just as it was then: the white town
> drowsing in the sunshine of a summer's morning; the
> streets empty, or pretty nearly so; one or two clerks
> sitting in front of the Water Street stores, with their
> splint-bottomed chairs tilted back against the walls,
> chins on breasts, hats slouched over their faces, asleep--
> with shingle-shavings enough around to show what broke
> them down; a sow and a litter of pigs loafing along the
> sidewalk, doing a good business in watermelon rinds and
> seeds; two or three lonely little freight piles scattered
> about the "levee"; a pile of "skids" on the slope of the
> stone-paved wharf, and the fragrant town drunkard asleep
> in the shadow of them; two or three wood flats at the
> head of the wharf, but nobody to listen to the peaceful
> lapping of the wavelets against them; the great Mississip-
> pi, the majestic, the magnificent Mississippi, rolling
> its mile-wide tide along, shining in the sun; the dense
> forest away on the other side; the "point" above the
> town, and the "point" below, bounding the river-glimpse
> and turning it into a sort of sea, and withal a very
> still and brilliant and lonely one. (*Life on the Missis-
> sippi* 32-33)

Such diction is evocative; we see the sights and colors, hear the sounds, and sense movements. It is all told in language

that is clear, vivid, lucid; in a style that is realistic and
factual, yet at the same time poetic, beautiful, and true.

In picturing his region Twain naturally introduced the
language of the black, which he depicted with an art, equaled
for accurate representation only by that of Joel Chandler
Harris and Thomas Nelson Page. Of course, it was with Jim,
Huck's companion on the raft, that Mark pictured the language
of the black of that time most fully. Huck with his untutored
speech, Jim with his slave dialect, Tom with the natural colloquial talk of a village boy never become confused in their
creator's mind, for the artist in Twain rendered dialogue as
truthfully as it presented human actions.

Structure

Mark Twain once spoke of Bret Harte "who trimmed and
trained and schooled me patiently until he changed me from an
awkward utterer of coarse grotesquenesses to a writer of para-
graphs and chapters that have found a certain favor in the eyes
of even some of the very decentest people in the land" (*Letters* 1: 182-83). Yet when Clemens came to write *The Innocents
Abroad* there was nothing of Harte's method in his architec-
tonics. Here, however, is the method Twain was to follow
generally throughout his career. Sam Clemens was even then,
despite fresh materials of the excursion, finding his deepest
reservoir in boyhood memories, the same that were to make *Tom
Sawyer*, *Huck Finn*, and the *Autobiography* great books. Yet as
Bernard DeVoto says, this is the method of genius, rather than
of a conscientious literary craftsman, and Twain often worked
on several projects at once, taking up whichever he found
stimulating, only to abandon it for another when enthusiasm
flagged. Sometimes a project would be laid aside for long
intervals; Twain returned to several manuscripts after twenty
years had lapsed, even taking up one thirty years later (*Mark
Twain at Work* 3). And always experience, unconscious absorp-
tion, played its role. Twain frequently reworked his own
materials; for instance there was the famous storm scene of
Following the Equator, given first in his speech on New England
weather. Then the final development of the "Boy's Manuscript"
of 1870 into *Tom Sawyer* shows the full extent to which Twain
could elaborate and improve his own suggestion.

Experience was the rough diamond; but the final artistic
embodiment came through the glow of imagination, which turned
actualities into the glorious world of dreams and fancy. And
this method held even for historical romance, where the tall

tale of frontier humor might intrude for no reason of history
or form.

In the preface to *Those Extraordinary Twins*, Mark made a
frank statement about the troublesome times arising when one
tries to build a novel. As the tale progresses and grows in
length the original motif often disappears, which happened in
Pudd'nhead Wilson, begun as a farce but changed to tragedy--
all without intent by the author. Twain, as he frankly tells
us, found himself with two plots on his hands, hopelessly
intermingled and cluttered, with no alternative save to separate
them, leaving tragedy dominant in *Pudd'nhead Wilson* and rele-
gating the farce to another story, *Those Extraordinary Twins*.
Into the farce about an Italian "freak," begun as extravaganza,
other characters began to intrude, Pudd'nhead Wilson, Roxana,
and Tom Driscoll, who pushed themselves so prominently into
the plot the others fell by the wayside.

Clemens also found that he had a defective plot, "two
stories in one, a farce and a tragedy." Intrusion of farce
upon serious plot recurred frequently with Clemens, as in *Joan
of Arc*, *The Prince and the Pauper*, and *A Connecticut Yankee*.
Here in this admixture, however, Twain managed to effect a
neat dichotomy, the result being the serious plot of *Pudd'nhead
Wilson* and the utter farce of *Those Extraordinary Twins*.

The mingling of diverse elements arose naturally in this
instance, as often in Mark Twain's writings, from the unchartered
manner of composition. In Twain's workshop the author held the
pen while the stories told themselves. This he believed the
only true art; of a writer who tried to substitute a fabricated
narrative for facts transfigured through imagination, Twain
said, "The result is a failure. It is a piece of pure literary manufacture and has the shopmarks all over it" (*Eruption*
244). Mark seldom knew where his plot was going, if we may
accept his own statement in the preface to *Those Extraordinary
Twins* that the author is unfamiliar with the future of his
tale, "and can only find out what it is by listening as it
goes along telling itself ..." (*Pudd'nhead Wilson* 207).

Fortunately for American letters, the boyhood period of
Hannibal recollected through a haze of memories and dreams
came to appeal more and more to the mature imagination of Samuel
Clemens. As Dixon Wecter tells us, the first hint occurs in
one of the New York letters to the *Alta California* during the
spring of 1867, a reference to the town drunkard, Jimmy Finn,
together with an account of the Cadets of Temperance, joined
by young Sam in order to wear a red scarf when marching in
funeral processions ("Mark Twain" 2: 929). This was to appear
later in *Tom Sawyer*. And several of Tom's adventures were in
a letter to Will Bowen, "My First, & Oldest & Dearest Friend,"
when on a February day of 1870 in Buffalo Mark Twain recalled

the old days and old faces from childhood (*Letters to Will
Bowen* 18-21).

Structurally *The Innocents Abroad* is a narrative of stories
strung on the autobiographical thread of a journey. The momentum of the narrative is one of travel, while the stories--
mostly in the manner of the frontier anecdote--are interspersed
with descriptive passages, some indeed of beauty. Bernard De-
Voto says of the burlesque passage on Heloise and Abelard,
which leads to the traditional attempt of a tourist to get an
American drink: "The passage is typical and the point need not
be labored; ... It is Mark discoursing in the manner of the
pilot house; he has found a technique completely adapted to his
qualities" (*Mark Twain's America* 246). A similar framework en-
closes the structure of *Roughing It*; yet here, too, it is travel
which takes the story forward, brings it to a close, and ener-
gizes throughout. When Twain came to write *A Tramp Abroad, Following the Equator*, and the first half of *Life on the Mississippi*, again movement from place to place supplied the framework.
Setting his characters on journeys supplies the structure or
channel for the narratives of *Huckleberry Finn, A Connecticut
Yankee, Joan of Arc*, and *The Prince and the Pauper*; only *Tom
Sawyer* and *Pudd'nhead Wilson* stand outside this device, and
even these not entirely.

For the rules of Aristotle, Twain had no regard; for rules
in general he held no brief: what he did seek consistently was
natural organic expression, not rules but natural laws. It was
his conviction that execution transcends design, that a tale
must tell itself, growing naturally from within until the ideal
narrative, informal like actual life or talk, flows along,
perhaps digressive yet ever fresh and vigorous. As Feinstein
observes, "Literary form is plainly for him a function of personality rather than of genre" (162). Thus it is true that
Life on the Mississippi, for instance, does not fit completely
into any category--history, travel, or novel--being more an
expression of Samuel Clemens' personality than anything else.[7]
Unity of time, place, or action means no more to Twain than it
did to Shakespeare, while the tonal unity of Hawthorne or Poe
struck him, it must be admitted, as artificial.

Yet Mark Twain did achieve a structural form, as the research of Trilling, Branch, Bellamy, and Blair reveals. It
has been the fashion, because of Twain's insistence upon natural,
organic outgrowth in expression, to say that his work is form-
less, but Walter Blair has demonstrated that *Tom Sawyer* has one
narrative, artistically developed: the growth of a boy from
adolescence toward maturity. Within this central theme are
four "units of narrative, the lines of action": (1) the story
of Tom and Becky, (2) the narrative of Tom and Muff Potter,
(3) the Jackson Island episode, (4) the series of happenings

which may be called the "Injun" Joe story. Of the thirty-five
chapters comprising the novel only four fail to deal with one
of these four plots, while eight chapters contain elements
uniting two of the lines of action. The theme of *Tom Sawyer*,
the single line of development, results in one main narrative:
the development of a boy from adolescence toward maturity, a
theme including the four threads of plot.

Mark Twain had in mind, then, the normal history of boyhood, and he worked out a "way of characterizing and a pattern-
ing of action which showed a boy developing toward manhood"
(Blair, "Structure" 85). Perhaps the simplest explanation of
the arrangement of the strands of narrative is, as Blair suggests, "a fictional working-out of the author's antipathy to
the conventional plot structure of juvenile tales" ("Structure"
83). In a word, Mark Twain, who had always disliked the unreal
stories of moral boys who prospered while the wicked perished,
probably decided that he would write a book about boys neither
angelic nor wicked--real boys possessing both virtues and flaws.
Disdaining burlesque, he turned to fictional representation of
boys who were real in their thoughts and actions, and thus came
naturally upon the unifying theme for his story: natural development opposed to the melodramatic sermonizing of the good-versus-
bad-boy tracts. With the four narratives bound together into
one plot, Twain takes his children through a series of happenings from the complete world of childhood at the opening into
the world of maturity which they enter at the close.

It has so long been the fashion to regard *Tom Sawyer* as
structurally superior to *Huckleberry Finn* that many readers
were surprised when Lionel Trilling declared, "In form and
style *Huckleberry Finn* is an almost perfect work" (Introduction
xv).[8] Even the elaborate game of Jim's escape, which concludes
the book, is defended by Trilling as an apt way of allowing
"Huck to return to his anonymity, to give up the role of hero,"
for Huck, modest as he is, would prefer to drop into the background, allowing Tom Sawyer to take the spotlight. As nearly
everyone must know, the form of *Huckleberry Finn* is the picar-
esque novel, its incidents depending on the hero's travels;
yet here, as Trilling illuminates, "... the road itself is the
greatest character in this novel of the road," for the road is
the great, moving, mighty river. Indeed, Trilling sees in
Huck's departures and returns to the river "a subtle and significant pattern" (Introduction xvi). The river is a place of
delight, yet one, also, of danger, and there is no elevation
of nature over human nature, for what Huck enjoys most is being
on the raft with Jim. Nevertheless, the Mississippi assumes
the qualities of a god, adored by Huck for its power, charm,
and beauty. In this way, river and narrative flow simultaneously, the whole structure being built around the Mississippi,

which furnishes the continuity and movement of the plot. And
the absolute freedom of the river-god in contrast to that of
Huck and Jim integrates it further with what Edgar M. Branch
calls the theme of the story--"the conflict between individual
freedom and the restraints imposed by convention and force; or,
within Huck's consciousness, the struggle between his intuitive
morality and his conventional conscience" ("Two Providences"
188).

   Both Trilling and Branch have seen the two unifying
threads: the river and the moral conflict, the latter interwoven in the moral nature suggested by the former. This is
further emphasized by an "ethical duality" in Huck's actions,
arising from moral intuition and conventional code, which leads
to his conflict "anchored in the duality of nature and dramatized through scenic analogues" ("Two Providences" 189).
Branch, also like Trilling, views the final scene of the book
as an integral part of the theme, significant because it is
the converse of Huck's internal struggle; the difference between Twain's two boys is explained: "Tom is the romantic,
working within the accepted social and moral framework; Huck
is the moral realist and individualist who goes beyond it"
("Two Providences" 192-93). And T.S. Eliot agrees that the
ending is right: "It is Huck who gives the book style. The
River gives the book its form" (Introduction xii). Eliot sees
the end as bringing us back to the mood at the beginning, and
adds that it is as impossible for Huck as for the Mississippi
itself to be confined within conventional limitations. In
fact, Eliot's praise for the way in which Twain concludes
Huck's saga is as high as his praise for the book as a whole,
which he declares a great masterpiece.

   In *Huckleberry Finn*, Twain achieved organic form in a
narrative that suited his ideas of storytelling, being alike
the most perfect expression for the thematic idea, and also a
mature expression of Twain's own personality. In a word, then,
the form found in Mark Twain's books is that found in life.
At least that is true of his successful ones. At times, however, as E.S. Fussell suggests, Twain's heart and his feelings for the individual were in disharmony with his philosophy.
Twain's humanity sometimes prevented a complete artistic inte-
gration, because he could never really feel as he said he believed about mankind. Fussell says that *The Mysterious Stranger*
is an example of Twain's failure to reconcile these conflicting
emotions and philosophizings (95-104).[9] But when heart and
head were as one, as in the books deriving from the Mississippi
Valley and the West, the artistic pattern was successful.

Origin of Humor

The origin of Mark Twain's humor is chiefly the humor of
the Old Southwest amid which he ripened and matured. But a
parallel source was the black slave, whose humor was made
known to the world by the creator of Uncle Remus. From the
blacks Twain must have first heard the narratives which later
went into such fabrications as the bluejay yarn of *A Tramp
Abroad*. The actual material is, of course, that of the bes-
tiary, stretching back before Chaucer, but preserved in Clemens'
youth by the black slaves, from whom he orally derived this
literary type. Into this story, as related by Twain, however,
comes the element of the tall tale, for the narrator, Jim
Baker, is present, alive and real, to convey fantasy through
an idiom, vivid and strong. Thus a narrative of utter fancy
is conveyed through a medium of complete reality.

Later, when a celebrity, Twain became a commentator on
political and social problems, again in the tradition of frontier humor, best exemplified by Abraham Lincoln. The backwoods philosopher in a leisurely but pragmatic manner took a
realistic approach to the problem, which was sure to impress
his audience as horse sense. As we have seen, this began in
the Snodgrass letters, developed steadily through Virginia
City correspondence, to flower in San Francisco, with only the
consummation of an art needed to lift it into the realm of
literature.

So much of Twain's humor derives from the folk that in
retelling "The Burning Shame," for instance, or the story of
Dick Baker and Tom Quartz, he was actually the folk bard in
operation, taking the story by word of mouth and passing it on
in print, often in prose of poetic quality. Though reality
is modified by imagination--thereby lifting it into literature--
the humorous tall tale also has historical value; for it reveals a heterogeneous people, so well known to Twain, engaged
in the characteristic activities of everyday life. In fact,
these anecdotes preserved by Clemens are a rich source of
stock characterizations and incidents set against a real background. One of the origins of Twain's humor, then, is his
realistic, truthful approach to life, seeing the gap between
life as it is and as it should be. As Pellowe states, "Humor
is sanity, a sense of perspective and proportion; it cannot
be misled in this valley of illusions. It sees things as they
are and keeps everything in its place--including the humorist
himself" (4).

Fantasy and realism exist side by side in the humor of
Mark Twain; burlesque and extravaganza derive from the former,
while the latter often produces satire. Burlesque and carica-

ture in frontier humor arose from exuberance, but as DeVoto
observes, "The desire to produce laughter is the motive that
begets the anecdote" (*Mark Twain's America* 242). Mark Twain
as a son of the frontier came naturally by his desire to create
laughter, for it was part of his tradition. In addition to
the word-of-mouth anecdote told by a narrator who skillfully
constructed a tall tale of impossible fancy, there was the
printed storehouse of native humor in newspapers, occasionally
even in books. And Samuel Clemens was heir to it all.

Going West, Twain became even more saturated with a comic
spirit of American origin; from the literary comedians came an
abundance of devices for producing laughter, such as the
description of the dragon in Chapter XVII of *A Tramp Abroad*,
or the doctor ("inspired idiot") of *The Innocents Abroad*.
Part of Western humor, and a very popular part, was shrewdness
veiled by an assumption of simplicity. This was the lecture
platform manner of Twain in his younger days, just as it had
been the manner of Artemus Ward before him.

There was still another link with the past, not frontier
humor or fun of the literary comedians, but the tradition of
Down East humor, which furnished him, though probably unconsciously, with Mrs. Partington as a model for Aunt Polly.
There was also the stream of humor in the genteel tradition,
which included the witty verse of Oliver Wendell Holmes, known
to Clemens from formative years. Yet, after all, the actual
origins of Samuel Clemens' humor seem to be in the kind of boy
he was born and and in the environments in which he spent his
adolescence and young manhood, the Mississippi Valley and the
far West.

A Study of Changing Style

Mark Twain's style is a study in evolution, beginning
with his first recorded appearance in print, "The Dandy
Frightening the Squatter," published in one of the lesser
humorous journals, *The Carpet-Bag*, May 1, 1852. He may have
written humorous verses about two marriage announcements in
Joseph P. Ament's *Courier* in 1849, while serving as printer's
devil, and he may have written humorously on the excellence
of a wedding cake for Orion's first Hannibal newspaper in
1850, but no definite proof has yet been established. And two
anecdotes said by Paine to have been published in 1851 have
not been located (Branch, "Chronological Bibliography" 113-14).
Hence "The Dandy" remains his first published writing.

There is nothing impressive about this account of an
Eastern dandy who tried to frighten a squatter for the amusement of the steamboat passengers and got the daylights knocked
out of him, but it shows young Sam Clemens retelling for a
Boston journal a rough, comic yarn, popular along the river.
The style is simple and direct with no more dialect than is
necessary for conversation.

When Orion left Sam in charge of the *Journal* during the
summer of 1852, however, his career of newspaper writing actually commenced. In July a mad dog conveniently caused enough
excitement in Hannibal to involve young Clemens in controversy
with a rival editor; Sam signed himself "A Dog-be-deviled
Citizen" and wrote flippantly in colloquialisms peppered with
an occasional pun. Then as "W. Epaminondas Adrastus Blab" he
engaged in humor more indicative of the future; such sentences
as "The first Blab lived in Adam's time," and "... honorable
mention was made of one of them in a book that was never published," show an advance over mere physical humor (Brashear
117-18). And though colloquial, the style is free of dialect.

A poem, *Love Concealed: To Miss Katie of H----l*, is a conventional bit of versifying, written by Clemens to provide a
series of exchanges purportedly by correspondents, though actually by himself. The opportunities of "H----l" for humorous
incongruities were worked to the fullest. Upon being dignified
by Orion with the title of assistant editor, Sam next turned
out three columns of miscellaneous squibbs on current events
in which humor mingles with moralizing. Again the style is
simple, direct, and free of dialect, though highly colloquial.

Following the subeditor period in Hannibal, *Mark Twain's
Letters in the Muscatine Journal* were written intermittently
during 1853 through 1855. Newsy with travel talk of Philadelphia, Washington, and St. Louis, they furnish Clemens' reactions to current events and a record of his leisure hours.
Though only five in number they reveal a growing interest in
economic, political, and social problems; and even if mainly
biographical, these letters for the Muscatine *Journal* reveal
a tendency to write succinctly.

Sam Clemens next wrote three letters for the Keokuk (Iowa)
Saturday Post which show gusto and robust humor. They are an
advance over the Muscatine correspondence, for here we have a
humorous character depicted and a narrative of his exploits.
These adventures, too, mark Clemens' sole excursion into the
realm of dialect spelling. Told through the mouth of Thomas
Jefferson Snodgrass, the yarns are narrated in the dialect of
a countryman, though the mixed spelling so disastrous to the
fame of George W. Harris is held to a minimum. It was a kind
of humor then in vogue, conveyed by peculiarities of spelling
and grammar.

These letters reveal some of the same delight in coarseness that poured forth later in Washoe. Snodgrass meets an
"indigent Irish woman--a widow with nineteen children and
several at the breast, accordin to custom"; and when he de-
cides to relate an unpleasant adventure of the previous evening
he confides, "... but drat if it don't work me worse'n castor
oil just to think of it" (*Snodgrass* 41). Left with a stranger's
baby on his hands Snodgrass "... walked it, and tossed it, and
cussed it, till the sweat run off my carcass to the amount of
a barl at least" (*Snodgrass* 46). And the brutality that has
been present in all primitive humor from Beowulf to Minsky's
burlesque appears here with the falsely accused "onnateral
father" seeking to extricate himself by "trying to poke the
dang thing through a hole in the ice" (*Snodgrass* 47).

Clemens' style is both vigorous and crude in these letters,
direct and realistic in detail, however fantastic the situations being narrated. By now he had advanced over the guide-
book imitation of the Muscatine letters, had created a character through whom he could give free expression to crudities--a
device he was to continue--and had embarked upon the journey
motif, which furnished the framework of his more mature efforts. When next he turned to Snodgrass, however, Clemens
changed the given name to Quintus Curtius and eschewed dialect
spellings. As befitted the more classical name, the style became more formal; perhaps Sam suspected that what might delight
Keokuk would be less acceptable for the more cosmopolitan
readers of the New Orleans *Daily Crescent*.[10]

Here Clemens wrote satire, describing first in mock-heroic
style the discomforts en route to capture the Federal garrison
at Baton Rouge. But he soon turned to parody--something Twain
was always inclined to do in his satire--making fun of the
Confederate *Manual of Arms* in a way to suggest personal famil-
iarity. The letters are presented to the reader "by the kind
permission of our friend Brown" to whom they were written by
Snodgrass. Unlike the humor of the earlier Thomas Jefferson
Snodgrass, who was in the tradition of the frontier, that of
his successor Quintus Curtius is more urbane and less boisterous. In the evolution of Mark Twain's style, the second series
of Snodgrass letters is more literary and mature than the earlier one. But the substitution of satire for exuberance, in
view of future developments, seems due to the medium rather
than to any fundamental change in Twain's character.

The next work of Samuel Clemens was for the Virginia City
Territorial Enterprise, the kind of writing the author of "The
Dandy" and the creator of Thomas Jefferson Snodgrass would take
to naturally--enthusiastic, spirited, and exuberantly masculine.
His audience, rough, energetic, frequently crude, was also
realistic, generous, and scornful of pretense. Humor here was

elemental, generally physical, often depending on horseplay.
An example of his Nevada style is the bloody massacre hoax,
coarse and gory in details, fantastic in exaggerations, its
satire and social reproof embedded in a native joke.[11] As a
piece of literary craftsmanship it has no value whatever.

When shortly thereafter the "wild humorist of the Sage
Brush Hills" journeyed to San Francisco to become the "Washoe
Giant," we find much the same style persisting, for many
readers of the *Golden Era* were themselves lately come from the
Stanislaus. If we recall Thomas Jefferson Snodgrass, we must
admit that the West only gave Twain freedom, the coarse inclinations, though dormant in the Muscatine and New Orleans
letters, now reappearing.

Though Clemens believed at one time that it was Bret
Harte who had trained and schooled him, what he wrote in San
Francsico justifies no such statement. What Sam Clemens
penned for the *Californian* differs little from what he wrote
for the *Enterprise*; his first contribution to the *Californian*,
October, 1864, combined a love letter with a soap boiler's ad-
vertisement. A week later he had a wonderful time describing
a stranded whale which "smells more like a thousand pole-cats"
(*Sixties* 128). Opening the story with references to seasick-
ness and bilious fever, Twain was soon happily describing the
long row of bottles behind the bar and the drunken attempts of
his comrade at speech. In this same sketch the law of compen-
sation is thus expounded, "Behold, the same gust of wind that
blows a lady's dress aside, and exposes her ankle, fills your
eyes so full of sand that you can't see it" (*Sixties* 127-28).

All are in the vein of Washoe: "Daniel in the Lion's Den--
and Out Again All Right" describes drinking and swapping lies
with stockjobbing brokers, introduces momentarily a "Snodgrass,"
and ends with the fantasy of St. Peter's admitting those Bulls
and Bears into Paradise. Later on, Twain, still practicing
mining camp puns, called the Great Bear the Great Menken--a
reference to the actress who appeared nearly nude; pictured a
drunk with a "wine-bred cauliflower" on his nose "spitting on
his shirt bosom and slurring it off with his hand"; and wrote
a jingle about a sow whose "swill is mine, and all my slops
her gain." Truly the mature style of Mark Twain seems little
influenced by the journalists of San Francisco's literary
frontier, for any refining influence Harte may have exerted is
unapparent. Indeed, the pieces collected in *Sketches of the
Sixties* and *The Washoe Giant in San Francisco* might well have
been written in Virginia City; the style is rough, physical,
and boisterous.

Shortly thereafter, when the Sandwich Islands correspondence
appeared in the Sacramento *Union*, Twain decided to express his
coarser humor through a character called Brown, thus using

crudity while absolving himself from censure. The primitive
delight in physical discomfort persists here in the seasick
passengers' vomiting while Brown comforted, "... it'll clean
you out like a jug, and then you won't feel ornery and smell
so ridiculous" (*Sandwich Islands* 3). Irreverence appears,
too, when Balboa becomes "like any other Greaser" and a "shame-
less old foreign humbug," deserving a blast to make his "old
dry bones rattle" for misnaming this violent ocean "Pacific."
Yet Twain seemed aware that his subject called for more dignity
than his former pieces for the *Golden Era* and the *Californian*
because the style is free of puns and illiteracies, and generally less colloquial.

These letters from the Sandwich Islands are Twain's first
sustained writing, an advance over the burlesque and satire of
previous unrelated sketches. Treating his subject comprehensively and informatively, Twain was entertaining, serious, or
light, as the material demanded. Here he combined factual
statements with passages of beautiful description, filled with
sense perceptions that conveyed vividly the sights and sounds
of nature; here, too, abundant humor bubbled forth in satire,
burlesque, and anecdote, while a propensity to moralize appeared
in the ridicule directed at petty politicians. It was his
first important reportorial assignment, and Twain worked hard
to make it a success. Though he was obligated to cover only
the sugar and whaling industries and the transportation problems, the artist in Twain pictured scenic beauty, while the
potential novelist described social, political, and religious
conditions. An interest in legends, personalities, and history of the islands, an acute foresight of their future importance, a delight in scenic grandeur--all spiced with abundant
humor--enlivened what might have been merely trade correspondence. The *Union* letters mark the transition from the rough
humor of the Western mining camp to the mature style of the
future. Not the cessation, however, for Twain's delight in such
humor was not to be so quickly stifled, remaining in abeyance
often to break forth in such unexpected places as *Joan of Arc*.

In this transition Brown figures prominently, for Twain
was writing for the West, and the realistic humor and unroman-
tic skepticism, often vulgar or irreverent, were to diminish
slowly as Twain found the East less inclined to approve. Brown
accompanied him through the letters for the San Francisco *Alta
California* in 1866 and 1867, describing adventures in Nicaragua,
Hannibal, and New York just prior to departure for Europe. Ir-
repressible as the humor he expressed, Brown's cynicism and
antiromantic nature intrude upon Mark's descriptions of the
voyage from San Francisco, the crossing of Nicaragua, the
cholera-stricken passage up the Atlantic, and arrival in New
York. The people, fashions, customs, and institutions of the

Eastern metropolis are described with an eye on his Western
audience, one quick to detect in Brown the alter ego of their
correspondent.

In these letters, written at the time Twain was abandoning
the California scene to embark upon the voyage that would produce *The Innocents Abroad*, the old delight in repulsive humor
remained. In fact, it might be said that the letters from
Honolulu show more refinement of style, for Clemens, with the
trip abroad ahead of him, was in a gay mood, one always leading into exuberant expression. And exuberance for Twain resulted in more than physical action; it generally led to the
roughness of humor to which he had become accustomed. Though he
was in New York, he was still writing for San Francisco; moreover
he had recently journeyed out to Hannibal, Keokuk, and Quincy.
A visit to the places of his youth must have refreshed his
memory of the humorists of the Old Southwest, who held so much
in common with the literary comedians and humorous lecturers
of the coast.

Soon he was able to write his third series of travel correspondence for Western readers, some fifty letters sent to the
Alta California during his excursion to Europe and the Holy
Land. But when prospects for a book appeared, Clemens realized
that he would be addressing a different audience; for six
months he revised, also converting the separate letters into a
unit. To Elisha Bliss, Jr., he wrote of weeding the letters
of "their chief faults of construction and inelegancies of expression" (*Letters* 1: 141), a task that would eliminate some
passages and necessitate creating new ones. Twain knew the
difference, even this early, between books and the "wind and
water" of newspaper matter. It was form, then, as well as
audience that demanded revision.

To adapt his writings to the more genteel taste of the
East, Clemens, depending less upon the extravagant, grotesque
situations so delightful to his former associates, sought a
more polite expression. Revising colloquialisms raised the
diction to a more literary level; he struck out many words and
references that might give offense. He deleted the word "mangy,"
substituted "donkey" for "jackass," and euphemized "lies" into
"exaggerations." "Bawdyhouse," "slimy cesspool," and "stink"
vanished with his Western audience; yet enough frontier irreverence remained to alarm the publishers with fear of foster-
ing a blasphemous enterprise.[12] Twain, however, had toned down
his newspaper version, omitting many criticisms of the church,
such as the "fat and greasy" Italian priests, who "would yield
oil like a whale"; he left out references to gambling like
"She [Venice] bets her all on St. Mark's"; and describing the
straight up view during the ascent of Vesuvius he refrained
from repeating "The ladies wore no hoops, which was well. They

would have looked like so many umbrellas" (qtd. in Dickinson 147).

Twain, moreover, revised some of the flippancies, omitted passages about the religious habits and beliefs of the pilgrims, as well as some questioning of their piety. And he gave up, no doubt reluctantly, the broad humor involving "Mr. Brown," who disappears from the book, his vulgar remarks generally being left out, while his purely ignorant ones are attributed to other pilgrims, usually to Blucher, sometimes to Jack. *The Innocents Abroad*, too, is less highly seasoned with slang than the *Alta* version, and in general the book is a stylistic improvement over the letters. For one thing, it is clearer; there is more continuity in paragraphing and smoother transition. The loose construction is tightened thereby; and when necessary whole scenes, such as the glove buying episode in Gibraltar, or the Parisian tour conducted by a guide christened Ferguson, were newly contrived. In these, Twain was on the way to becoming a novelist, for he replaced the satirical humor at the narrator's expense--so prevalent in the letters--with detailed situations involving several characters who express themselves through dialogue. An air of reality is achieved as episodes are particularized and characters come to life. And in defense of San Francisco, be it said, not all of the passages needed revision; the description of the Parthenon by moonlight--one of the finest Twain ever wrote--was scarcely altered a word (*Innocents* 2: 54-57). Even if Twain's Western audience had been predominantly masculine, and the newly sought Eastern one greatly dominated by feminine taste, both could sometimes enjoy the same material.

When *Roughing It* appeared in 1872, Twain incorporated about one-third of the Sandwich Islands correspondence into it. Much of this text remains unchanged; in fact, the best passages in the Sandwich Islands sections of *Roughing It* were taken practically verbatim from the originals. Of course, Brown's crude humor disappears here, just as it did from *The Innocents Abroad*, but the descriptive passages and the observations on native character and custom were little changed. Though discarding about two-thirds of the letters, what Mark did carry over remained practically the same. By now Twain had achieved maturity of style, he addressed an audience on both sides of the Atlantic, and there was to be a steady progression until with *The Mysterious Stranger* even the colloquial was forsaken.

Though maturity of style was established with *The Innocents Abroad*, Twain frequently submitted manuscripts to Howells and Livy, generally with the result that they were improved. Twain was a Victorian, one who might indulge in an Elizabethan freedom of expression in his unpublished manuscripts, but who in print observed the conventions. And it was just as well that

he did; no editor would have wished to offend his readers, and
one need no more expect Mark Twain to write with the verbal
freedom of a Caldwell or Farrell than he might expect Robert
Browning to exercise the same realism as Chaucer. Though the
unpublished manuscripts of the Mark Twain Estate contain
lengthy discussions of sexual intercourse, revealing a very
un-Victorian frankness about its physical delight to women,
when he published, Twain wrote for his age--just as Chaucer and
Shakespeare wrote for theirs.

In a word, Twain wrote in the style best suited to his
audience. Yet there remained, always in abeyance, a natural
delight in rough humor; for as late as 1896, Twain wrote that
Bourget had charged him with preferring "the manure pile to
the violets" ("A Little Note" 181-86). That Twain sometimes
enjoyed a vulgar joke cannot be denied, but that he realized
the impropriety of bringing smoking-room humor into the drawing
room is equally evident. In brief, Twain had the good taste to
realize that a time and place exists for everything. It is
evidence of the inclusiveness of the man that his appreciation
ranged broadly from the fastidious to the bawdy, without, however, lacking the essential good taste to perceive which was
which. Many present-day readers find pleasure in these over-
flowings of the Victorian dikes of propriety; we frankly delight
in much that offended past sensibilities, even as our own taste
will perhaps amuse posterity.

Mark Twain's mature style is vivid, direct, and accurate,
for he disliked pretension in writing, even as he did in human
beings. Twain gives us clear and specific detail to convey
accurate description of person or place, an accuracy which
demanded American colloquial speech and dialect. Yet his prose,
simple, lucid, and graceful--if one looks beyond the dialect--
is the result of a conscious, literary effort. It was this
knowledge of the actual speech of America that influenced Ernest Hemingway to say, "... all modern American literature
comes from one book by Mark Twain called *Huckleberry Finn*"
(22). What lifts Twain's prose to the highest literary level
is not alone his vivid accuracy, but passages also of poetic
sense perceptions.

Twain's figurative language may take the form of a pretty
simile: "At half-eclipse the moon was like a gilded acorn in
its cup" (*Following the Equator* 1: 44) or it may be humorous:
"... the house was as empty as a beer closet in premises where
painters have been at work" (*The Mysterious Stranger* 323). But
in every instance a clear-cut impression is conveyed to the
reader, one imparting perception of beauty or causing the smile
of humor--and always precise. The changing style of Mark Twain
retained the humor, realism, and accuracy of the humorists of
the Old Southwest and the literary comedians of the Pacific

coast, but it went beyond them because its creator was an artist of rare perception, sensitive to beauty. When the author desires, there is a harmony between subject matter and manner that is compatible as nature; and when incongruity of manner and matter is introduced for comedy the art of disparity is quite as great. Mark Twain was an artist born, conditioned by environment, but potentially endowed to grow beyond his originals. Style is the man, and the style of Mark Twain contains those same qualities of truth, beauty, humor, and humanity that made Samuel Clemens great as a man.[13]

NOTES

1. Moore also believes that Cervantes influenced *The Innocents Abroad*, *Life on the Mississippi*, *Tom Sawyer*, and *A Connecticut Yankee* ("Mark Twain and Don Quixote" 324-46).

2. These traditions and superstitions, which West wisely distinguishes from those of Twain's early environment, appear largely in *Following the Equator*, *A Tramp Abroad*, *A Connecticut Yankee*, *The Prince and the Pauper*, and *Joan of Arc*.

3. Alan Gribben, in *Mark Twain's Library: A Reconstruction* (1980), lists several thousand books known to have been in Clemens' library. In addition there are numerous commentaries included, some extensive. Gribbens' book is highly useful for the study of Mark Twain's mind and art.

4. Bryant Morley French's *Mark Twain and the Gilded Age* (1965) is a comprehensive study of Clemens' collaboration with Charles Dudley Warner. French sees *The Gilded Age* as an early example of realism in American literature, a *roman à clef* with characters and incidents accurately drawn from the times.

5. To what extent Clemens drew his sources from life, of course, remains a lively issue. Walter Blair, in *Mark Twain and Huck Finn* (1960), for example, treats in detail the genesis, composition, publication, reception, and popularity of *Huckleberry Finn*. While including a perceptive analysis of Clemens as a creative artist from 1876 through 1883, Blair contends that visits to France, Germany, and England; involvements in political battles of the postwar era; and a hectic business career all shaped *Huckleberry Finn* in vital ways. A similar contention exists in *Mark Twain on the Damned Human Race* (1962), a collection of Clemens' most pessimistic topical writings on aggression, imperialism, and exploitation in the United States, Spain, France, Italy, the Belgian Congo, Imperial

Russia, and England. Edited by Janet Smith and containing
an introduction by Maxwell Geismar, *Mark Twain on the Damned
Human Race* is ultimately about how Twain's personal observations and his reading of history made their way into everything
he wrote.

On the other hand, the sources need not be from the life
of a cosmopolitan. *Mark Twain's Hannibal, Huck and Tom* (1969),
edited by Walter Blair, is a collection of previously unpublished manuscripts about what has come to be known as the
Matter of Hannibal. Blair's effort is to document Twain's
adult preoccupation with his childhood, including the years
on the river as apprentice and pilot. After Twain's calamities,
contends Blair, he needed to return to a less complicated world,
and the result was a renewed effort to recreate Hannibal. In
The Innocent Eye: Childhood in Mark Twain's Imagination (1961),
Albert E. Stone, Jr., also examines Twain's return to childhood. Hawthorne's "The Gentle Boy" (1832), says Stone, "may
be taken as a landmark in a new literary genre" (viii). After
the Civil War all major American novelists followed Hawthorne's
example, and Mark Twain, who "devoted a career to writing about
childhood" (ix), stood at the center of this literary development. Stone accounts for the theme of childhood throughout the
Twain canon, but the significant thing about Stone's book is
that he sees Twain conducting a search similar to that conducted by Melville, a search which led him from maturity back into
youth, from the man to the child. Although Stone views Twain's
"boy's-life" material as part of a larger interest in the romantic image of childhood, his explanation of how Twain used
the mask of childhood to view "the matter of Adam" is, in fact,
another explanation of how Twain drew sources from life.

6. Fred W. Lorch points out ten parallel passages to show
how Clemens substitutes direct expression for the florid style
of R.A. Smith's *Philadelphia as It Is in 1852* ("Mark Twain's
Philadelphia Letters in the Muscatine *Journal*" 348-51).

7. One of the most thorough and convincing of recent
studies on structure in *Life on the Mississippi* is that of
Horst H. Kruse, *Mark Twain and Life on the Mississippi* (1981).
Admitting that Twain had difficulty in completing *Life on the
Mississippi*, Kruse, however, rejects the usual notion that the
second part of the book is a failure. On the contrary, he contends, Twain was able to continue the narrative he had begun;
he simply "conceived and designed it [part two] as a comple-
ment and in such a way that both parts together should result
in the standard work he had intended *Life on the Mississippi*
to be from its inception" (130).

8. In *Twentieth Century Interpretations of Adventures of
Huckleberry Finn* (1968), Claude M. Simpson, the editor, has

collected some of the best essays available on the structure
and meaning of *Huckleberry Finn*. Especially useful for the
undergraduate student engaged in research on *Huckleberry Finn*,
and especially valuable to students enrolled in colleges and
universities with limited library facilities, *Twentieth Century Interpretations of Adventures of Huckleberry Finn* includes
a chronology of important dates and a selected bibliography.

   9. For a detailed study of structure in *The Mysterious
Stranger*, three books appear to be indispensable: John S.
Tuckey, *Mark Twain and Little Satan: The Writing of the Mysterious Stranger* (1963); John S. Tuckey, ed., *Mark Twain's
The Mysterious Stranger and the Critics* (1968); and William M.
Gibson, ed., *Mark Twain's Mysterious Stranger Manuscripts*
(1969). The conclusions reached by Gibson are largely those
reached by Tuckey, and the gist of the matter is this: Because
The Mysterious Stranger is the most important literary creation
of the later period, it is essential to understanding the later
life and work of Twain. Three versions of the mysterious
stranger story, in Twain's handwriting, existed when he died in
1910. Having named and catalogued the three versions, Bernard
DeVoto died before he could write a book on Twain's writing of
the manuscripts, and the result was that uncertainty remained
over "the direction and tendency" of drafts that Twain left.
DeVoto thought Twain wrote the "Hannibal" version first, the
"Print Shop" version next, and the "Eseldorf" version last,
but when *The Mysterious Stranger* was published, six years after
Twain died, the editors, Albert Bigelow Paine and Frederick
Duneka, based it on the "Eseldorf" version and added a chapter
Paine found among Mark Twain's papers. Tuckey contends that
DeVoto's assumptions about the various versions were wrong,
and that the chronology is the reverse of what DeVoto supposed.
Thus Paine and Duneka published the wrong version of *The Mys-
terious Stranger* and in doing so misrepresented Mark Twain's
intentions.

   10. This second series of Snodgrass letters was first discovered by Minnie Brashear, who reprinted one and described
three others (*Mark Twain, Son of Missouri* 180-92). Six additional letters were later discovered by Ernest Leisy, who
edited the entire series, *The Letters of Quintus Curtius Snodgrass*.

   11. The version copied from the *Enterprise* by the San Francisco *Bulletin*, October 31, 1863, is probably verbatim. The
later one, given to us by Paine, shows emendations. In "My
Bloody Massacre," *Sketches New and Old*, Mark adds some touches
not found in the original.

   12. For a full study of Clemens' efforts to achieve a more

polite expression see Leon T. Dickinson ("Mark Twain's Revisions in Writing *The Innocents Abroad*" 139-57).

13. In the last twenty-five years much has been written
about the evolution of Mark Twain as a writer in terms of
structure, humor, and style.   In his excellent book *Mark
Twain and Southwestern Humor* (1959), for example, Kenneth S.
Lynn contends that Southwestern humor arose out of conflict
and resulted in two radically different styles in an effort
to account for tension between what is (realism) and what
should be (romanticism).   Lynn's book is an attempt to record
how Twain handled that tension.   On the other hand Franklin
R. Rogers, in *Mark Twain's Burlesque Patterns* (1960), sees
burlesque at the center of Twain's art.   As Fielding, Jane
Austen, and Thackeray moved from burlesque to the writing of
fiction, says Rogers, so did Twain.   Rogers traces Twain's
growth as a literary artist through three stages to prove that
his structural patterns derived from burlesque.   Pascal
Covici, Jr., in *Mark Twain's Humor* (1962), takes a slightly
different tack.   Twain, argues Covici, transcended the humor
of the Old Southwest, and when he did humor became a technique
rather than an end in itself.   One of the most effective forms
of humor used by Twain was the hoax: "Twain's humor at its
core is organized around the hoax which operates to reveal to
ourselves the discrepancy between what we assume we are and
what we are in truth" (182).   Twain is seriously concerned with
the problems of existence, contends Covici, and the hoax "takes
one to the center of Twain's thought" (216).   James M. Cox,
in *Mark Twain: The Fate of Humor* (1966), uses still a different approach.   Twain's humor did not exist for the sake of
seriousness, says Cox; it always evaded seriousness and reverence.   Clemens created Mark Twain for the purpose of "investing
the world with an absurd humanity" (12) to reveal the discrepancy
between illusion and reality, and he ended by finding the world
more absurd than he had ever dreamed.

Mark Twain's Satires and Burlesques (1967), edited by
Franklin R. Rogers, follows the contentions in *Mark Twain's
Burlesque Patterns* concerning the evolution from burlesque to
accomplished works of art.   According to Rogers, Twain early
created a fictional world, using Hannibal as its basis, and
his village world was essential to correcting injustices in
the actual world.   In demonstrating Twain's evolution from
writer of burlesque to writer of serious fiction, Rogers examines twelve previously unpublished Twain pieces.   Finally,
David E.E. Sloane, in *Mark Twain as a Literary Comedian* (1979),
examines possible influences on Mark Twain's development as a
humorist.   In addition to humor of the Old Southwest, Sloane
sees influences of British and Irish humor as well as humor of

the Northeast. But Twain, argues Sloane, borrowed extensively from a tradition of literary humor which informed his
writing with social viewpoints of the 1850–1870 era: "To deny
the significance of the tradition of literary comedy in the
development of the Twain canon ... is to deny most of the
ethical and social basis of his philosophy" (195).

WORKS CITED

Blair, Walter. *Mark Twain and Huck Finn*. Berkeley: U. of
    California Press, 1960. A monumental work of critical
    scholarship.

————. *Native American Humor*. New York: American, 1937.
    Excellent discussion of Twain in relation to our native
    traditions in frontier humor.

————. "On the Structure of *Tom Sawyer*." *Modern Philology*
    37 (1939): 75–88. One of the most important treatments of
    Twain's art.

Branch, Edgar M. "Chronological Bibliography." *American
    Literature* 18 (1946): 113–14.

————. "The Two Providences: Thematic Form in *Huckleberry
    Finn*." *College English* 11 (1950): 188–95. Illuminating
    study of form and thought.

Brashear, Minnie. *Mark Twain, Son of Missouri*. Chapel Hill:
    U. of North Carolina Press, 1934.

Browne, J. Ross. *Yusef*. New York: Harper & Brothers, 1853.

Buxbaum, Katherine. "Mark Twain and American Dialect."
    American Speech 2 (1927): 233–36. Reveals the vigor of
    Twain's dialect.

Carkeet, David. "The Dialects in *Huckleberry Finn*." *American
    Literature* 51 (1979): 315–32. A fine analysis.

Covici, Pascal, Jr. *Mark Twain's Humor: The Image of a World*.
    Dallas: Southern Methodist U. Press, 1962. Contends that
    for Twain humor became a technique and not an end in it-
    self.

Cox, James M. *Mark Twain: The Fate of Humor*. Princeton:
    Princeton U. Press, 1966. Traces the forms of Twain's humor
    from the beginning to the end of his career.

DeVoto, Bernard. *Mark Twain's America*. Boston: Little, Brown,
    1935. Traces the frontier influence. Important.

————. *Mark Twain at Work*. Cambridge: Harvard U. Press, 1942. Important contribution.

Dickinson, Leon T. "Mark Twain's Revisions in Writing *The Innocents Abroad*." *American Literature* 19 (1947): 139–57. Reveals Twain's revisions as he made the *Alta* letters into a book.

Eliot, T.S. Introduction. *The Adventures of Huckleberry Finn*. By Mark Twain. New York: Chanticleer, 1950. vii–xvi.

Feinstein, George. "Mark Twain's Idea of Story Structure." *American Literature* 18 (1946): 160–63. Shows individualized form of Twain.

Ferguson, DeLancey. *Mark Twain: Man and Legend*. Indianapolis: Bobbs–Merrill, 1943.

Fiske, Samuel. *Mr. Dunn Browne's Experiences in Foreign Parts*. Boston: Jewett, 1857.

French, Bryant Morley. *Mark Twain and the Gilded Age: The Book that Named an Era*. Dallas: Southern Methodist U. Press, 1965. Full treatment of the Clemens–Warner novel.

Fussell, E.S. "The Structural Problem of *The Mysterious Stranger*." *Studies in Philology* 49 (1952): 95–104. Discusses Twain's attempt to reconcile his humanitarian feeling for the individual with his philosophy.

Gribben, Alan. *Mark Twain's Library: A Reconstruction*. 2 vols. Boston: G.K. Hall, 1980.

Hawthorne, Nathaniel. "The Gentle Boy." *The Token*. Ed. Samuel G. Goodrich. Baltimore: Goodrich, 1832. 193–240. *The Token* was a gift annual.

Hemingway, Ernest. *The Green Hills of Africa*. New York: Scribner's, 1935.

Holmes, Oliver Wendell. *The Autocrat of the Breakfast Table*. 1900. Rpt. New York: Heritage, 1955.

Johnson, Merle. *A Bibliography of the Works of Mark Twain, Samuel Langhorne Clemens. A List of First Editions in Book Form and of First Printings in Periodicals and Occasional Publications of His Varied Literary Activities*. New York: Harper & Brothers, 1935.

Kipling, Rudyard. *From Sea to Sea*. 2 vols. New York: Doubleday, 1899.

Kruse, Horst H. *Mark Twain and Life on the Mississippi*. Amherst: U. of Massachusetts Press, 1981. Exhaustive account of the genesis of *Life on the Mississippi*.

Lewis, Oscar. *The Origin of the Celebrated Jumping Frog of Calaveras County*. San Francisco: Book Club of California, 1931.

Long, E. Hudson. "Sut Lovingood and Mark Twain's *Joan of Arc*." *Modern Language Notes* 64 (1949): 37-39. Shows that George W. Harris' yarn "Sicily Burns' Wedding" was used in Chapter Thirty-Six of *Joan of Arc*.

Lorch, Fred W. "Mark Twain's Philadelphia Letters in the Muscatine *Journal*." *American Literature* 17 (1946): 348-51.

Lynn, Kenneth S. *Mark Twain and Southwestern Humor*. Boston: Little, Brown, 1959. Sees Twain as a conscious and deliberate artist deriving from an artistic tradition of humor.

McKeithan, D.M. "Mark Twain's *Tom Sawyer Abroad* and Jules Verne's *Five Weeks in a Balloon*." University of Texas *Studies in English* 28 (1949): 257-70. Points out a number of similarities.

Miller, Michael G. "Geography and Structure in *Huckleberry Finn*." *Studies in the Novel* 12 (1980): 192-209. Maps the raft journey.

Moore, Olin H. "Mark Twain and Don Quixote." *PMLA* 37 (1922): 324-46. Traces supposed influence of Cervantes.

Paine, Albert Bigelow. *Mark Twain: A Biography*. 4 vols. New York: Harper & Brothers, 1912. Indispensable for the study of Twain as an artist.

Pellowe, William C.S. *Mark Twain: Pilgrim from Hannibal*. New York: Hobson, 1945.

Rogers, Franklin R. *Mark Twain's Burlesque Patterns as Seen in the Novels and Narratives 1855-1885*. Dallas: Southern Methodist U. Press, 1960. Examines the place of literary burlesque in the evolution of Twain as a writer.

Rourke, Constance. *American Humor, a Study of the National Character*. New York: Harcourt, Brace, 1931. Relates Twain to the native tradition.

Sherman, Stuart P. "Mark Twain." *The Cambridge History of American Literature*. Ed. William Peterfield Trent, et al. 4 vols. New York: Putnam's, 1921. 3: 1-20. Contains a good estimate of Twain's place in literature at the time.

Simpson, Claude M., ed. *Twentieth Century Interpretations of Adventures of Huckleberry Finn: A Collection of Critical Essays*. Englewood Cliffs: Prentice-Hall, 1968. Essays addressing the major critical and textual issues concerning *Huckleberry Finn*.

Sloane, David E.E. *Mark Twain as a Literary Comedian*. Baton Rouge: Louisiana State U. Press, 1979. Examines possible influences on Twain's development as a humorist.

Stone, Albert E. *The Innocent Eye: Childhood in Mark Twain's Imagination*. New Haven: Yale U. Press, 1961. Explores Twain's uses of the mind of a child as an ideal mask for art.

Trilling, Lionel. Introduction. *The Adventures of Huckleberry Finn*. By Mark Twain. New York: Rinehart, 1948. v–xviii.

Tuckey, John S. *Mark Twain and Little Satan: The Writing of The Mysterious Stranger*. West Lafayette: Purdue U. Studies, 1963. Analyzes genesis of *The Mysterious Stranger*.

————, ed. *Mark Twain's The Mysterious Stranger and the Critics*. Belmont: Wadsworth, 1968.

Twain, Mark [Samuel Langhorne Clemens]. *The Adventures of Huckleberry Finn*. New York: Harper & Brothers, 1918.

————. *The Adventures of Thomas Jefferson Snodgrass*. Ed. Charles Honce. Chicago: Covici, 1928.

————. *The Adventures of Tom Sawyer*. New York: Harper & Brothers, 1922.

————. *A Connecticut Yankee in King Arthur's Court*. New York: Harper & Brothers, 1917.

————. *Following the Equator*. 2 vols. New York: Harper & Brothers, 1925.

————. *The Innocents Abroad*. 2 vols. New York: Harper & Brothers, 1911.

————. *Joan of Arc*. 2 vols. New York: Harper & Brothers, 1924.

————. *The Letters of Quintus Curtius Snodgrass*. Ed. Ernest E. Leisy. Dallas: Southern Methodist U. Press, 1946.

————. *Life on the Mississippi*. New York: Harper & Brothers, 1917.

————. "A Little Note to Paul Bourget." *In Defense of Harriet Shelley*. New York: Harper & Brothers, 1925. 181–86.

————. *The Love Letters of Mark Twain*. Ed. Dixon Wecter. New York: Harper & Brothers, 1949.

————. *Mark Twain in Eruption: Hitherto Unpublished Pages about Men and Events*. Ed. Bernard DeVoto. New York: Harper & Brothers, 1940.

————. *Mark Twain on the Damned Human Race.* Ed. Janet Smith. New York: Hill and Wang, 1962.

————. *Mark Twain's Autobiography.* Ed. Albert Bigelow Paine. 2 vols. New York: Harper & Brothers, 1924.

————. *Mark Twain's Hannibal, Huck and Tom.* Ed. Walter Blair. Berkeley: U. of California Press, 1969.

————. *Mark Twain's Letters.* Ed. Albert Bigelow Paine. 2 vols. New York: Harper & Brothers, 1917.

————. *Mark Twain's Letters from the Sandwich Islands.* Ed. G. Ezra Dane. Stanford: Stanford U. Press, 1938.

————. *Mark Twain's Letters in the Muscatine Journal.* Ed. Edgar M. Branch. Chicago: Mark Twain Association of America, 1942.

————. *Mark Twain's Letters to Will Bowen, "My First, & Oldest & Dearest Friend."* Austin: U. of Texas, 1941.

————. *Mark Twain's Mysterious Stranger Manuscripts.* Ed. William M. Gibson. Berkeley: U. of California Press, 1969. Analyzes manuscripts in relation to the text of *The Mysterious Stranger*.

————. *Mark Twain's Notebook.* New York: Harper & Brothers, 1935. A storehouse of information about Twain's mind and art.

————. *Mark Twain's Satires and Burlesques.* Ed. Franklin R. Rogers. Berkeley: U. of California Press, 1967. Examines Twain's evolution from writer of burlesques to writer of accomplished works of art.

————. "My Bloody Massacre." *Sketches New and Old.* New York: Harper & Brothers, 1917. 293-97.

————. *The Mysterious Stranger.* New York: Harper & Brothers, 1922.

————. *The Prince and the Pauper.* New York: Harper & Brothers, 1909.

————. *Pudd'nhead Wilson.* New York: Harper & Brothers, 1922.

————. *Roughing It.* 2 vols. New York: Harper & Brothers, 1913.

————. *Tom Sawyer Abroad.* New York: Harper & Brothers, 1917.

————. *A Tramp Abroad.* 2 vols. New York: Harper & Brothers, 1921.

————. *The Washoe Giant in San Francisco*. Ed. Franklin
Walker. San Francisco: Fields, 1938.

Twain, Mark and Bret Harte. *Sketches of the Sixties*. Ed. John
Howell. San Francisco: Howell, 1926. Rev. 1927.

Twain, Mark and Charles Dudley Warner. *The Gilded Age*. 2
vols. New York: Harper & Brothers, 1915.

Wagenknecht, Edward. *Mark Twain: The Man and His Work*. New
Haven: Yale U. Press, 1935. Important examination of
Twain's mind and work.

Walker, Franklin. "An Influence from San Francisco on Mark
Twain's *The Gilded Age*." *American Literature* 8 (1936):
63-66. Actual experiences of Laura D. Fair which parallel
those of Laura Hawkins in this book.

Wecter, Dixon. "Mark Twain." *Literary History of the United
States*. Ed. Robert E. Spiller, et al. 2 vols. New York:
Macmillan, 1948. 2: 917-39.

West, Victor R. *Folklore in the Works of Mark Twain*. Studies
in Language, Literature and Criticism 10. Lincoln: U. of
Nebraska, 1930.

Williams, Mentor L. "Mark Twain's *Joan of Arc*." *Michigan
Alumnus Quarterly Review* 54 (1948): 243-50. Important
study of the sources.

Chapter 5

FUNDAMENTAL IDEAS

Though Mark Twain was fully aware of his deficiencies in
formal learning, he nevertheless seems to have taken himself
seriously as a "philosopher." An early tendency to moralize
appears in his subeditor writings at Hannibal; before leaving
San Francisco he was introduced as "The Moralist of the Main";
satire mingles with moralizing as his work matures, until
finally we have the expounding of his "Gospel" in *What Is Man?*
Lacking any inclination to be the founder of a definitely
formalized system of thought, having none of the mystical approach, Twain perhaps does not deserve the title of philosopher
at all. Yet if to reason upon the purpose of man in this universe, to ponder the question of his existence and the meaning
of life, entities one to be called *thinker*, then surely Mark
Twain was that.[1]

The questions engaging Twain, however, were ethical, moral,
and practical rather than mystical, speculative, or dialectical. Growing up in a religious household in a religious community, where the law-abiding were in the majority, Clemens'
early religious beliefs came from a normal, healthy background, which as readers of *Tom Sawyer* may perceive, included
fun, play, and amusement. Hannibal valued religion as a guide
to life, not as speculative theology, and if one were a true
Christian his acts would show it.[2] If Sam's father embraced
"village-lawyer agnosticism," bequeathing to his son the
"will to disbelieve," never at any time did he reject Christian ethics. On the contrary, his ethical character seems to
have been transmitted to the future author, who had in his
father an example of high ideals and morality. It was not the
ethics of Christianity, then, nor the purpose of Christ that
Twain was later to assail, but actually the superstitions and
dogmas that may accompany any religion. For the code of Christ
Clemens had nothing save reverence, and for those who lived by
it nought but admiration and respect. But he reserved the
privilege to determine his own personal habits and tastes.
In other words, the code by which Samuel Clemens lived partook

of the philosophy of John Stuart Mill: "The only freedom which deserves the name, is that of pursuing our own good in our own way, so long as we do not attempt to deprive others of theirs, or impede their efforts to obtain it" (*On Liberty* 18).

Yet for those who admired Christian ethics and who held to their high standards Twain felt comradeship. The many clergymen who were his friends understood his nature and furnished him spiritual and intellectual companionship. Though reared in the Sunday school, Sam Clemens, with the example of his father before him, was too skeptical to accept a fundamentalist interpretation of the Scriptures. There was, moreover, the subsequent influence of the Scotchman named Macfarlane, who had anticipated Darwin's theory, and whose conclusions left their impress upon Clemens for life (Paine 1: 115).[3] At the fundamentalist then, at the God of the Old Testament, Twain uttered impieties. Twain inherited, also, the spontaneous irreverence of the frontier, an irreverence so natural it could become all-embracing.

The frontier, deep down under, had an immature dislike of authority and restraint; ministers and schoolteachers, as well as law enforcement officers, fell into this category. Not Sut Lovingood and Simon Suggs alone indulged in acts toward the clergy of prodigious disrespect, for the humor of the Old Southwest abounds with examples of this attitude. Along with the skepticism of his father, Samuel Clemens inherited, then, this impious attitude as part of his regional environment, acquiring it by a kind of frontier osmosis. And he never outgrew it. But his disregard was not really for the cloth, for Joseph Twichell remained as valued a friend as Twain ever had.

As already indicated, Twain's dislike was not for the ethics of the Christian faith, but for what he regarded as ignorance and superstition. He had once wondered if God were actually aware of man's existence at all. And, moreover, he could not countenance man's reducing the greatness of God to the level of triviality by talking about "special providence" for himself, a belief he felt gave man a position of too extreme importance. Indeed, he had never accepted the Bible as a guide to spiritual salvation, for large portions of it seemed nothing more than fables and mythology. To Livy, who insisted upon Bible readings during the early days of their marriage, he declared that much of it contradicted his reason. It was not the idea of God that he resisted, but the Old Testament account, which he felt distorted a grand and noble concept.

His belief in a "just and fair" God was not constant; for the "hell" that man lives in "from the cradle to the grave" assumed larger proportions in Twain's thinking as his personal adversities increased. Twain stated his convictions about Christ in a letter to Orion: "Neither Howells nor I believe in

hell or the divinity of the Savior, but no matter, the Savior
is none the less a sacred Personage, and a man should have no
desire or disposition to refer to him lightly, profanely, or
otherwise than with the profoundest reverence" (*Letters* 1:
323). Neither did he desire to mock at any sincere expression
of religious faith, such for instance as prayer. Yet his
honesty precluded any pretense on his part, leading him once
to confess to Twichell that he did not believe the Bible to
be inspired by God.[4]

So profound was Clemens' belief in a larger God than the
one of the Old Testament, in a greater mind governing the
immutable laws of time and change, that eventually he converted
his wife. In his philosophy the individual became merely a
unit in the larger scheme of life--if at all times he remained
even that--a belief which destroyed all illusions of a personal
God. Nevertheless, Twain insisted upon a divine spirit. "No
one who thinks can imagine the universe made by chance," he
once observed. "It is too nicely assembled and regulated.
There is, of course, a great Master Mind, but it cares nothing
for our happiness or our unhappiness" (qtd. in Paine 4: 1353).
Declaring the Old Testament portrait of a wrathful God to be
merely "a portrait of a man, if one can imagine a man with
evil impulses far beyond the human limit," Clemens found it
"the most damnatory biography that ever found its way into
print" (qtd. in Paine 4: 1354).

As Mark grew older he became increasingly preoccupied with
evil in the universe; of that he was as acutely conscious as
Hawthorne or Melville. And in his gropings for an answer he
came, more and more, to disparage whatever creative force might
be blamed; he declared at the same time that regret filled his
mind over the lip service which alone was so often paid to the
teachings of Christ. Yet he often talked with his biographer
about the unseen forces of creation, those immutable laws
holding the planets to their courses and bringing the seasons
with their miracles of diversity and beauty. Such Twain designated "The Great Law," whose principle seemed to be unity, and
whose outward expression was revealed in the beauties of nature.
As to the moral laws from which the legal laws governing man's
conduct are devised, Clemens expressed belief that they came in
no manner from the Deity but were "the outcome of the world's
experience" (qtd. in Paine 4: 1583).[5]

His final statement on immortality, however, is revealed
indirectly at the time of Livy's fatal illness. With remorse
at having destroyed her own faith, Clemens wrote his wife,
"Dear, dear sweetheart, I have been thinking & examining, &
searching & analyzing, for many days, & am vexed to find that
I more believe in the immortality of the soul than misbelieve
in it" (*Love Letters* 344). As expected her reply was one of

pleasure. The clue to his actual convictions, however, appears penciled on the back of the envelope containing Livy's letter: "In the bitterness of death it was G.W.'s chiefest solace that he had never told a lie except this one" (*Love Letters* 345).

As Twain aged, however, and as the human race continued its course toward two destructive world catastrophes, blasphemous convictions grew that God was not good but wicked. Indeed, he came to blame God for all disease, pestilence, crime, and war. For instance, Twain took the housefly, disease carrier of filth, to charge that the Creator of the universe was not kind or good, but really man's enemy, devising this affliction to bring upon the human race ill health and death. Thus in the darkness of despair we find him actually going back to the wrathful, vengeful God of the Old Testament he had so often repudiated as a myth.

Yet it would seem that Mark Twain rejected the idea of the divine inspiration of the Scriptures and the divinity of Christ; he rejected all belief in special providences; he rejected as fables or myths the ideas of hell, Satan, and a heaven of harp-playing angels. But he did believe in God as a "Larger Law" governing the universe and all that is in it. Ethically he was a Christian; for truth, honor, and lofty ideals were the fabric of his character. No one ever held a greater admiration for the ideals of Christianity than Twain, nor ever felt more remorse when those principles were degraded.

Mark Twain's political views were closely allied with his concept of Christian ethics.[6] Though frequently active on behalf of good government, Clemens was himself entirely without political ambition. And when an editorial writer suggested that Twain, "the greatest man of his day in private life," merited consideration as a presidential candidate, Twain did not even offer the encouragement of a jest (Paine 3: 1201). Yet since the days when he had attacked municipal corruption on the coast, Twain had worked for good government. It was the good of the nation that he sought, not the entrenchment of any political faction. To Howells he wrote in 1884, "It is not *parties* that make or save countries or that build them to greatness—it is clean men, clean ordinary citizens, rank and file, the masses" (*Letters* 2: 445). Clemens, moreover, practiced his own preaching in politics.

With a firm belief that the duty of every citizen was first of all to "his own honor," loyalty to his country coming second, and the party last, Twain outlined a plan for a "Casting-Vote party"; it would nominate no candidates but support the better man nominated by either the Democrats or Republicans, thereby forcing the two major parties to select men of honest purpose. For those who felt that their loyalty was

to a party, first and last, Twain stated, "I prefer to be a
citizen of the United States" (*Notebook* 203). He felt that
independence of mind was a personal privilege, and Clemens
echoed the sentiments of Thoreau that he alone could determine
what was patriotic for himself.

The intimate relationship between Twain's politics and his
devotion to Christian ethics is made clear in the following
passage:

> A man can be a Christian *or* a patriot, but he can't
> legally be a Christian *and* a patriot—except in the
> usual way: one of the two with the mouth, the other with
> the heart. The spirit of Christianity proclaims the
> brotherhood of the race and the meaning of that strong
> word has not been left to guesswork, but made tremendously
> definite....
>
> The spirit of patriotism in its nature jealous and
> selfish, is just in man's line, it comes natural to him—
> he can live up to all its requirements to the letter;
> but the spirit of Christianity is not in its entirety
> possible to him. (*Notebook* 332-33)

Twain was opposed to violence, a believer in law and
order in contrast to unreason and emotion, and he thought all
cruelty should be punished. Believing that right should appropriate might, that the weak need protection against the
strong, Twain looked upon the rising labor unions, such as
the Knights of Labor, as equalizing power between the forces
of capital and the workers. To Howells he sent an essay ex-
tolling the unionized workman as "the greatest birth of the
greatest age the nations of the world have known," one who
"has before him the most righteous work that was ever given
into the hands of man to do; and he will do it" (qtd. in Paine
3: 850). In this opinion Twain did not change, for in the year
of his death he defended unions as "the only means by which
the workman could obtain recognition of his rights" (Paine 4:
1557).

And the Connecticut Yankee conversing in the realm of
Arthur told the working men that the laborer should have something to say about his wages, for a day will come, he foretold,
when "... all of a sudden the wage-earner will consider that a
couple of thousand years or so is enough of this one-sided sort
of thing; and he will rise up and take a hand in fixing his
wages himself. Ah, he will have a long and bitter account of
wrong and humiliation to settle" (*Connecticut Yankee* 332).[7]

In his autobiographical papers Twain spoke of what he
termed "constitutional monarchy, with the Republican party
sitting on the throne." It is clear that Mark Twain abhorred
"monarchy," as he styled "dictatorship," and though he does

not seem to have considered the idea of any absolute rule by
the proletariat--only that of an oligarchy or plutocracy--he
does have this to say on the economics of communism:

> Communism is idiocy. They want to divide up the
> property. Suppose they did it. It requires brains to
> keep money as well as to make it. In a precious little
> while the money would be back in the former owner's
> hands and the communist would be poor again. The
> division would have to be remade every three years or
> it would do the communist no good. (qtd. in Paine 2:
> 644)

Twain's politics thus takes human nature into account;
and while Mark was concerned with economic betterment for the
masses, he was also passionately devoted to the ideal of freedom. When the Spanish-American War opened, Clemens wrote to
Joe Twichell:

> I have never enjoyed a war--even in written history--
> as I am enjoying this one. For this is the worthiest
> one that was ever fought, so far as my knowledge goes.
> It is a worthy thing to fight for one's freedom; it is
> another sight finer to fight for another man's. And
> I think this is the first time it has been done. (*Let-
> ters* 2: 663)

But jubilation was to change quickly to despair as he watched
the war for freedom appear in its true guise of imperialism
and exploitation. Like Emerson, Twain was never frightened
by the hobgoblin of foolish consistency, and he now denounced
this "wanton war and a robbing expedition" (qtd. in Paine 3:
1165).

Indeed, as the new century dawned Twain looked about with
bitterness. All about him in New York was municipal corruption, war raged in South Africa, American troops were conquer-
ing the Philippines, Leopold of Belgium was coercing natives
in the Congo, and most of the Christian powers were fighting
the Chinese for trade rights. Twain was angered, disappointed,
and embittered by betrayal in so many ways of all Christian
principles. The fact that bad as our imperialism was, that
of Russia and Germany was even worse, furnished small consolation.[8]

It was monarchy, or as we say, "dictatorship" that Twain
detested; to remove that, to set up a truly democratic republic, he felt the remedy for political woes. And he so frequently particularized the evils of a system in an individual.
Just as it was the Czar who drew his wrath, so was it "Boss"
Croker that he denounced, and Cecil Rhodes of whom he wrote,
"I admire him, I frankly confess it; and when his time comes

I shall buy a piece of the rope for a keepsake" (*Following the Equator* 2: 378).

With interest in the individual went an insistence upon personal independence; regretting the misuse so often made of the idea of "loyalty" Twain stated in a note made while writing *A Connecticut Yankee*:

> The first thing I want to teach is *disloyalty*, till they get used to disusing that word *loyalty* as representing a virtue. This will beget independence--which is loyalty to one's best self and principles, and this is often disloyalty to the general idols and fetishes. (*Notebook* 199)[9]

Yet Twain knew the price that one must pay for insisting upon freedom of thought for himself in any age and any clime.

Clemens, as his own actions show, valued this independence greatly, placing it above purely physical benefits, though he realized the importance of the latter. We find him saying, "That government is not best which best secures mere life and property--there is a more valuable thing--manhood" (*Notebook* 210). And in another place Twain records that only in independence does he find "spiritual comfort and a peace of mind quite above price" (*Autobiography* 2: 15).

Like Whitman and Melville, Mark Twain was a democrat; he was not a leveler. Moreover, his conception of democracy embodied a firm insistence on the rights of others, minorities included. Thus indignation mingled with shame for the human race when he once reported, "As I write, news comes that in broad daylight in San Francisco, some boys have stoned an inoffensive Chinaman to death, and that although a large crowd witnessed the shameful deed, no one interfered" (*Roughing It* 2: 105-06).

And along with this humanity went an utter contempt for snobbery. During his Buffalo days of writing for the *Galaxy* Twain heard that the Reverend Talmage, an immensely popular minister, had preached against the right of workingmen to attend service at fashionable churches. Twain immediately spoke for human justice, suggesting that the minister in question would have objected to the original twelve disciples because "... he could not have stood the fishy smell of some of his comrades who came from around the Sea of Galilee" (qtd. in Paine 2: 405).

Clemens' democracy, like his politics, derived largely from Christian ethics. His chief objection to monarchy was the advantage given the fortunate, aversion to an artificial system requiring "the misery of the many for the happiness of the few, the cold and hunger and overworking of the useful that the useless may live in luxury and idleness" (*Notebook*

197). And Twain's democracy was more than a matter of theory;
it was something to practice, as at the funeral of his coachman, Patrick McAleer, when Clemens was asked to serve as pallbearer with his old gardener (*Autobiography* 2: 202). Always
there is insistence by Mark Twain upon the worth of the individual, regardless of race, creed, or station.

Yet in essence the democracy of Mark Twain was more that
of Shakespeare and Chaucer, the similarity being that each
realized he was but human. Like the Whitman who sang the song
of mankind as his own, Clemens said, "... in myself I find in
big or little proportion every quality and every defect that
is findable in the mass of the race" (*Eruption* xxix). So
great was his humility in this regard that he even enrolled
himself among the cowards and fools.[10]

His democracy, moreover, was essentially that of the
natural gentleman. "Good breeding," Twain tells us humorously, "consists in concealing how much we think of ourselves
and how little we think of the other person." But circumstances
of environment and heredity are not ignored. Though born without wealth, a self-made man in every detail of the American
success story, Samuel Clemens was never an inverted snob of
the kind which dislikes wealth, social position, and their
holders, per se. Rather we find him calmly evaluating each
person individually for his spiritual, moral, and intellectual
worth. In *Huckleberry Finn*, Jim, through those natural qualities of kindness, generosity, and consideration for others,
so evident in his concern for Huck, rises to a natural dignity
commanding our respect. Here on the raft a black slave and a
white outcast enacted an everlasting drama of democracy in
practice. Like Burns, Twain looked beyond externals to perceive the natural man. Here is the English concept of democracy, which has for so long been ours, that the individual by
his own worth and his opportunities may rise or fall in the
scale.

Twain, by early associations, was of the people himself,
but he valued the aristocratic tradition, something he never
attacked as he did royalty and plutocracy, because it was
based upon consideration, enlightenment, and good taste.
Naturally, Clemens abhorred any racial oppression or any other
unfair discrimination, for he judged each individual, regardless of all else, upon his own worth. He was opposed to anything destroying personal liberty or restricting the right to
improvement and progress. And he held no prejudices based on
the color of a person's skin; yet he seems ever the individualist, endorsing fair play and equal opportunity rather than
artificial forcing of equality. In his introduction to *The
Portable Mark Twain* Bernard DeVoto finds Twain's first importance in American literature to be the "democratizing effect

of his work" (25), reminding us that "Mark Twain was the first
great American writer who was also a popular writer" (26), and
pointing out moreover that Twain's democracy was both "impli-
cit and explicit." The books of Samuel Clemens were at once
great art and at the same time, as DeVoto claims, "... the
first American literature of the highest rank which portrays
the ordinary bulk of Americans, expresses them, accepts their
values, and delineates their hopes, fears, decencies, and in-
decencies as from within" (26).

Naturally Twain was interested in education as a means of
improving the human mind. The Yankee in Arthur's realm found
that the brightest intellect in the kingdom could not perceive
beyond the bounds of its knowledge. We find him saying, "Arguments have no chance against petrified training; they wear
it as little as the waves wear a cliff" (*Connecticut Yankee*
143). The only way then to combat ignorance and superstition
was through education. One should train in the right direction, which to Twain meant proper morality in one's relationships. In *What Is Man?* we are told, "Inestimably valuable is
training, influence, education, in right directions--*training
one's self-approbation to elevate its ideals*" (*What Is Man?* 9).
The importance of education in Twain's whole philosophical concept of man is here stated. Since each acts according to his
nature, seeking his own self-approval, then it becomes necessary to establish standards on a high ethical plane. Only by
education of the common mind can this be accomplished. While
granting that people with property generally have a greater
stake in the community than those with no material responsi-
bilities, Twain still tips the scales in the direction of
knowledge. "Learning goes usually with uprightness, broad
views, and humanity;" he tells us, "so the learned voters, possessing the balance of power, became the vigilant and efficient
protectors of the great lower rank of society" (*Curious Republic* 3-4).

Twain, we may repeat, saw no virtue in mere lack of wealth.
Yet he was never a materialist. It was, for instance, his
belief that the motto "In God We Trust" should be removed from
our coins because it "stated a lie." And to Andrew Carnegie
he said, "If this nation has ever trusted in God, that time
has gone by; for nearly half a century almost its entire trust
has been in the Republican party and the dollar--mainly the
dollar" (*Eruption* 50). Practicality, however, was never absent
from his thinking. For the most part Twain thought nobilities
are foolish, but as he recognized, "We have to worship these
things and their possessors, we are all born so and we cannot
help it.... In America we manifest this in all the ancient
and customary ways" (*Eruption* 64). In short, we worship money
and its possessors. In a letter to Twichell (1905) Twain de-

plored the lack of human advancement in matters of the heart
and mind, refusing to take comfort in mankind's colossal
material progress.

As he grew older Twain gradually developed a philosophy
of determinism based upon the concept of an inexorable chain
of events. He exists for us, therefore, not alone as a great
creative artist, but like Melville and Hawthorne in kinship
with serious thinkers who have concerned themselves with the
basic problems of man's destiny. Mark's idealism did not deny
evil as it did not deny the reality of life, a concept making
him alike the romanticist and idealist on one hand, the satirist and pessimist on the other. Thus Clemens could delight
naturally in material possessions, while at the same time
placing as high a value upon spirituality as the most abstract
philosopher. He saw no reason why physical comfort should
mean loss of soul. In fact, Twain took a broad view of life,
one based upon comprehension of the shrewd and vicious, the
stupid and gullible, the helpless and innocent, even as it
embraced the wise and noble. If Twain gradually transferred
his early distrust of the Creator to his creation, man, he
nevertheless continued to approach the problem of evil through
introspection. Pondering such problems as the ambiguity of
good and evil, how man's effort to do good, although well
meant, often produces evil, Mark Twain represents a philosophical and ethical maturity.

In seeking truth, Clemens felt compelled to account for
the fact that man is so often tragically afflicted. The
answer of Calvinism, the doctrine of original sin, was one
early rejected. Finally, as revealed by the unpublished papers
of his estate, Twain dropped the plummet deeper into the well
of speculation in search for a final sounding. Yet concern
over evil never remained purely philosophical with him, for
he held a practical, reforming interest. And because he con-
centrated on matters agitating him at the moment, he was often
led astray from the basic philosophical problem. Clemens,
moreover, sensitive by nature, was profoundly shocked because
civilization, which should have been a blessing, now appeared
an evil. His visit to the Sandwich Islands, like Melville's
sojourn in the South Seas, showed civilization bringing degradation, rather than spiritual improvement. In his personal
life, there was firsthand knowledge of human suffering and
cruelty, derived from his experiences on the river and in the
mining camps. Then, too, there were the family misfortunes--
loss of loved ones and financial disaster.

Twain speculated on the tragic flow of events; yet like
the Greek dramatists he sought the vulnerable crack in the
protagonist's armor that allowed fate to set the furies on
his track. There could be one's own guilt, his own fatal

determination or lack of it, which led Twain at first out of
natural humility to blame himself for his woes. Thinking,
then, on this problem, he evolved his own concept of evil in
the world, facing it with Promethean courage, a good warrior
to the end.

In a speech to the Monday Evening Club (1883) Clemens had
pointed out that selfishness may be of two kinds: "... brutal
and divine; that he who sacrifices others to himself exempli-
fies the first, whereas he who sacrifices himself for others
personifies the second--the divine contenting of his soul by
serving the happiness of his fellow-men" (Paine 2: 744). Because of misunderstanding of his philosophy, no doubt, Twain
made this clarification:

> Diligently train your ideals upward, and still upward
> toward a summit where you will find your chiefest
> pleasure in conduct which, while contenting you, will
> be sure to confer benefits upon your neighbor and the
> community. (qtd. in Paine 2: 744)

"The Facts Concerning the Recent Carnival of Crime in
Connecticut" (1876) had previously set forth Twain's ideas on
conscience, something which was to play so important a part in
Huckleberry Finn. In this paper, read before the Monday
Evening Club, Twain elaborated on the differences in individuals, showing how a good man with a weighty conscience might
suffer remorse for an innocent act, while a scoundrel might
commit crimes without a twinge. In this imaginary interview
between Clemens and his own conscience, the former complains:

> "Smith is the noblest man in all this section, and
> the purest; and yet is always breaking his heart because
> he cannot be good! Only a conscience *could* find pleasure
> in heaping agony upon a spirit like that." (*Tom Sawyer
> Abroad* 321)

His own conscience, indeed, plagued Samuel Clemens through
life. In *Huckleberry Finn* circumstance and temperament in
Huck produce a clash between sympathy and will to freedom,
on one hand, and custom and law, on the other; for in this
book conscience is the agent of law and custom, and it is only
when Huck rises superior to it that he wins the battle.

The interest in man's duality which had led Twain to publish "The Recent Carnival of Crime in Connecticut" continued
to influence his thoughts. January 7, 1897, found him attempt-
ing to account for the seeming presence of two persons in
each individual.[11] This duality meant the presence in each
"of *another* person; not a slave of ours, but free and independent, and with a character distinctly its own." At first
Twain conceived of this other person as our conscience, but

he came to modify this as erroneous. He believed that Robert
Louis Stevenson's concept of the duality of man's nature, each
with its own conscience, was nearer the truth, but he thought
Stevenson's plot rang false in having the two separate natures
aware of each other's presence. Twain came finally to believe,
as he expressed it: "Inborn nature is Character, by itself in
the brutes--the tiger, the dove, the fox, etc. Inborn nature
and the modifying Conscience, working together make Character
in man." Conscience then is not another self; yet each person does have duality of character, each character possessing
its own conscience.

Clemens came finally to divide his own character into the
physical self and the "spiritualized self." It was common
memory that made him aware of the oneness of his spiritual
and physical selves, which he explains:

> Now, as I take it, my other self, my dream self, is
> merely my ordinary body and mind freed from clogging
> flesh and become a spiritualized body and mind and with
> the ordinary powers of both enlarged in all particulars
> a little, and in some particulars prodigiously. (*Note-
> book* 350)

For once, here, Twain becomes the utter mystic, saying: "Waking
I move slowly; but in my dreams my unhampered spiritualized
body flies to the ends of the earth in a millionth of a second.
Seems to--and I believe, *does*" (*Notebook* 350). And the most
definite expression that Twain has made upon spiritual immortality occurs in this philosophy of duality: "When my physical
body dies my dream body will doubtless continue its excursion
and activities without change, forever" (*Notebook* 351).

Three years earlier (1894) he had written to Mrs. Fairbanks on her husband's death: "I am sorry for you--very, very
sorry--but not for him nor for any body who is granted the
privilege of prying behind the curtain to see if there is any
contrivance there that is half so shabby & poor & foolish as
the invention of mortal life" (*Mrs. Fairbanks* 274-75). And
generally Clemens saw no hope beyond. "One of the proofs of
the immortality of the soul is that myriads have believed
it," he says, only to add, "They also believed the world was
flat" (*Notebook* 379). No doubt, it was the attempt of each
person to win his own self-respect in a material world that
caused Twain to state the same thought expressed by his admired
poet Robert Browning, that the failure is in having too-easily-
achieved ideals, not striving ever upward for the unattainable.
Inherited traits engrossed him at times, leading him to declare, "We don't create any of our traits; we inherit all of
them. They have come down to us from what we impudently call
the lower animals. Man is the last expression, and combines

every attribute of the animal tribes that preceded him" (qtd. in Paine 4: 1296).

Another facet of his thought was that the moral idea is constantly undergoing change; that what was in earlier days considered highly immoral may no longer be so. This was to Clemens further evidence of the general scheme of things, arising from some primal cause and developing upward. DeLancey Ferguson has called our attention to the conversation between Clemens and Kipling at the full tide of Twain's powers to show that it was not personal misfortune but life itself that caused his pessimism (*Man and Legend* 242). In a note made probably for *The Mysterious Stranger* Clemens indicated the lack of spiritual progress he found so distressing: "... the little stinking human race, with its little stinking kings and popes and bishops and prostitutes and peddlers" (*Notebook* 337).[12]

Twain's explosions against the human race finally drew this remonstrance from Livy, "Does it help the world to always rail at it? There is great & noble work being done, why not sometimes recognize that? Why always dwell on the evil until those who live beside you are crushed to the earth & you seem almost like a monomaniac" (*Love Letters* 333). The nobility of human nature was recognized at times by Twain. Once when a particularly brutal act of imperial despotism had occurred in Russia, he declared that all over Russia "... a myriad of eyes filled with tears"; and he concluded, "If I am a Swinburnian--and clear to the marrow I am--I hold human nature in sufficient honor to believe there are eighty million mute Russians that are of the same stripe, and only one Russian family that isn't" (*Letters* 2: 538).

We may seek an explanation of Twain's pessimism, then, from a number of causes. Twain, like his predecessors Hawthorne and Melville, was profoundly aware of evil in the world. Moreover, while growing to maturity on the river and as a young man in Washoe he saw life at its worst, and this never makes for optimism. His personal life, though ultimately one of worldly success, was actually filled with sickness, loss of loved ones, and temporary disaster. And as he watched the trend of world affairs, at home and abroad, doubts increased for the future, doubts now justified by a world of strife, uncertainty, and wars. An idealist who saw ideals betrayed, one sensitive to suffering, a Christian in the best sense of ethical conduct, Twain often felt cause for pessimism. Nevertheless, he had an intense sense of justice, hatred of wrong, and admiration for nobility of action. It was the ignorance, cowardice, and stupidity of the human race in contrast to the noble actions of individuals that he deplored. His strong sense of justice made him sensitive to any deviation,

large or small. In his books we see humanity in the mass
struggling through ignorance, stupidity, and cowardice, sometimes accompanied by crime, but we see, also, the noble actions of individuals: perchance a Huck or Jim, perhaps a Joan
of Arc. And it is upon these great in soul that hopes for the
future must rest.

NOTES

1. About Theodor Mommsen, the German historian and archeol-
ogist, Mark wrote, "Been taken for Mommsen twice. We have
the same hair, but upon examination it was found that our brains
were different" (*Notebook* 222). When Twain saw Mommsen at a
celebration in honor of another scientist he said, "I could
have touched him with my hand—Mommsen—think of it!" (qtd. in
Paine 3: 938). As for the existence of man, Paine states that
Mark repeatedly emphasized his doctrine of man as an irresponsible machine, saying that it covered everything like the sky;
"... you can't break through anywhere" (qtd. in Paine 4: 1322).

2. The attitude is expressed in John Hay's poem *Jim Bludso
of the Prairie Belle.*

3. As explained in Chapter 2, Paul Baender has questioned
the existence of Macfarlane in "Alias Macfarlane: A Revision
of Mark Twain Biography" (187-97). Baender argues that the
philosophy attributed to Macfarlane was Twain's, but that
likely makes little difference. If Twain could create Macfarlane, he could just as reasonably create Macfarlane's
philosophy. Created or not, Twain gave Macfarlane a real and
necessary place in his thinking about philosophical matters.

4. For an excellent study of this matter see Allison Ensor's *Mark Twain and the Bible* (1969). According to Ensor
"irreverence" is the word most characterizing Twain's attitude
toward the Bible. Although Twain thought he was telling the
world the truth about the Bible, contends Ensor, he failed to
comprehend its full content because he had gaps in his reading
and his knowledge. Ensor concludes that Twain was a literary
genius, but a "feeble Bible scholar" (101).

5. Concerning the "legal laws governing man's conduct" see
D.M. McKeithan, *Court Trials in Mark Twain and Other Essays*
(1958). McKeithan describes the trials of Laura Hawkins in
The Gilded Age, Muff Potter in *Tom Sawyer*, Luigi Capello in
Pudd'nhead Wilson, Joan of Arc in *Joan of Arc*, Silas Phelps in
Tom Sawyer, Detective, and Father Peter in *The Mysterious*

Stranger. Twain's interest in court trials persisted throughout his career, and that it did leads McKeithan to conclude,
"The court trials in Mark Twain reveal his permanent interest
in the administration of justice and his concern for justice"
(114).

6. Louis J. Budd, in *Mark Twain: Social Philosopher*
(1962), has made an assessment of Mark's interest in politics.
Budd sets aside the popular image of Twain as avid crusader
and defender of American virtues in favor of an image of one
who studied politics. Through Mark's thinking on politics,
according to Budd, we have access to his thinking on many
other issues of his time.

7. Henry Nash Smith assesses the political and economic
ideas of Mark Twain's *Connecticut Yankee* in *Mark Twain's Fables
of Progress* (1964). Smith writes, "*A Connecticut Yankee in
King Arthur's Court* (1889) is one of the most characteristic
productions of the decade when Americans generally first
realized they were entering the modern world" (6). Continues
Smith, Mark Twain

> ... found it impossible to show how the values represented
> by his vernacular protagonist could survive in an indus-
> trial society ... Frustrated by his attempt to come to
> terms with the industrial revolution, he gave up the
> modern world for lost, and during the rest of his career
> devoted most of his energy to composing variations on the
> theme expressed in his slogan of "the damned human race."
> (107-08)

8. In his *Mark Twain: An American Prophet* (1970) Maxwell
Geismar views Twain as similar to Whitman in being one criti-
cally aware of America's shortcomings and at the same time
caught up in a "dark fantasy of civilizational collapse." In
making his case for Twain as polemicist and radical social
critic Geismar writes, "Fundamentally Mark Twain was not a
novelist or a fiction writer at all. As I am forced to repeat,
he was a poet-prophet on the model of Walt Whitman even more
than that of Melville" (442). The whole late nineteenth century world, according to Geismar, worshiped Mark Twain "... as
a social and moral voice of justice and humanity whose humor
made the lesson more effective" (510). Philip S. Foner also
writes about Mark Twain as moralist and social critic in *Mark
Twain: Social Critic* (1958). Like Geismar, Foner sees Twain
as a great force for freedom and democracy everywhere, a true
patriot who never gave up in exposing the evils he saw in
American society. Contending that no writer has ever been
more dedicated to the welfare of his fellow man, Foner writes,
"Mark Twain was our greatest social critic. As such he speaks

to us with an immediacy that surmounts the barriers of time"
(313).

9. According to Thomas Blues, in *Mark Twain and the Community* (1970), in the novels of the 1870s and 1880s Twain was
concerned about the fate of the individual who triumphs over
the community. That is, he sees a pattern in which the individual is allowed to rebel against the community and at the
same time continue to operate within it. In short, the individual enjoys a triumph over the community but his relationship to the community is not endangered. Blues sees *A Connecticut Yankee in King Arthur's Court* as pivotal, however,
because for the first time Twain fails to restore the protagonist to the community. From the time of *A Connecticut
Yankee* Twain would increasingly rage against the "damned human
race" while unleashing his pessimism and determinism: "In his
disillusionment following *A Connecticut Yankee* Mark Twain excoriated the community from a detached and cynical point of
view" (77).

10. "The human race is a race of cowards; and I am not
only in that procession but carrying a banner" (*Eruption* xxix).
"Ah, well, I am a great and sublime fool. But then I am
God's fool, and all his work must be contemplated with respect"
(qtd. in Paine 2: 609).

11. This theme was used, of course, by Robert Louis Stevenson in *Dr. Jekyll and Mr. Hyde* (1886) and in *Markheim* (1884);
it was used by Edgar A. Poe in *William Wilson* (1840).

12. Mark Twain's commentaries on "the little stinking human
race" abound. See, for example, *A Pen Warmed-up in Hell: Mark
Twain in Protest* (1972), a collection of manuscripts on the
"damned human race" edited by Frederick Anderson. Or see *Letters from the Earth* (1962), the first part of which consists
of a treatment of biblical themes and characters as commentary
on Twain's own world of the late nineteenth and early twentieth
centuries. In *Letters from the Earth*, edited by Bernard DeVoto,
Twain is aiming his arrows at the "damned human race." Likewise, *Mark Twain's Fables of Man* (1972), edited by John S.
Tuckey, consists of thirty-six selections which treat outdated
ideas about the nature of man and the universe, the possibilities of true brotherhood among human beings, and the coming
of a dark age when religious beliefs will again enslave mankind.
Finally, *Mark Twain's Which Was the Dream? and Other Symbolic
Writings of the Later Years* (1967), edited by John S. Tuckey,
contains selections which were all written between 1896 and
1905, the period in which Twain produced the "Great Dark"
manuscripts. Closely related to *The Mysterious Stranger* in
theme and style, the selections in this volume give us Mark's
final observations on the "damned human race."

As for *The Mysterious Stranger*, in *Mark Twain and the Backwoods Angel* (1966) William C. Spengemann traces Twain's changing attitudes toward "the matter of innocence" throughout the Twain canon. Twain was increasingly convinced that evil rules the world, and Spengemann views *The Mysterious Stranger* as the logical conclusion to Mark's pursuit of innocence. Rather than offering solutions in *The Mysterious Stranger*, Twain succeeds only in advancing his pessimism and determinism. Roger B. Salomon, in *Twain and the Image of History* (1961), cites the upheavals brought on by the years 1860 to 1868 in America in Twainian terms of what happened to the individual; for Twain history was what happened to the individual, a kind of revelation of human nature. Beginning with *The American Claimant* (1892), according to Salomon, Twain undertook a con- scious and radical reformulation of his interpretation of his- tory, which Salomon traces through *Joan of Arc*, *Following the Equator*, and other sources. What Twain was working toward in *Following the Equator*, writes Salomon, he developed explicitly and at length in *The Mysterious Stranger*: that history has no teleological significance (200). The theme of *The Mysterious Stranger* is the meaninglessness of life (207); Twain had reached the position of the absurd. His final image of history is one in which life and the universe are both without meaning.

WORKS CITED

Baender, Paul. "Alias Macfarlane: A Revision of Mark Twain Biography." *American Literature* 38 (1966): 187-97.

Blues, Thomas. *Mark Twain and the Community.* Lexington: Uni- versity Press of Kentucky, 1970. Proposes that Twain's attitudes toward the relation of the individual to the com- munity influences both the meaning and direction of his fiction.

Boller, Paul F. "Mark Twain's Credo: A Humorist's Fatalistic View." *Southwest Review* 63 (1978): 150-63.

Brodwin, Stanley. "The Theology of Mark Twain: Banished Adam and the Bible." *Mississippi Quarterly* 29 (1976): 167-89.

Budd, Louis J. *Mark Twain: Social Philosopher.* Bloomington: Indiana U. Press, 1962. An assessment of Twain's interest in politics.

DeVoto, Bernard. Introduction. *The Portable Mark Twain.* By Mark Twain. New York: Viking, 1946. 1-34.

Ensor, Allison. *Mark Twain and the Bible.* Lexington: Univer-
    sity Press of Kentucky, 1969. Treats Twain's position on
    the Bible and Christianity as one of duality.

Ferguson, DeLancey. *Mark Twain: Man and Legend.* Indianapolis:
    Bobbs-Merrill, 1943. Sound conclusions on Twain's thought.

Foner, Philip S. *Mark Twain: Social Critic.* New York: Inter-
    national Publications, 1958. Examines Twain's thinking on
    major social, political, and economic issues.

Geismar, Maxwell. *Mark Twain: An American Prophet.* Boston:
    Houghton Mifflin, 1970. Makes a case for Twain as a
    polemicist and radical social critic.

McKeithan, D.M. *Court Trials in Mark Twain and Other Essays.*
    The Hague: Nijhoff, 1958. Explores Twain's interest in
    court trials.

Mill, John Stuart. *On Liberty.* London: Oxford U. Press, 1933.

Neider, Charles. "Reflections on Religion." *Hudson Review* 16
    (1963): 329-52. Five dictations from 1906 by Clemens.

Paine, Albert Bigelow. *Mark Twain: A Biography.* 4 vols. New
    York: Harper & Brothers, 1912. Important for Twain's
    philosophy and religious thought.

Salomon, Roger B. *Twain and the Image of History.* New Haven:
    Yale U. Press, 1961. Traces changes in Twain's image of
    history.

Smith, Henry Nash. *Mark Twain's Fable of Progress.* New Bruns-
    wick: Rutgers U. Press, 1964. Assesses political and
    economic ideas in Twain's *A Connecticut Yankee in King
    Arthur's Court.*

Spengemann, William C. *Mark Twain and the Backwoods Angel:
    The Matter of Innocence in the Works of Samuel L. Clemens.*
    Kent: Kent State U. Press, 1966. Traces Twain's changing
    attitudes toward innocence.

Twain, Mark [Samuel Langhorne Clemens]. *The Adventures of
    Huckleberry Finn.* New York: Harper & Brothers, 1918.

————. *The Adventures of Tom Sawyer.* New York: Harper &
    Brothers, 1922.

————. *The American Claimant.* New York: Harper & Brothers,
    1924.

————. *A Connecticut Yankee in King Arthur's Court.* New
    York: Harper & Brothers, 1917.

————. *The Curious Republic of Gondour and Other Whimsical
    Sketches.* New York: Boni and Liveright, 1919.

————. *Following the Equator*. 2 vols. New York: Harper & Brothers, 1925.

————. *Joan of Arc*. 2 vols. New York: Harper & Brothers, 1924.

————. *Letters from the Earth*. Ed. Bernard DeVoto. New York: Harper & Row, 1962. A collection of materials on the "damned human race."

————. *The Love Letters of Mark Twain*. Ed. Dixon Wecter. New York: Harper & Brothers, 1949. Especially valuable on religion and politics.

————. *Mark Twain in Eruption: Hitherto Unpublished Pages about Men and Events*. Ed. Bernard DeVoto. New York: Harper & Brothers, 1940. Valuable contribution to our knowledge of Twain's mind and thought.

————. *Mark Twain to Mrs. Fairbanks*. Ed. Dixon Wecter. San Marino: Huntington Library, 1949. Interesting correspondence adding to our knowledge of Twain's mind.

————. *Mark Twain's Autobiography*. Ed. Albert Bigelow Paine. 2 vols. New York: Harper & Brothers, 1924. Selected from Twain's autobiographical papers.

————. *Mark Twain's Fables of Man*. Ed. John S. Tuckey. Berkeley: U. of California Press, 1972. Materials on man and the universe, the possibility of a true brotherhood, and the coming of a dark age.

————. *Mark Twain's Letters*. Ed. Albert Bigelow Paine. 2 vols. New York: Harper & Brothers, 1917. By no means complete, but important.

————. *Mark Twain's Notebook*. New York: Harper & Brothers, 1935. Brief and sketchy, but important.

————. *Mark Twain's Which Was the Dream? and Other Symbolic Writings of the Later Years*. Ed. John S. Tuckey. Berkeley: U. of California Press, 1967. Materials presenting Twain's final observations about man and his place in the universe.

————. *The Mysterious Stranger*. New York: Harper & Brothers, 1922.

————. *A Pen Warmed-up in Hell: Mark Twain in Protest*. Ed. Frederick Anderson. New York: Harper & Row, 1972. A collection of Twain's criticism of the "damned human race."

————. *Pudd'nhead Wilson*. New York: Harper & Brothers, 1922.

————. *Roughing It*. 2 vols. New York: Harper & Brothers, 1913.

————. *Tom Sawyer Abroad*. New York: Harper & Brothers, 1917.

————. *What Is Man?* New York: Harper & Brothers, 1917.

————. *The Works of Mark Twain: What Is Man? and Other Philosophical Writings*. Ed. Paul Baender. Berkeley: U. of California Press, 1973.

Twain, Mark and Charles Dudley Warner. *The Gilded Age*. 2 vols. New York: Harper & Brothers, 1915.

Chapter 6

MARK TWAIN'S PLACE IN LITERATURE

The United States

The early literary reputation of Samuel Clemens, one in
fact continuing into his maturity, was that of literary
comedian. As Dixon Wecter says, "... his reputation throughout
life kept returning to that of a 'phunny phellow' turning cartwheels to captivate the groundlings" ("Mark Twain" 2: 922).
Mark Twain, we must remember, grew up amid the flowering of
the Old Southwestern humor; his first book featured a comic
story picked up from a miner on Jackass Hill, while his first
best seller mingled irreverent Washoe guffaws with brash con-
templation of European culture. No wonder nineteenth-century
criticism, accustomed to the genteel tradition, failed readily
to perceive the greatness of Twain's stature, even as academi-
cians of that period failed to evaluate Whitman fairly, and in
America, at least, Melville went his way unnoticed.

When *The Innocents Abroad* (1869) appeared, it was reviewed
in the *Nation* as typical of our humorists, the unsigned critic
failing, however, to accord the book literary status, even
though enjoying its fun. William Dean Howells, who acclaimed
The Innocents Abroad for its humor, limited his praise to
saying that Twain was now worthy to rank among the best of
"the humorists California has given us." With the reading
public, notwithstanding, it suddenly brought what Carl Van
Doren called "explosive fame," and Oliver Wendell Holmes wrote
the author a complimentary acknowledgment. But it was humor
and fun that brought responsive sales; readers did not dream
that Twain was a serious artist.

When *Roughing It* (1872) was published, though in general
the leading journals took no notice of what seemed another
funny, journalistic effort, Howells remarked upon its verisimi-
litude expressed through grotesque exaggeration and irony. It
was still the fun maker, nevertheless, that Twain remained,
not social historian, or literary artist. Many readers con-

tinued to echo J.G. Holland's comment on *The Innocents Abroad*
that its author was a "mere fun-maker of ephemeral popularity"
(Paine 1: 382). As more books continued to appear, critical
evaluation altered slightly. Richard Watson Gilder paid his
respects to Twain as a "humorous storyteller" and "homely
philosopher," saying it was because Twain was a satirist and
a philosopher that his humorous books and speeches had met
with wide favor. Yet Gilder felt, as he said of *The Prince
and the Pauper* (1882), that Clemens could not successfully
produce a work after the older models. Critics who did like
The Prince and the Pauper--and it appears to have been liked
better than Twain's earlier books--approved because it complied
with conventional ideas of literature. Here was less originality and more of those qualities of the genteel tradition,
which if less vigorous, at least could be evaluated on critical
scales adjusted for historical romance in Old England (Vogelback, "A Study" 48-54).

    Across the Atlantic, John Nichol, professor of English
literature in the University of Glasgow, found Twain master of
a "degenerate style," one who has "done perhaps more than any
other living writer to lower the literary tone of English
speaking people" (426). Nichol declared Twain a joker, who
could not be a fine writer, because he turned everything to
jest. But the succeeding year another English writer, Haweis,
dealt more kindly: "Mark Twain's strong points are his facile
but minute observation, his power of description, a certain
justness and right proportion, and withal a great firmness of
touch and peculiar--I had almost said personal--vein of humor"
(167). And in America *Harper's* finally decided to recognize
Clemens' existence with a review of *Life on the Mississippi*
(1883), though even then it was historical and regional interest which drew the reviewer rather than literary quality
("Editor's Literary Record" 799).

    With the appearance of *Huckleberry Finn* (1885) there was
slight critical acclaim. T.S. Perry, reviewing it in the
Century did little more than praise the plot; Charles F.
Richardson placed its creator in a chapter headed "Borderlands
of American Literature," while writing of Charles D. Warner and
Oliver Wendell Holmes as having "actually contributed to literature." Arthur L. Vogelback finds that Twain's masterpiece
"received at the time practically no critical attention in
America," despite the fact that "Of all Clemens' books published up to 1885, *Huckleberry Finn* received the greatest pre-
and post-publication notice" ("Publication" 260-72). In spite
of this, however, it appears that Twain's work in general continued to be widely popular with the reading public; and French
translations appeared in 1883 and during 1884-86. In 1890
William Dean Howells praised Clemens for "the delicious satire,

the marvellous wit, the wild, free, fantastic humor" found in
his writings. Comparing Twain with Cervantes, he said, "the
two writers are of the same humorous largeness." Howells then
lauded Clemens' writings for being "true to human nature" and
declared that "his fun is unrivaled" because of the "right
feeling and clear thinking" that it contains (Review 145-49).
One year later, however, Henry A. Beers found Twain nothing
more than an able jokester, below the literary level of Lowell
and Holmes, one destined to last only through his humor (188).
However, in England, Andrew Lang perceived that *Huckleberry
Finn* was "a nearly flawless gem of romance and humor," though
even he qualified his praise by assertion that "Mark Twain
often sins against good taste" (45).

As time went on, Twain's importance as social historian
impinged even more on critical consciousness. Charles M.
Thompson said he had "recorded the life of certain southwestern
portions of our country, at one fleeting stage in their development, better than it is possible it will ever be done
again" (488). To this Henry C. Vedder added, in 1898, an appreciation of Twain's "broad humanity, his gift of seeing far
below the surface of life, his subtle comprehension of human
nature, and his realistic method" (138). Just one year later,
Brander Matthews, writing a preface to a collected edition of
Clemens' works, declared:

> At how long an interval Mark Twain shall be rated
> after Moliere and Cervantes it is for the future to de-
> clare. All that we can see clearly now is that it is
> with them that he is to be classed--with Moliere and
> Cervantes, with Chaucer and Fielding, humorists all of
> them, and all of them manly men. ("An Appreciation"
> xxx)

Higher praise was to come in 1900, and from whence least expected, Barrett Wendell of Harvard, who designated *Huckleberry
Finn* "a book which in certain moods one is disposed for all
its eccentricity to call the most admirable work of literary
art as yet produced on this continent" (503).

Two other historians of the same year failed to see
Clemens with Wendell's perception; Henry S. Pancoast grouped
Twain with the literary comedians, dismissing *The Innocents
Abroad* with this comment: "... but to some of us even shallow
raptures are better than a cynical levity" (329); at the same
time, Walter C. Bronson briefly placed Clemens with Harte and
Miller, and while complimenting the originality and imagination
of this "greatest writer of the West" (286), treated him in
less than a page. William P. Trent, only three years later,
though designating Twain a "socio-political humorist," nevertheless rated him below Holmes and Lowell (518), while George

E. Woodberry said that Clemens missed being a national author
because he belonged to a "provincial caste"--that is, the West
(206).

In 1904 Richard Burton stated that we possessed "One living
writer of indisputable genius ... Mark Twain" (312). Thus by
the last years of his life the literary reputation of Samuel
Clemens had risen from the lowly status of a mere "funny man"
to that of a major figure in the eyes of some initiated critics.
Such, for instance, was the opinion of William Lyon Phelps of
Yale, who wrote: "Indeed, it seems to me that Mark Twain is
our foremost living American writer" (542).

John Macy, a few years after Clemens' death, spoke of
Huckleberry Finn as our "greatest piece of American fiction"
(290). Waldo Frank, however, that same year called Huck Finn
importance to social history, realism, true chivalry, breadth
of knowledge; then he said: "Mark Twain's mind was of universal proportions; he meditated on all the deep problems, and
somewhere in his work he touches upon most of the vital things
that men commonly think about and wonder about" (274). Macy
concludes by calling Twain's portrait of mankind "the greatest
canvas that any American has painted" (275).

Yet there were those who still voiced adverse opinions;
"... the verdict of time," said Walter C. Bronson, "will be
that he could see and describe far better than he could think"
(290). Waldo Funk, however, that same year called Huck Finn
"the American epic hero" and acclaimed, "... the soul of Mark
Twain was great" (38). Official academic sanction was placed
upon his literary reputation when *The Cambridge History of
American Literature* (1921) appeared; it represented something
in the nature of a final court of scholarly judgment. Here
Stuart P. Sherman praised Mark for "his exhibition of a masterpiece or so not unworthy of Le Sage or Cervantes." And added,
"He is a fulfilled promise of American life" ("Mark Twain"
3: 1). Brander Matthews in a reissue of an earlier appraisal
affirmed that Twain's "place in the English literature of the
nineteenth century is with its leaders" (*Introduction* 226).
But even as a position of security seemed to have been reached,
a damaging frontal attack occurred; Van Wyck Brooks decided
upon a Freudian analysis of Twain's writings to prove that he
had failed to become a serious, mature artist. Briefly the
thesis ran: Mark Twain was born with potentialities which were
not realized, because of his environment and his lack of courage.
"Mark Twain's attack upon the failure of human life was merely
a rationalization of the failure in himself," Brooks concludes,
"And this failure was the failure of the artist in him" (313).
Then he dismisses Clemens' books by calling their appeal
"largely an appeal to rudimentary minds" (28).

Thus the general line was established for a school of criticism which misunderstood the frontier, deplored humor, and demanded that all literature devote itself to political and sociological problems. Though students of the frontier, such as Lucy Lockwood Hazard, saw the complete misunderstanding in all this, the idea swept across critical ranks like prairie fire.[1]

A leading exponent was Lewis Mumford, who saw Mark Twain "caught as deeply in the net of the industrialist and the pioneer as any of his contemporaries" (170). Believing with Brooks that Clemens as a pilot most fully realized his capabilities, Mumford found him unaware of the "black squalor of the new immigrant workers" (172). In a word, the Twain pictured here liked industrialism because it brought him personal comfort and accepted unthinkingly the values of the Gilded Age.

To Vernon L. Parrington, Mark Twain was the answer to Walt Whitman's query about the absence of a fresh, courageous, Western writer: "Here at last was an authentic American—a native writer thinking his own thoughts, using his own eyes, speaking his own dialect—everything European fallen away, the last shred of feudal culture gone, local and western yet continental" (3: 86). To Parrington, Clemens was "an embodiment of three centuries of American experience," born and reared on the frontier, inheriting all its vigor, exuberance, and folkways. Yet because of his frontier origin Twain suffered from a lack of spiritual, intellectual, and cultural background, never achieving an "untroubled, conscious integrity" as did Emerson and Whitman. And Brooks is termed partly right about Twain's bitter pessimism arising from surrender to the ideals of the Gilded Age; however, Parrington credits the "inevitable toll exacted by the passing years" with exerting an equal influence, until we have a slow change from the gaiety of youth to the "fierce satire of disillusion." Parrington believed that Clemens wished to be a satirist, but refrained because "... the wares of the satirist were not in demand at the barbecue" (94), yet Parrington sees at the heart of Mark Twain's philosophy "the individual will in opposition to society" (95). Thus he finds Mark turning within and escaping reality.

Soon, however, Constance Rourke in a penetrating analysis of American humor as a revelation of national ideals and character also showed the talent of Twain to be "consistently a pioneer talent." Mark Twain, Rourke stated, was not a failure as an artist; rather he was a "great repository" for all the national moods, attitudes, and legends; for Clemens had "achieved scale, with the gusty breadth astir in the country as the Pacific was reached" (218-19). The difference here in critical attitudes arose, it might be said, from what the critic expected, or valued, in Twain's subject matter. At the

same time, a balanced, penetrating commentary on Twain appeared
by C. Hartley Grattan, in which Mark's ability to gather up
into himself "more elements of the life of his day than any
other writing man of the time" was stressed. In contradiction
of the Brooks-Mumford thesis, Grattan found Twain "an idealist
of a most uncompromising sort" (274). Declaring that *The
Gilded Age*, *Huckleberry Finn* and *Pudd'nhead Wilson* reveal
Twain's true attitude toward the America of his day, Grattan
found no cause for wonder over the bitter books of later years.

Another important estimate was that of Ludwig Lewisohn,
who saw Twain as the "bardic type of artist" speaking with
understanding to the people, one who did possess an awareness
of the "dark and desperate problems of humanity." Lewisohn
doubted the "ordeal" or frustration, for he found instead the
artist, whose material was that "inimitable American civilization which Mark Twain not only recorded as in its living character it was, but which he raised, by the heightening and isolation of art, into a permanent realm of the human imagination"
(232).

Also refuting the failure of Twain, V.F. Calverton declared
that perhaps *The Innocents Abroad* might be justly termed our
first American book because Mark's democracy was more than
political; it was economic, and here it even carried into art.
And Calverton met the Brooks attack squarely with the denial,
"... at no time did he 'sell out' his philosophy to the upper
bourgeoisie of the East" (327). Yet Granville Hicks kept the
frustration theory current. "The frontier humorist and realist
might have become a great social novelist," he said, adding,
"In minor ways Mark Twain made progress, but he never transcended the limitations of his tradition" (46). And Hicks dismissed Twain from literature: "He was and knew he was, merely
an entertainer" (46).

Then Newton Arvin, adapting social or class attitudes to
literature, criticized Clemens: "He should have remained true
to the best traditions of his family and his class, or have
gone beyond them. He did neither" (126). Clemens wrote for
the vast majority with whom he was popular, and Arvin, following
in part the Brooks thesis, seemed to believe such books could
not really be good. Yet "stultification was never complete"
and Twain, however much edited by Howells and Livy, retained
enough "original freedom of spirit" at times to write literature,
though Arvin even dismisses much of *Huckleberry Finn* from that
realm. Gradually, through the efforts of DeVoto, Ferguson,
Wecter, and Trilling, informed opinion came to agree with
James T. Farrell that "... too much of the critical writing
on Mark Twain has stressed his failure and his limitations" (25).

Virtually no one any longer questions the place of Mark
Twain in American literature, or in international literature.

On the other hand, Newton Arvin's accusation that Clemens
wrote "for the vast majority with whom he was popular" was
published in 1935, and *The League of Frightened Philistines*
by James T. Farrell was published in 1945. When in 1948
Dixon Wecter observed that Clemens' reputation throughout his
life "kept returning to that of a 'phunny phellow' turning
cartwheels to captivate the groundlings" (2: 922), he seemed
to be suggesting that the issue of the popular writer and
speechmaker versus the man of letters did not die with Clemens
in 1910. Hal Holbrook's dramatizations of Mark Twain on stage,
the popular reception of Mark Twain films, and a variety of
critical concerns over the last thirty years would bear that
out.

Although critics over the last thirty years have not questioned Mark Twain's place in literature, they have examined a
variety of issues in an effort to account for that place.
Much of the criticism has been discussed in previous chapters,
but a brief chronological survey of additional sources in this
concluding chapter might serve to remind the reader that Mark
Twain's place in literature is still being discussed. For
example, one of the approaches to accounting for Twain's place
in literature is to trace changes in critical attitudes toward
him, that is, to trace the growth of his literary reputation,
and this is well done in *Mark Twain: Selected Criticism*
(1955), edited by Arthur L. Scott. Especially interesting in
this collection are essays by Brander Matthews, William Lyon
Phelps, John Macy, and Lionel Trilling.

Henry Nash Smith, in *Mark Twain: The Development of a
Writer* (1962), uses the same approach. He considers problems
of style and structure Twain confronted at the outset of his
career and then traces the author's handling of these problems
through nine major works. Smith sees a conflict in cultures
at the center of Twain's development as a writer. He charac-
terizes the traditional culture as dominated by "the pale
negations and paler affirmations of the genteel tradition"
(11) coming to America by way of Europe. The term *vernacular*,
on the other hand, he sees as characterizing the ethical and
aesthetic assumptions as well as the language of the nineteenth-
century backwoodsman or frontiersman. Mark Twain, says Smith,
was hostile toward the dominant culture; it had "lost its power
to relate its values to actual experience" (20). What Smith
accomplishes in examining Twain's style and structure is a
record of changing attitudes toward conflicting cultures, and
it was in his handling of the conflict between cultures, concludes Smith, that Twain became a writer worthy of attention.
The approach was successful enough that Smith relied on it
again when he edited *Mark Twain* (1963). Recognizing that the
Brooks controversy, brought on by *The Ordeal of Mark Twain*

(1920), dominated the first phase of Twain criticism in this
century, and that Roger Asselineau, in the introduction to
The Literary Reputation of Mark Twain from 1910 to 1950
(1954), thoroughly documented critical opinion about Mark
Twain to the middle of the century, Smith chose essays written
for the most part after 1950 and arranged them according to
the chronological order of the works by Mark Twain with which
they deal. Smith tried to include discussions of all of
Twain's major works, the best recent criticism representing a
variety of critical methods and approaches, and commentary on
the successive stages of Twain's career.

Other approaches to accounting for Twain's place in literature are equally impressive. Robert Regan, in *Unpromising
Heroes: Mark Twain and His Characters* (1966), relies on folklore for his explanation. Regan is not merely interested in
the recurrences in Twain's fiction of what folklorists know as
the Unpromising Hero. Rather he sets out to demonstrate that
"... the same psychological imperatives which we may easily
discover in fairy tales operate in such books as *Tom Sawyer* and
Pudd'nhead Wilson" (x). Using folklore studies as a means of
examining the literature and Twain's life, Regan traces through
both what he calls Twain's "visions of himself as Unpromising
Hero" (26). Whether Twain created his literary heroes as a
means of handling his personal feelings of inferiority or not,
the issue of the popular writer versus the man of letters
seems at the heart of Regan's approach.

Arthur L. Scott uses an even different tack in *On the
Poetry of Mark Twain: With Selections from His Verse* (1966).
Twain wrote more than 120 poems, and using the unpublished as
well as the published ones Scott constructs a history of
Twain's interest in poetry which in many ways parallels his
interest in prose. Asserting that Twain's interest in poetry
was far more extensive than has been imagined, Scott concludes
that we should not take seriously Twain's "literary declaration" about detesting poetry. On the contrary, argues Scott,
Mark Twain loved poetry and that should be taken into consideration more than it has been in considering his place in
literature. A similar argument exists in *Mark Twain as Critic*
(1967) by Sydney J. Krause, except that Krause's purpose is
to demonstrate that Twain's literary criticism should be considered more in evaluating his place in literature. According
to Krause, Twain's moral and social criticism spilled over into
his criticism of literature providing a systematic way of
looking at the world as well as at literature. Contending
that Twain wrote a large amount of literary criticism and disguised it in his work, Krause says that in writing the early
criticism Twain used the mask of the fool or "muggins" and that
in the later criticism he used the mask of the rebel or

"grumbler," the latter being an extension of the former.
Krause also discusses what he calls Mark Twain's "appreciative
criticism" as it relates to such people as Macaulay, Howells,
Howe, Zola, and Wilbrandt. Although it has not been the habit
among Twain scholars to praise Twain as a literary critic,
Krause contends that his criticism is more important to his
place in literature than we have recognized.

In *The Art of Mark Twain* (1976), William M. Gibson surveys
form and technique used in various genres by Twain and ultimately arrives at the idea that Twain developed one of the
great styles in the English language because he had a firm
grasp of the American vernacular. Out of his "oral style,"
says Gibson, Mark Twain created a new language for prose (5),
and that language was his source of power in attacking life's
absurdities. The argument is strikingly similar to that in
Henry Nash Smith's *Mark Twain: The Development of a Writer*,
except that Gibson seems not to place as much emphasis on a
conflict of cultures. William R. Macnaughton, by contrast,
isolates a particular time period in Twain's career as a writer
and argues for its significance in discussing Twain's place in
literature. In *Mark Twain's Last Years as a Writer* (1979),
Macnaughton concentrates on the period coming after the completion of *Following the Equator* in the summer of 1897; the
consensus about Twain as a writer during that period of approximately thirteen years is that he was a failure, according
to Macnaughton. Critics have generally ignored the period,
and few journal articles have been written about it. Macnaughton disagrees with Hamlin Hill's suggestion in *God's Fool*
that in these last years Twain was "frequently out of control"
(6), and in doing so he sets out to demonstrate that much of
what Twain wrote between 1897 and 1910 has more value toward
considering his place in literature than has been recognized.
Macnaughton examines one work after another and concludes that
"... in overall quality, Mark Twain's output between 1897 and
1910--and in particular between 1897 and 1906--is not markedly
inferior to the writing that he produced in any comparable
period during his career" (242).

Macnaughton's estimate of Twain's last years as a writer
seems much in accord with John S. Tuckey's purpose in editing
The Devil's Race-Track: Mark Twain's Great Dark Writings
(1980), especially when one considers that all the selections
included were written after Mark Twain passed the age of sixty
and that they had been printed previously in two volumes of the
Mark Twain Papers series, *Which Was the Dream?* (1967) and
Fables of Man (1972), both by the University of California
Press and edited by Tuckey. Their importance to Twain's place
in literature seems the most likely reason for republishing
them so soon after their appearance in the other volumes.

In *Our Mark Twain* (1983), Louis J. Budd analyzes Mark
Twain's status as a cultural hero, including Twain's efforts
to shape, protect, and elevate that status. According to
Budd, Twain skillfully engineered the "windings of publicity"
to project a public personality that would endear him to the
American people as well as generate a sizeable income (xiii).
Mark Twain as clown, buffoon, and comic; Mark Twain as moralist, sage, and reformer--Budd discusses all of these roles and
more. He also considers Mark Twain's popularity since his
death in 1910 and cites Hal Holbrook's one-man show as the
"strongest popularizing influence since around 1960" (237).
But the popularity remains, and as Budd explains, Mark Twain's
posturing "worked and gave us both his writings and his public
personality. We would not have those writings as they now
stand if he had shaped a substantially different life" (xiv).
Just as Budd is interested in the image-making process, and
how Mark Twain's literary images overlapped images from his
life, *The Mythologizing of Mark Twain* (1984), edited by Sara
deSaussure Davis and Philip D. Beidler, focuses on similar
interests. If one substitutes Budd's term "image-making" for
the term "myth-making" used by Davis and Beidler, he quickly
learns that both books examine Mark Twain as cultural hero and
in doing so raise the issue once again of the popular writer
and speechmaker versus the man of letters. Both *Our Mark Twain*
and *The Mythologizing of Mark Twain* remind us of Dixon Wecter's
observation about "turning cartwheels to captivate the groundlings," but they also remind us that Mark Twain's place in
literature is still being discussed.

Other Countries

In the future anyone who attempts to assess Mark Twain's
place in literature abroad will have to examine *Mark Twain
International* (1982), compiled and edited by Robert M. Rodney.
Most of Rodney's book--262 pages--is comprised of a bibliography of domestic editions for the years 1867 through 1976.
Preceding the bibliography is a forty-page section titled
"Introduction and Interpretation of the Bibliography," in which
Rodney discusses the scope of Mark Twain's international
audience, his popularity in various parts of the world, the
diversity of cultures to which he has appealed, trends in the
growth of his popularity, the comparative popularity of his
major works, his competition in the form of other major
American writers in the middle of this century, his work among
the best sellers of this century, and his role in shaping the
"American image" abroad.

Near the end of his introductory essay, Rodney states his purpose: "The purpose of the present work is not to evaluate Twain's literary achievement, but rather to provide a survey of his extensive publication and offer an interpretation of its significance" (lvii). *Mark Twain International* is a landmark in Twain bibliography with copious statistical tables to substantiate the findings discussed in "Introduction and Interpretation of the Bibliography." Rodney's book should prove invaluable to anyone interested in Mark Twain as an international figure, but for a critical estimate of Twain's literary achievement abroad one must look elsewhere.

Because of limitations of space, the purpose here is not to discuss in detail Mark Twain's place in literature abroad. The most that can be hoped for is some minor observations indicating the nature of his reputation in only a few countries. In his introduction Rodney states, "The geographical extent and high degree of Mark Twain's popularity are phenomena that have been too long overlooked. A measure of that popularity, however approximate, can supply a much-needed dimension to Twain's stature" (xxi). One cannot argue with such a statement. That Mark Twain is popular is obvious. The extent of his popularity in various parts of the world is another matter.

England

In *Tom Sawyer Abroad*, Mark Twain has Tom say, "Why, look at England. It's the most important country in the world; and yet you could put it in China's vest pocket" (80). And in *What Is Man?*, there is this explanation of Shakespeare: "In England he rose to the highest limit attainable through the *outside helps afforded by that land's ideals, influences, and training*" (9). Furthermore, Twain himself wrote to Howells in 1897, "This has been a bitter year for English pride, and I don't like to see England humbled—that is, not too much. We are sprung from her loins, and it hurts me. I am for republics, and she is the only comrade we've got, in that" (*Letters* 2: 643). Another time he wrote to Twichell that poor as our civilization is, it is "better than *real* savagery," adding, "And so we must not utter any hurtful word about England in these days, nor fail to hope that she will win in this war, for her defeat and fall would be an irremediable disaster for the mangy human race" (qtd. in Paine 3: 1096).

Before 1880 Twain's work had appeared in England, along with other American authors, in a "Select Library of Fiction," one of the titles, *Funny Stories and Humourous Poems* by Mark Twain and O.W. Holmes, indicating British delight in different aspects of American humor. When Chatto and Windus took over

many of the items pirated by John C. Hotten, they soon issued
a "Popular Novels" series at two shillings each; three were
by Mark Twain (Gohdes, *American Literature* 24). The earlier
writings of both Twain and Harte appeared regularly in these
cheap editions, a popularity never granted either Howells or
James. During the last two decades of the century at least
sixty editions or issues of books by Clemens appeared, stimulated in part by the large number of subscribers to Mudie's
circulating library (Gohdes, "British Interest" 356-62).

The English *Review of Reviews*, started as a monthly in
January, 1890, ran a condensed version of *A Connecticut Yankee*
in the February number. Indeed, Clemens' popularity had long
been so great that prior to the copyright act of 1891 he had
protected himself with previous publication in London. Though
the *Jumping Frog* appeared first in America, an authorized
version was published by Routledge in England only a few months
later. Such were the possibilities following the reception of
the *Jumping Frog* that John C. Hotten, the literary pirate, not
only reprinted it, but with an eagle eye on the cash drawer,
had an unauthorized edition of *The Innocents Abroad* on the market
before the legitimate publisher, Routledge, could issue his.
This literary buccaneering was so lucrative that the greedy
Hotten, intent upon turning more ink into gold, reached for
the "Memoranda" from the *Galaxy*. By the time Twain visited
England in 1872 he was fully aware of his financial loss from
inability to collect royalties on his increasing sales; it was
then that the idea of prepublication in England was adopted as
a solution. Indeed, Routledge and Hotten, between them, had
published twelve separate books by Twain during 1871-72, and
several other items appearing at the same time represented
combinations of some of those titles (Gohdes, *American Literature* 89-90).

By 1883 Thomas Hardy asked Howells why people did not
realize Twain was more than a great humorist, indicating how
critical appreciation in England was keeping step with general
popularity (Howells, *Life in Letters* 1: 349). And this popularity increased as his books continued to appear there;
Andrew Lang received *Huckleberry Finn* as "a nearly flawless
gem of romance and humor" (Lang 45), a critical dictum more
concretely expressed by the large numbers who read it.

When Rudyard Kipling called on Clemens during the summer
of 1889, he found no disillusion with "this man I had learned
to love and admire fourteen thousand miles away" (2: 171).
More than a decade later Kipling wrote to his publisher, Frank
Doubleday:

> I love to think of the great and godlike Clemens.
> He is the biggest man you have on your side of the water
> by a damn sight, and don't you forget it. Cervantes was
> a relation of his. (qtd. in Paine 3: 1208)

No higher praise, nor from a more acceptable source, could
have come to Twain than William Archer's dictum on *Huckleberry
Finn*: "If any work of incontestable genius, and plainly predestined to immortality, has been issued in the English language during the last quarter of a century, it is that brilliant romance of the Great Rivers" (Archer 178-79). Yet
Clarence Gohdes finds such appreciation scant among run-of-
the-mill critics in England, who continued to regard Clemens
as "too vulgar, irreverent, and eccentric" for admission into
the front rank of authors (*American Literature* 129). Despite
this, however, Mark Twain, according to Gohdes, probably had
more articles written about him for the British journals than
were devoted to any of his American contemporaries (139).
Twain was entertaining; moreover, he represented the United
States--so well that George Bernard Shaw wrote him: "I am persuaded that the future historian of America will find your
works as indispensable to him as a French historian finds the
political tracts of Voltaire" (qtd. in Paine 4: 1398). Always
popular in England, at the time of his death Clemens was honored
by a Mark Twain number of the London *Bookman* (June, 1910), to
which several distinguished literary men contributed.[2]

Since Twain's death English criticism has divided somewhat
on his place in literature--perhaps the influence of Brooks
across the Atlantic. D.H. Lawrence in his *Studies in Classic
American Literature* (1923), of course, does not even mention Mark Twain, although he includes both Melville and Whitman. A.C. Ward in a treatment of American letters, which becomes at times rather supercilious, deplores Twain's lack of
taste and insight, especially in *The Innocents Abroad* and the
Connecticut Yankee: "... at his worst," says Ward, "he was a
rhinoceros among porcelain" (55). Ward followed Brooks in believing Twain was "chafed" and restrained, though he does perceive the "complexity and subtlety" of his work, realizing that
"... *Tom Sawyer* and *Huckleberry Finn* are among the few humorous
masterpieces in world literature" (61). Indeed, Ward finally
praises Twain for his independent vision and for dealing freely
with human experience.

George Stuart Gordon, Merton Professor of English Literature, later president of Magdalen College, writing of Clemens
in *Anglo-American Literary Relations* (1942), calmly declared
him an "authentic man of genius" and *Huckleberry Finn* "among
the great books of the world" (109). And this dictum would
seem justified by the continuing numbers of its readers in
Great Britain. Twelve years later, in 1954, Marcus Cunliffe,
lecturer in American Studies at Manchester University, commented
on the "warmth and accuracy" of Clemens' best works, saying,
"But *Huckleberry Finn*, apart from the Tom-Sawyerish rescue of
Jim, is perfect, the unforgettable portrait of a frontier boy"

(167). And Cunliffe calls Mark Twain "a great artist whose
touch is sure."

More recently, in *Mark Twain and John Bull: The British
Connection* (1970), Howard G. Baetzhold appears to have presented all that is known about Clemens' visits to England, his
friends and associates, his publishing relations, English criticism of his works, and his popularity with English readers.
Using a chronological approach, Baetzhold shows how Twain's
opinions continued to change on political and social problems,
and he questions whether Clemens ever became an absolute determinist. Baetzhold's discussion of literary influences on
Twain's work is convincing, influences coming from such writers
as Browning, Tennyson, Dickens, Byron, Wordsworth, Kipling, and
Stevenson. Also important as an influence is the philosophy of
W.E.H. Lecky, who advocated that conscience is "original,"
that it comes entirely from within as opposed to being trained
or conditioned by the community. Baetzhold sets out to examine
the influence of Clemens' relationship with Britain on his
thought, and near the end of his study Baetzhold concludes
about Clemens, "What he borrowed from books, he often adapted
so skillfully that we have been a long time discovering his
debts and are still a long way from identifying all of them"
(319). Despite evidence to the contrary, Baetzhold makes a
good case for the idea that Twain hoped for humanity to improve its moral stature.

France

In France recognition came first from Marie Thérèse Blanc
(Th. Bentzon), whose significant estimate of Twain in 1872
appeared in the *Revue des Deux Mondes* ("Les Humoristes américains" 313-35). Blanc, wishing to popularize American literature in her native country, translated the *Jumping Frog*, which
Twain later playfully retranslated into English. Misunderstanding much of Twain's humor, such as his pretended naive aston-
ishment, she did see the extravaganza therein and also his
democratic qualities, even if not granting them entire critical
approval. Three years later, this same critic wrote an elaborate review of *The Gilded Age* including lengthy quotations from
it ("L'Age doré en Amérique" 319-43). Though failing to appreciate the character of Colonel Sellers, Blanc did praise
Mark's accuracy as a reporter; and her strictures upon the
collaboration from the standpoint of art are just. It was
through her quotations of long passages from *The Innocents
Abroad*, and *The Gilded Age*, together with the whole of the
Jumping Frog, that Mark Twain was first introduced to the French

people, an introduction, it must be admitted, which presented
him more as a wild and untamed funster than a civilized man
of letters.

Émile Blémont next continued the introduction of Mark's
work to French readers with *Esquisses Américaines de Mark
Twain* (1881), a volume of translations of some of Mark's lighter
sketches. More important, Eugène Forgues contributed a summation of French critical attitudes toward Twain in "Les Caravanes
d'un humoriste" published in *Revue des Deux Mondes* (1886), to
which was added several lengthy quotations from *Life on the
Mississippi.* Forgues, however, was unfriendly in his esti-
mates; with his admiration for form he could see little to
praise in Twain's writings, abounding, so they seemed, with
brutal wit and lack of taste (874-918).

The attempts made, up to then, to popularize Clemens' work
in France had failed because the French did not like the
roughness and blatancy of his humor; however, the success that
had been achieved--and there had been some--came through the
penetrating observation with which Twain looked at life, together with his art for evoking scenes and situations.

Archibald Henderson tells us, notwithstanding, that eventually Twain's comedy "won its way with the *blasé* Parisians"
who gradually began to purchase the copies of *Roughing It* appearing in the bookstalls (*Mark Twain* 137). And by the time
the authoritative edition of Twain's work appeared in English,
Gabriel de Lautrec in the *Mercure de France* paid him surprising
tribute as probably the greatest humorist then living ("Mark
Twain" 69-82). Yet even so, shortly after Clemens' death
(May 7, 1910), *Le Figaro* pointed out that Twain's popularity in
France would probably remain restricted, even as that of La
Fontaine in America, for there is a difference between wit and
humor, though both are based upon good sense.

And so it seems, for four years later, H. Houston Peckham
could find only the following translations (382-88): Émile
Blémont (Paris, 1881), Paul Largillière (Paris 1883), W. Hugues
(Paris, 1884, 1886). In 1920 the Professor of American Literature and Civilization at the Sorbonne overlooked Mark Twain
entirely in a survey of our literature which treated Whitman
adequately and mentioned Bret Harte favorably (Cestre 85-89).
And in a summary of French studies from 1923 through 1933,
Jean Simon, though finding critical works on major figures and
even some American authors of second rank, cites no material
whatever on Clemens (176-90).

In June, 1935, Maurice Le Breton stated that Mark Twain was
hardly known in France and never read since the greater part of
his writings remained untranslated, the great public judging
him entirely on certain extracts which did not reveal him at
his best (401). Adding that Twain had never excited in France

the same interest as had Fenimore Cooper and Bret Harte, who
were more respectful of conventions, Le Breton then said, however, that Twain's book represented America no less than the
lyric work of Whitman. Commenting briefly on the Van Wyck
Brooks thesis, which he rejects, Le Breton says in contradiction that the American West of 1840 to 1870 remained the source
of Mark's inspiration. And he sees the individualism in his
work, the idealism joined to an awareness of reality, while
the whole Brooks following is dismissed. After discussing the
two veins in Clemens' humor, pure fantasy arising spontaneously and the serious side based on reflection, Maurice Le Breton
praises him. Le Breton finds Twain to be the poet of a phase
unique in the experience of America and his books to be original
and lasting (418).

Léon Lemonnier contributed a biographical sketch of Samuel
Clemens' youth to *La Grande Revue* (1935) in which he followed
Paine's account. At times sentimental in tone and somewhat
distorted, as when Poe and Dickens are presented as Twain's
favorite authors, the sketch is otherwise a good, flowing
narrative ("Les débuts d'un humoriste" 76-88). Also, in this
centenary year, Gabriel de Lautrec, who a quarter of a century
earlier had praised Twain in the *Mercure de France*, now wrote
a further appreciation for that same journal. De Lautrec
praised Twain's courage which led him to attack any and all
persons and things he thought deserved it. Moreover, de Lautrec
like Le Breton sees Twain as the supreme literary example of
the prodigious development of the American continent and declares, "Mark Twain est Américain" ("Mark Twain" 80). A sensitive humorist who resents cruelty and has compassion, Samuel
Clemens the man appeals to de Lautrec equally as much as Twain
the author. It seems strange, nevertheless, that in this article filled with praise for both the man and the author none
of Twain's great books are mentioned.

Another critic, John Charpentier, returned almost full
cycle to the first French impressions of Clemens; for Charpentier, Twain is the "enfant sauvage de l'Ouest" (490), one so
natural, energetic, so representative of the American people
it was fitting that President Roosevelt in Washington should
touch the button to open the centennial celebration at Hannibal.
In brief, too, Charpentier views Twain as the "incarnation of
an art where the muscle participates equally with the intelli-
gence" (500). Little indeed is said about any of Twain's
great works; rather his popularity with the masses in America
is dwelt upon.

It remained for Léon Lemonnier to write an adequate appreciation of Clemens, *Mark Twain: L'Homme et Son Oeuvre*
(1946). Lemonnier understands the personalized, organic nature
of Twain's literary expression. And Twain's humor receives

sympathetic appreciation. Lemonnier also shows sound critical judgment; while calling *Tom Sawyer* one of Twain's major
works, he says of *Huck Finn*, "C'est sans doute le meilleur
roman de Mark Twain" (114). Indeed, Lemonnier's discussion
of Twain's pessimism is one of the most logical, taking into
account his temperament, inheritance, and the tragic happenings
of his life calculated to produce such an outlook.

Roger Asselineau has written a perceptive appreciation of
Clemens' work in *The Literary Reputation of Mark Twain from
1910 to 1950* (1954), which contains a very useful bibliography
of books and articles from European and American sources.
Asselineau, however, limits his study to American criticism
of Twain's books because he believes that no major critical
contribution has come from any other country. Though never
so popular in France as in England and Germany, Twain has
gained readers there, even as he has received more attention
from the critics. Asselineau concludes, "This gradual discovery of the merits of Mark Twain's works, this constantly
deeper and better-motivated appreciation of his books is the
best guarantee that his literary reputation will suffer no
eclipse in the coming years" (65).

For the most part Asselineau's estimate of Clemens remains
valid more than thirty years later, and perhaps part of the
reason "that no major critical contribution has come from any
other country" has been explained by Robert M. Rodney in *Mark
Twain International*. Although Rodney cites 5,344 editions of
Mark Twain and locates them in and among fifty-five countries,
the pessimistic writings of Mark Twain--published after 1899--
did not extend beyond Great Britain until the middle of the
twentieth century. Hence the popular conception of Twain persisted (xxviii); he gained much of his international audience
after his death in 1910 (xxxv). It should not be surprising
that Rodney found 1,291 international editions of *Tom Sawyer*
and only nine of *What Is Man?* (265).

L. Clark Keating, in "Mark Twain and Paul Bourget," views
Twain's cautious acceptance in France from another angle. Says
Keating, early nineteenth-century Americans were still conscious of the their debt to France for France's role in the
American Revolution, and Frenchmen were also still aware of
their role. In time, however, mutual admiration weakened and
Americans reared on the frontier became skeptical of all things
foreign. Keating sees Mark Twain as typical of the American
tendency to ridicule Europe beginning with Twain's observations
in *The Innocents Abroad* (342). Keating also sees Paul Bourget
as typical of the French to ridicule the United States. The
two formed a "perfect antithesis," contends Keating. Bourget
was afraid of what American democratic principles and material-
ism might do to harm Europe. Neither writer was an impartial

observer; both were narrow (343). As Keating explains, Bourget's conclusions seem to be full of paradoxes (347); the frontier, however, remains a real difference in the experience and
the literature of the two countries.

Germany

It was due to the success of Bret Harte in German translation that Mark Twain first appeared in that language; the
steady sale of *The Tales of the Argonauts* caused the publishers
to expect a similar interest in other Western stories. Within
a brief four years Wilhelm Grunow in Leipzig brought forth *The
Jumping Frog, Roughing It and Other Sketches* (1874), *The Innocents Abroad* (1875), *The Gilded Age* (1876), *The Adventures of
Tom Sawyer* (1876), and *Sketches New and Old* (1877), all translated by Moritz Busch, who was a strong exponent of republican-
ism (Hemminghaus 9-10). These translations were so popular
that Tauchnitz at once issued *Tom Sawyer* in 1876, following it
with other Mark Twain volumes as they appeared, these, of
course, being in English. Though Tauchnitz made Twain available to those who could read English, it was, naturally,
through translations that the bulk of the reading public came
to know him. *Life on the Mississippi* appeared in 1888, soon
followed by *Huckleberry Finn*, translated by a capable short-
story writer, Henny Koch (Hemminghaus 13).
    Archibald Henderson tells us of the unprecedented manner
of Clemens' reception in Vienna (*Mark Twain* 142), and it was
an Austrian critic and literary historian, Anton Emanuel
Schönbach, who first accorded Twain full critical treatment,
an appraisal more favorable than otherwise, but one placing
him below Bret Harte (Hemminghaus 16). Some of the journalists,
on the other hand, failed completely to appreciate Twain's
humor. Yet the extensive publications of his writings in Germany at least impressed the critics, so that gradually informed opinion began to view Clemens as a literary personality
worth serious attention (Hemminghaus 30).
    The years 1892-1904 witnessed numerous reprints of Twain's
books, publication of new works, and a steady growth of public
interest; the resulting literary prestige led Robert Lutz in
1892 to undertake a six-volume edition of selected writings
(Hemminghaus 31). During these years German critical opinion
divided on Clemens, many seeing him as a mere buffoon, working
without any moral or artistic purpose, while others began to
view him, in the words of an anonymous critic, as one who "in-
structs and educates as well as amuses and cheers" (Hemminghaus
49).

During the closing years of Clemens' life some German
critics pointed out the "glorious unconstraint and wholesome-
ness of the era in which he lived" (Hemminghaus 57) as one
reason for the unique quality of his output. Another element
in his art, later recognized, was "the strongly human appeal
of his colorful career" (Hemminghaus 58), one so closely interwoven into the web of his fiction as to become at times indis-
tinguishable. Finally the "heroic honesty and iron diligence"
of Clemens' personal dealings in business contributed to his
general popularity. The reading public, as repeated publications demonstrated, admired most the *Sketches*, *Tom Sawyer*, and
Huck Finn. During the years immediately following Clemens'
death and through the first world conflict, no German critic
of note had anything much to say about him, although there
were a few magazine articles now and then, with an occasional
review in an educational journal. *The Deutsche Revue* in 1911
carried an important article on Mark Twain by Archibald Henderson of the University of North Carolina, whose books on
Ibsen, Shaw, and other contemporary dramatists were well-known
abroad. Henderson, pointing out that the fame of no single
international figure in literature rests on humor alone, emphasized the basic seriousness and moral conviction in Twain's
writings, notably in *Huckleberry Finn* ("Mark Twain als Philosoph" 189-205). This recognition of Twain as a philosopher
and sociologist, though not entirely new to the Germans, suggested a fresh appraisal of this aspect of his work. But of
even more importance were the lectures delivered in German at
the University of Berlin by C. Alphonso Smith, serving there
as Roosevelt Professor of American History and Institutions
while on leave from the University of Virginia, where he was
the first Edgar Allan Poe Professor of English. Smith, observing
that Twain had enjoyed more numerous opportunities for viewing
human life in all aspects than any other American author, advanced the opinion that Twain's ultimate purpose was to express the truth as he found it.[3] Meanwhile popular demand had
caused the issuing of *Tom Sawyer* and *Huck Finn* together in a
single volume, while *The Prince and the Pauper* and *Tom Sawyer*
were published in textbooks for school instruction. In 1914,
Grace I. Colbron found *Tom Sawyer* and *Huckleberry Finn* to be
especially popular with German novel readers, so much so that
among American writers Twain's popularity was second to none
save Bret Harte (45-49).

During the summer of 1921 *The Adventures of Tom Sawyer*
reappeared, this time in a new jacket designed to catch the
imagination of spring buyers at the Leipzig Fair, where advance orders for Christmas quickly demonstrated its popularity
for juveniles. This led six months later to a new edition of
Huckleberry Finn, which soon proved popular with adults as well

as children. A demand for other works brought *A Tramp Abroad*,
Roughing It, and a selection of *Sketches* in cheap editions, a
revival due, it should be said, to Georg Steindorff, who made
modernized translations of *Tom Sawyer* and *Huckleberry Finn*
designed for popular appeal. Success of the Steindorff translations caused others, a new volume of selections from *The
Innocents Abroad* coming from the press in 1924, followed by
several other Twain items during 1925. And this latter year,
also, saw the appearance of the most important German book on
Mark Twain, Friedrich Schönemann's *Mark Twain als literarische
Persönlichkeit*. Schönemann began his study with a refutation
of Van Wyck Brooks' *Ordeal of Mark Twain* before proceeding
to an analysis of Twain's nature, which he found a "combination
of barbaric force and intense sweetness," leading to inner conflict, a duality of romantic and antiromantic tendencies (61-
72). Schönemann's constructive contribution to an understanding
of Twain's literary personality apparently helped to intensify
German interest. Yet by the end of the twenties, the vogue
enjoyed by Twain in Germany was drawing to a close; Hemminghaus
concluded on the basis of published criticism that Mark's popularity there was "gradually on the decline" (131). Though the
one-hundredth anniversary of Clemens' birth was commemorated
in Germany, the scale was much smaller than elsewhere. For
the more penetrating German readers, Hemminghaus believes Twain
is valued most as a "realistic chronicler of an important era
of original American life" (137).

In *Mark Twain International* Rodney lists 104 German editions of Mark Twain between 1970 and 1976 (90-120), but many
of those are collections of stories and sketches. Of the
novels appearing in German editions the most frequent were
Tom Sawyer, *Huckleberry Finn*, *The Prince and the Pauper*, and
A Connecticut Yankee in King Arthur's Court. As for East
German interest in Mark Twain, it is well illustrated in Karl-
Heinz Schönfelder's *Mark Twain: Leben, Persönlichkeit und Werk*
(1961), which Henry A. Pochmann from the University of Wis-
consin reviewed for *American Literature*. Writes Pochmann:

> The East German orientation of the book is betrayed
> by the author's overemphasis of Mark Twain's attacks on
> capitalism—numerous and extensive though these are in
> what he said and wrote. What is annoying is the heavy-
> handed seriousness which makes Mr. Schönfelder take at
> face value everything Mark Twain said, whether he meant
> it or not—not realizing that Mark Twain enjoyed talking
> through his hat and sometimes out of both sides of his
> mouth. (542)

What Schönfelder failed to recognize, says Pochmann, is that
Twain himself was a capitalist. Pochmann finds in Schönfelder's

book the kind of criticism of Clemens we have come to expect
of the Soviets, the kind in which a writer is exploited for
the ideological purposes of the state.

In still other countries Twain's literary reputation has
varied. For example, Latin countries in general seem to have
paid little or no critical attention to Clemens, but his books
have been translated into Spanish and Italian.[4] On the other
hand, in Scandinavia, where a general interest in American
letters exists, Twain enjoyed an individual popularity. The
chief librarian of the Royal Swedish Library records learning
Huckleberry Finn almost by heart after receiving it for a
birthday present (Cowley 2: 1383). Before Clemens' death a
Danish critic and novelist, Johannes von Jensen, demanded a
more serious consideration of Twain as an author, his own evaluation being translated into German (Hemminghaus 61). Ivan
Benson has found that the copies of Twain on the shelves of
the Stockholm City Library are numerous, and although generally
in English, are read enough to demand frequent rebinding (4).
Tom Sawyer and *Huckleberry Finn* were early translated into
Swedish (4). *Pudd'nhead Wilson*, too, made its way into that
language. An interesting study of Mark Twain is S.B. Liljegren's *The Revolt Against Romanticism in American Literature
as Evidenced in the Works of S.L. Clemens*, a study which places
Mark in the cultural tradition of Europe, one altered by
American environment, but nevertheless basically the same.
Liljegren claims that Clemens' literary roots go back to Beowulf rather than Franklin, his revolt against the romanticism
of Scott and the others being but the transatlantic aspect of
the same attitude in Thackeray (50-51). The Scandinavian scholar
disagrees with Parrington and others who find the Western
influence strongest in Twain's literary development, pointing
out Mark's "essential mental refinement, culture, and poetic
sense of values" (51). While Liljegren undervalues the Western
influences, both social and literary, in the development of
Twain's art, he does remind us once more of the European tradition which, as Brashear proved earlier, played an important
part in the shaping of Samuel Clemens as a man of letters.[5]

In the year of Twain's centenary a Swiss scholar named
August Hüppy issued a small study designed to show Clemens'
interest in Switzerland as the cradle of liberty (*Mark Twain
und die Schweiz* 1935). Telling of Mark's first visit there in
1878, and the later ones of 1891 and 1897, the book contributes
nothing to Twain criticism, nor does it add any new biographical facts, its interest being only in its appreciation of
Clemens as a glorifier of the Alps. Of considerable importance, however, is Mark Twain's reception in Russia, which
began there prior to 1910, for Clemens followed Cooper, Harriet
Beecher Stowe, and Bret Harte in winning favor with Russian

readers (Cowley 2: 1385).   The first of his stories to appear
was the *Jumping Frog*, published in the St. Petersburg *Stock
Exchange News* (1872), accompanied by an article praising Twain
for "a highly original gift molded under the influence of the
completely new life now springing up in the deserts of California and the mountains of Sierra Nevada."   Though warning readers not to expect literary finesse, Twain's "inexhaustible
supply of humor, vivid imagination, powerful fantasy, and un-
affected gaiety" received praise (qtd. in Magidoff 11).   From
then on Twain appeared in newspapers and magazines, his first
magazine appearance being in *Homeland Notes* in 1877 (Magidoff
11).

Before the revolution the Czar's subjects apparently liked
American books that were "realistic or humorous or heroic in
treatment, if they were democratic in sentiment, if they dealt
with life in a great city or, still better, with adventures
on the frontier, and if the characters were representative of
the American masses" (Cowley 2: 1384-85).   Mark Twain, like
O. Henry, another favorite in Russia, easily fitted into this
pattern for popularity.   Twain was widely enough read to make
his own way into Ukrainian or Little Russian dialect (Yarmolinsky 47).   Among his books *The Prince and the Pauper* seems to
have been read more often even than *Tom Sawyer* and *Huckleberry
Finn*, and the purely humorous sketches, issued sometimes in
"cheap yellow-covered brochures," enjoyed a good sale (Yarmolinsky 47).

When control of the publishing industry in Russia passed
into the hands of the Soviet, there was apparently no great
change in the reading taste of the people, although many books
were kept out of the country for political reasons.   Of all
American authors in the Soviet Union only Jack London is more
widely read than Clemens, whose books sold 3,100,000 copies
between 1918 and 1943 (Cowley 2: 1386).   This popularity has
led to a multitude of translations of Twain into Russian, each
one of which, naturally enough, reflects the political and
nationalistic leanings of the translator.   For instance, a
version of *The Innocents Abroad* published during the Czarist
regime expounded the beneficence of the upper classes, whereas
a later version prepared by the Leninites satirizes the former
Russian nobility (Parry 1).   A fine edition of Mark Twain's
complete works has been issued, along with nineteen separate
printings of his most popular books.   During World War II
Soviet publishing houses printed several editions for the
Russian army and navy publishing branches.[6]   Soviet criticism
has since followed an underlying theme of patriotism, a
nationalistic attitude the disillusioned Twain could never
hold (Manning 218).

Although it is becoming dated, *A Guide to Soviet Russian Translations of American Literature* (1954) by Glenora Brown and Deming B. Brown remains interesting not so much because of its listing of translations but because of such discussions as that of Soviet literary taste (3-27) and the softening of Soviet literary policy in the thirties leading to publication of some of the best of American literature in the thirties and forties (22). The differences of taste held by Russian and American critics, nonetheless, was brought sharply into focus when Charles Neider published *Mark Twain and the Russians* (1960), a fascinating exchange of views about Mark Twain between Neider and editor Yan Bereznitsky of the Soviet publication *Literaturnaya Gazeta*. An exchange of letters between the two critics, reprinted in *Mark Twain and the Russians*, was prompted by the appearance of Neider's edition of *The Autobiography of Mark Twain* in an American exhibit in Moscow. The gist of Bereznitsky's dissatisfaction with Neider's edition is that Neider left out much of the didactic work in favor of demonstrating Twain's ability as a fabulist and master of anecdote. Nieder holds that in literature the aesthetic element is primary (27). On the contrary, Bereznitsky holds that Twain's interests and feelings are best expressed in the political writings; they contain his pronouncements on democracy and capitalism. Even Bereznitsky finally admits that the dispute was about opposed tendencies in literary scholarship over social content (23).

Two years later, in *Soviet Attitudes Toward American Writing* (1962), Deming Brown published an excellent analysis of the political implications of literature in Russian society. Of criticism he writes, "Soviet criticism is in the main a tightly organized, disciplined body of thought and prejudice. In a very real sense there has been no 'independent' Soviet criticism since the late 1920's" (9). The interests of Soviet critics are confined to "critical realism" and "socialist realism," says Brown, an emphasis on social experience and rational recognition of reality. Contending that Russian critics are "inspectors of ideology," and that they frequently misinterpret to force conformity to ideology, Brown concludes, "The overwhelming defect of Soviet criticism has been its insistence that there is only one correct way for the artist to perceive life" (323). By contrast, in a collection of essays titled *20th Century American Literature: A Soviet View* (1976), Ronald Vroon, the translator, believes that the October Socialist Revolution marked a turning point in the Russian view of American literature. Treating a plethora of American writers, the collection also contains essays on genres and movements in America. This collection in itself is evidence that American literature is much read and discussed in the Soviet Union.

As might be expected, Mark Twain has not made great in-
roads in the Far East. In *Mark Twain International* Rodney
lists total single editions by country as follows: Philippines,
1; Thailand, 2; China, 10; Hong Kong, 19; Japan, 77; Korea, 6;
and Taiwan, 15 (273). As for Mark Twain's place in literature in Japan, Shunsuke Kamei assesses it in "Mark Twain in
Japan." The first work of Twain to appear in Japanese, says
Kamei, was probably *The Prince and the Pauper*, translated by
Sazanami Iwaya and two of his literary disciples and published
in 1899. Then Hoichian Hara published three Twain stories in
Western Strange Stories in 1903. Other translation efforts
followed; "... Kuni Sadaki was perhaps the one who most dedicated himself to Twain" (10). Even though Twain's influence
on Japanese juvenile and humorous literature is substantial,
he seems not to have made a great difference in other ways.
Kamei cites the only noteworthy Japanese study of Mark Twain,
Masajiro Hamada's *Mark Twain: His Characters and Works* (1955):

> Since they determined to absorb Western civilization in
> the 1850's and 60's, the Japanese have most highly re-
> spected English culture and have learned foreign litera-
> ture mainly from the English point of view. Accordingly
> they have not favored Twain's rustic, contradictory, and
> continental character. Moreover, the Japanese from
> their country's start have hardly experienced a frontier
> life, so they have not felt sympathy with the life of
> wandering and strife which Twain describes. (11)

Although Hamada's estimate is "partly legitimate," concludes
Kamei, the real reason Mark Twain has not been very influential
is that he has not been introduced to the Japanese sufficiently.
    The reasons for Twain's lacking a great audience in the
Far East are complex, and probably more so than Kamei's analysis indicates. On the other hand Mark Twain still enjoys a
large audience abroad as well as at home, and that he does
should not be surprising. He was an internationally minded
thinker, one who had resided in or visited all the great
countries of Europe. Travel in foreign lands, residence
abroad, contact with the most intellectual and cultured society on both sides of the Atlantic gave him a cosmopolitan
vision. Even his Americanism was continental in scope rather
than sectional. The native Southwesterner, born in a Missouri
slaveholding community, of Virginia and Kentucky parentage,
soon transformed himself into the Westerner, then into the
resident of New England--finally to become the complete cosmopolitan of New York, London, and the continent. Yet,
withal, he remained the typical American--indeed, the boy from
Hannibal--until the end of his days. So substantial and
strong was the base of Twain's character that the superstruc-

ture of later experience only added to his intellectual height and breadth; the soundness of heart and mind were native. Mark Twain was an artist of great human spirit, devoted to honor and truth, whose concern for his fellow-man was profound and universal.

NOTES

1. Hazard, in *The Frontier in American Literature*, credits Mark with writing of the Gilded Age with a "fierce undercurrent of savage criticism" (220). She also says that he exposed "the relation of Big Business to the government" (228).

2. A list of contributions is conveniently found in Archibald Henderson (*Mark Twain* 228-29).

3. Smith's lectures on American literature were published in *Die Amerikanische Literatur* (Berlin, 1912).

4. Although he discusses a number of American writers in detail in *American Literature: Essays and Opinions* (1970), Cesare Pavese treats Twain only tangentially. He sees Twain as writing in the American vernacular tradition, and he labels *Tom Sawyer* and *Huckleberry Finn* "heroic fables." About the matter of language he writes:

> The dialect quality of the short stories from Mark Twain to O. Henry comes from the need to speak to a rather democratic public (miners, sometimes), and in any case always to speak to a bourgeoisie which tends toward solidity and wants to understand and to recognize itself in newspapers. Because of course from Mark Twain to O. Henry all the literature that lives is journalistic. (83).

5. Liljegren is particularly interested in Twain's burlesque poetry, and this reveals that he had literary ideals of his own.

6. Some volumes have been illustrated. Magidoff reproduces an interesting illustration by Fedor Konstantin for "Journalism in Tennessee" ("American Literature in Russia" 10). As for editions of Mark Twain's works, Robert M. Rodney reports in *Mark Twain International* that 317 single editions had been published in Russia by 1976 (270).

WORKS CITED

Archer, William. *America To-day*. London: Heinemann, 1900.
    An affirmation of Twain's genius.

Arvin, Newton. "Mark Twain: 1835-1935." *New Republic* 83
    (1935): 125-27. Sees Clemens surviving more as a legendary
    figure than as a literary man.

Asselineau, Roger. *The Literary Reputation of Mark Twain from
    1910 to 1950*. Paris: Librairie Marcel Didier, 1954.
    Sound criticism. Contains useful bibliography.

Baetzhold, Howard G. *Mark Twain and John Bull: The British
    Connection*. Bloomington: Indiana U. Press, 1970. Valua-
    ble for the British influence on Twain.

Beers, Henry A. *Initial Studies in American Letters*. New
    York: Chautauqua, 1891.

Benson, Ivan. "From Our Stockholm Correspondent." *Twainian*
    os 2.5 (1940): 3-4.

Bentzon, Th. "L'Age doré en Amérique." Review of *The Gilded
    Age* by Mark Twain. *Revue des Deux Mondes* 45 (1875): 319-
    43.

————. "Les Humoristes américains: I. Mark Twain." *Revue
    des Deux Mondes* 100 (1872): 313-35. An article introducing
    Twain to the French.

Bronson, Walter C. *A Short History of American Literature*.
    New York: Heath, 1900.

Brooks, Van Wyck. *The Ordeal of Mark Twain*. Rev. ed. New
    York: Dutton, 1933. Revised edition varies slightly from
    the 1920 edition. Failed to see Twain's greatness.

Brown, Deming B. *Soviet Attitudes Toward American Writing*.
    Princeton: Princeton U. Press, 1962. Political implica-
    tions of literature in Russian society.

Brown, Glenora W. and Deming B. Brown. *A Guide to Soviet
    Translations of American Literature*. New York: King's
    Crown Press, Columbia U. Press, 1954. Treats Soviet
    literary tastes.

Budd, Louis J. *Our Mark Twain*. Philadelphia: U. of Pennsyl-
    vania Press, 1983. Analyzes Twain's status as a cultural
    hero.

Burton, Richard. *Literary Leaders of America*. New York:
    Scribner's, 1904.

Calverton, V.F. *The Liberation of American Literature.* New York: Scribner's, 1932.

Charpentier, John. "Humour Anglais et Humour Américain. À Propos du centenaire de Mark Twain." *Mercure de France* 264 (1935): 475-500. Views Twain as the Western savage.

Cestre, Charles. "American Literature Through French Eyes." *Yale Review* ns 10 (1920): 85-98.

Colbron, Grace I. "The American Novel in Germany." *Bookman* 39 (1914): 45-49.

Cowley, Malcolm. "American Books Abroad." *Literary History of the United States.* Ed. Robert E. Spiller, et al. 3 vols. New York: Macmillan, 1948. 2: 1374-91.

Cunliffe, Marcus. *The Literature of the United States.* London: Penguin, 1954. Interesting criticism on Twain.

Davis, Sara deSaussure and Philip D. Beidler, eds. *The Mythologizing of Mark Twain.* University: U. of Alabama Press, 1984. Contains eight essays on myth-making.

De Lautrec, Gabriel. "Mark Twain." *Mercure de France* 264 (1935): 69-82. Praises Twain but cites none of his great work.

"Editor's Literary Record." *Harper's Magazine* 67 (1883): 799.

Farrell, James T. *The League of Frightened Philistines.* New York: Vanguard, 1945.

Forgues, Eugène. "Les Caravanes d'un humoriste." *Revue des Deux Mondes* 56 (1886): 874-918. An adverse estimate.

Frank, Waldo. *Our America.* New York: Boni and Liveright, 1919.

Gibson, William M. *The Art of Mark Twain.* New York: Oxford U. Press, 1976. Surveys form and technique used in various genres by Twain.

Gohdes, Clarence. *American Literature in Nineteenth Century England.* New York: Columbia U. Press, 1944.

———. "British Interest in American Literature During the Latter Part of the Nineteenth Century as Reflected by Mudie's Select Library." *American Literature* 13 (1942): 356-62.

Gordon, George Stuart. *Anglo-American Literary Relations.* London: Oxford U. Press, 1942. Sees Twain as a genius who wrote one of the world's great books.

Grattan, Hartley. "Mark Twain." *American Writers on American Literature, by Thirty-Seven Contemporary Writers.* Ed.

John Macy. New York: Liveright, 1931. 274-84. Valuable estimate. Still of interest.

Haweis, H.R. *American Humorists*. London: Chatto and Windus, 1883.

Hazard, Lucy Lockwood. *The Frontier in American Literature*. New York: Crowell, 1927. Twain's attitude toward big business and government.

Hemminghaus, Edgar H. *Mark Twain in Germany*. New York: Columbia U. Press, 1939. A definitive study. Contains bibliography.

Henderson, Archibald. *Mark Twain*. New York: Stokes, 1911. Contains some early English comments on Twain's books.

————. "Mark Twain als Philosoph, Moralist un Soziologe." *Deutsche Revue* (Stuttgart and Leipzig) 36 (1911): 189-205.

Hicks, Granville. *The Great Tradition*. New York: Macmillan, 1933.

Hill, Hamlin. *Mark Twain: God's Fool*. New York: Harper & Row, 1973.

Howells, William Dean. *Life in Letters of William Dean Howells*. Ed. Mildred Howells. 2 vols. Garden City: Doubleday, 1928.

————. Review of *A Connecticut Yankee in King Arthur's Court*. By Mark Twain. *Harper's Monthly* 80 (1890): 319-21. Rpt. in *My Mark Twain*. By Howells. New York: Harper & Brothers, 1910. 145-49.

Hüppy, August. *Mark Twain und die Schweiz*. Zurich: Reutimann, 1935. A Swiss compliment to Twain.

Kamei, Shunsuke. "Mark Twain in Japan." *Mark Twain Journal* 12.1 (1963): 10-11, 20. Analyzes Twain's place in literature in Japan.

Keating, L. Clark. "Mark Twain and Paul Bourget." *French Review* 30.5 (1957): 342-49. Examines Twain's acceptance in France.

Kipling, Rudyard. *From Sea to Sea*. 2 vols. New York: Doubleday, 1899.

Krause, Sydney J. *Mark Twain as Critic*. Baltimore: Johns Hopkins U. Press, 1967. Makes a case for Twain as literary critic.

Lang, Andrew. "The Art of S.L. Clemens." *Illustrated London News* 98 (1891): 222. Rpt. as "Mr. Lang on the Art of Mark

Twain." *The Critic* Mar. 7 1891: 130 and July 25 1891: 45-46.

Le Breton, Maurice. "Un Centenaire: Mark Twain." *Revue Anglo-Américaine* 13 (1935): 401-19. A sound critical evaluation.

Lemonnier, Léon. "Les Débuts d'un Humoriste." *La Grande Revue* 149 (1935): 76-88. Biographical rather than critical.

————. *Mark Twain: L'Homme et Son Oeuvre.* Paris: Librairie Artheme Fayard, 1946. A full, lengthy study. Sound in judgment.

Lewisohn, Ludwig. *Expression in America.* New York: Harper & Brothers, 1932.

Liljegren, S.B. *The Revolt Against Romanticism in American Literature as Evidenced in the Works of S.L. Clemens.* Upsala: Lundequistka Bokhandeln, 1945. Relates Clemens to the stream of European realism.

Macnaughton, William R. *Mark Twain's Last Years as a Writer.* Columbia: U. of Missouri Press, 1979. Makes a case for the value of Twain's later writing.

Macy, John. *The Spirit of American Literature.* New York: Doubleday, 1913.

Magidoff, Robert. "American Literature in Russia." *Saturday Review of Literature* 29.44 (1946): 9-11, 45-46.

Manning, Clarence A. "Socialist Realism and the American Success Novel." *South Atlantic Quarterly* 48 (1949): 213-19.

Matthews, Brander. *Introduction to American Literature.* New York: American, 1896. Rev. 1923. Contains an appreciation of Twain's place in literature.

————. "An Appreciation." *Europe and Elsewhere.* By Mark Twain. New York: Harper & Brothers, 1923. vii-xxx. First printed as an introduction to the Uniform Edition of Mark Twain's Works, published in 1899.

Mumford, Lewis. *The Golden Day.* New York: Boni and Liveright, 1927.

Neider, Charles. *Mark Twain and the Russians.* New York: Hill and Wang, 1960. Valuable international exchange of views concerning Twain.

Nichol, John. *American Literature: an Historical Sketch 1620-1880.* Edinburgh: Balc, 1882. Views Twain as a jester.

Paine, Albert Bigelow. *Mark Twain: A Biography.* 4 vols. New

York: Harper & Brothers, 1912. The authorized life.
Still an indispensable storehouse of information.

Pancoast, Henry S. *An Introduction to American Literature.*
New York: Holt, 1900.

Parrington, Vernon L. *Main Currents in American Thought: An
Interpretation of American Literature from the Beginnings
to 1920.* 3 vols. New York: Harcourt, 1930.

Parry, Albert. "Mark Twain in Russia." *Books Abroad* 15
(1941): 168-75.

Pavese, Cesare. *American Literature: Essays and Opinions.*
Trans. Edwin Fussell. Berkeley: U. of California Press,
1970. Treats Twain only tangentially.

Peckham, H. Houston. "Is American Literature Read and Respected in Europe?" *South Atlantic Quarterly* 13 (1914): 382-
88. Found Twain little read in France.

Phelps, William Lyon. "Mark Twain: Humorist and Philosopher."
North American Review 185 (1907): 540-48.

Pochmann, Henry A. Review of *Mark Twain: Leben, Persönlichkeit
und Werk.* By Karl-Heinz Schönfelder. *American Literature*
33 (1962): 541-42. East German orientation toward Twain.

Regan, Robert. *Unpromising Heroes: Mark Twain and His Characters.* Berkeley: U. of California Press, 1966. Study of
the idea of the Unpromising Hero as it relates to Twain's
life and work.

Rodney, Robert M., ed. *Mark Twain International.* Westport:
Greenwood, 1982. Indispensable for editions of Twain published abroad. International bibliography and interpretation of Twain's popularity abroad.

Rourke, Constance. *American Humor.* New York: Harcourt, Brace,
1931.

Schönemann, Friedrich. *Mark Twain als literarische Persön-
lichkeit.* Jena: Verlag der Frommanschen Buchhandlung,
Walter Biedermann, 1925. Most important German study of
Twain.

Scott, Arthur L. *On the Poetry of Mark Twain: With Selections
from His Verse.* Urbana: U. of Illinois Press, 1966.
Surveys Twain's interest in poetry.

————, ed. *Mark Twain: Selected Criticism.* Dallas: Southern
Methodist U. Press, 1955. Traces changes in critical attitudes toward Twain and the growth of his literary reputation.

Sherman, Stuart P. "Mark Twain." *The Cambridge History of American Literature*. Ed. William Peterfield Trent, et al. 4 vols. New York: Putnam's, 1921. 3: 1-20.

Simon, Jean. "French Studies in American Literature and Civilization." *American Literature* 6 (1934): 176-90.

Smith, C. Alphonso. *Die Amerikanische Literatur*. Berlin: Weidmann, 1912. Lectures at the University of Berlin.

Smith, Henry Nash. *Mark Twain: The Development of a Writer*. Cambridge: Belknap Press of Harvard U. Press, 1962. Traces Twain's handling of problems of style and structure through nine major works.

————, ed. *Mark Twain*. Englewood Cliffs: Prentice-Hall, 1963. Essays written largely after 1950.

Thompson, Charles M. "Mark Twain as an Interpreter of American Character." *Atlantic* 79 (1897): 443-50.

Trent, William. *A History of American Literature, 1607-1865*. New York: Appleton, 1903.

Twain, Mark [Samuel Langhorne Clemens]. *The Adventures of Huckleberry Finn*. New York: Harper & Brothers, 1918.

————. *The Adventures of Tom Sawyer*. New York: Harper & Brothers, 1922.

————. *The Celebrated Jumping Frog of Calaveras County and Other Sketches*. New York: Webb, 1867.

————. *A Connecticut Yankee in King Arthur's Court*. New York: Harper & Brothers, 1917.

————. *The Devil's Race-Track: Mark Twain's Great Dark Writings*. Ed. John S. Tuckey. Berkeley: U. of California Press, 1980. Selections written after Twain turned sixty.

————. *The Innocents Abroad*. 2 vols. New York: Harper & Brothers, 1911.

————. *Life on the Mississippi*. New York: Harper & Brothers, 1917.

————. *Mark Twain's Fables of Man*. Ed. John S. Tuckey. Berkeley: U. of California Press, 1972.

————. *Mark Twain's Letters*. Ed. Albert Bigelow Paine. 2 vols. New York: Harper & Brothers, 1917.

————. *Mark Twain's Which Was the Dream? and Other Symbolic Writings of the Later Years*. Ed. John S. Tuckey. Berkeley: U. of California Press, 1967.

————. *The Prince and the Pauper*. New York: Harper & Brothers, 1909.

————. *Pudd'nhead Wilson*. New York: Harper & Brothers, 1922.

————. *Roughing It*. 2 vols. New York: Harper & Brothers, 1913.

————. *Sketches New and Old*. New York: Harper & Brothers, 1917.

————. *Tom Sawyer Abroad*. New York: Harper & Brothers, 1917.

————. *Tom Sawyer Abroad, Tom Sawyer, Detective, and Other Stories*. New York: Harper & Brothers, 1896.

————. *A Tramp Abroad*. 2 vols. New York: Harper & Brothers, 1921.

————. *What Is Man?* New York: Harper & Brothers, 1917.

Twain, Mark and Charles Dudley Warner. *The Gilded Age*. 2 vols. New York: Harper & Brothers, 1915.

Vedder, Henry C. *American Writers of Today*. New York: Silver, Burdett, 1898.

Vogelback, Arthur L. "*The Prince and the Pauper*: A Study in Critical Standards." *American Literature* 14 (1942): 48-52.

————. "The Publication and Reception of *Huckleberry Finn* in America." *American Literature* 11 (1939): 260-72.

Vroon, Ronald, ed. *20th Century American Literature: A Soviet View*. Moscow: Progress Publications, 1976.

Ward, A.C. *American Literature 1880-1930*. London: Methuen, 1932. Inclines toward the Brooks theory.

Wecter, Dixon. "Mark Twain." *Literary History of the United States*. Ed. Robert E. Spiller, et al. 3 vols. New York: Macmillan, 1948. 2: 917-39. Sound, critical estimate.

Wendell, Barrett. *A Literary History of America*. New York: Scribner's, 1900.

Woodberry, George E. *America in Literature*. New York: Harper & Brothers, 1903.

Yarmolinsky, Abraham. "The Russian View of American Literature." *Bookman* 44 (1916): 44-48. Contains interesting facts up to 1916.